SSL and TLS

Theory and Practice

For quite a long time, computer security was a rather narrow field of study that was populated mainly by theoretical computer scientists, electrical engineers, and applied mathematicians. With the proliferation of open systems in general, and of the Internet and the World Wide Web (WWW) in particular, this situation has changed fundamentally. Today, computer and network practitioners are equally interested in computer security, since they require technologies and solutions that can be used to secure applications related to electronic commerce. Against this background, the field of computer security has become very broad and includes many topics of interest. The aim of this series is to publish state-of-the-art, high standard technical books on topics related to computer security. Further information about the series can be found on the WWW at the following URL:

http://www.esecurity.ch/serieseditor.html

Also, if you'd like to contribute to the series by writing a book about a topic related to computer security, feel free to contact either the Commissioning Editor or the Series Editor at Artech House.

For a listing of recent titles
in the *Artech House Information Security and Privacy Series*,
turn to the back of this book.

SSL and TLS

Theory and Practice

Rolf Oppliger

ARTECH HOUSE
BOSTON | LONDON
artechhouse.com

Library of Congress Cataloging-in-Publication Data
A catalog record for this book is available from the U.S. Library of Congress.

British Library Cataloguing in Publication Data
A catalogue record for this book is available from the British Library.

ISBN-13 978-1-59693-447-4

Cover design by Igor Valdman

© 2009 ARTECH HOUSE
685 Canton Street
Norwood, MA 02062

Printed and bound in the United States of America. No part of this book may be reproduced or utilized in any form or by any means, electronic or mechanical, including photocopying, recording, or by any information storage and retrieval system, without permission in writing from the publisher. All terms mentioned in this book that are known to be trademarks or service marks have been appropriately capitalized. Artech House cannot attest to the accuracy of this information. Use of a term in this book should not be regarded as affecting the validity of any trademark or service mark.

10 9 8 7 6 5 4 3 2 1

To my parents

Contents

Foreword		xi
Preface		xv
Acknowledgments		xxi

Chapter 1	Introduction			1
	1.1	OSI Security Architecture		1
		1.1.1	Security Services	4
		1.1.2	Security Mechanisms	8
	1.2	Security Definition		11
	1.3	Final Remarks		14
		References		15

Chapter 2	Cryptography Primer			17
	2.1	Introduction		17
		2.1.1	Preliminary Remarks	17
		2.1.2	Cryptographic Systems	19
		2.1.3	Classes of Cryptographic Systems	21
		2.1.4	Secure Cryptosystems	22
		2.1.5	Historical Background Information	24
		2.1.6	Legal Situation	26
	2.2	Cryptosystems Overview		28
		2.2.1	Unkeyed Cryptosystems	28
		2.2.2	Secret Key Cryptosystems	35
		2.2.3	Public Key Cryptosystems	45
	2.3	Final Remarks		59
		References		60

Chapter 3	Transport Layer Security		65
	3.1	Introduction	65

	3.2	Protocol Evolution	68
	3.3	Final Remarks	73
		References	73
Chapter 4	SSL Protocol		75
	4.1	Introduction	75
	4.2	Protocols	87
		4.2.1 SSL Record Protocol	87
		4.2.2 SSL Handshake Protocol	94
		4.2.3 SSL Change Cipher Spec Protocol	117
		4.2.4 SSL Alert Protocol	118
		4.2.5 SSL Application Data Protocol	120
	4.3	Traffic Analysis of an SSL Session	121
	4.4	Security Analysis	125
	4.5	Final Remarks	129
		References	130
Chapter 5	TLS Protocol		133
	5.1	Introduction	133
		5.1.1 TLS PRF	136
		5.1.2 Generation of Keying Material	139
	5.2	TLS 1.0	141
		5.2.1 Cipher Suites	141
		5.2.2 Certificate Management	144
		5.2.3 Alert Messages	145
		5.2.4 Other Differences	146
	5.3	TLS 1.1	147
		5.3.1 Preliminary Remarks	147
		5.3.2 Cipher Suites	149
		5.3.3 Certificate Management	150
		5.3.4 Alert Messages	151
		5.3.5 Other Differences	151
	5.4	TLS 1.2	152
		5.4.1 TLS Extensions	153
		5.4.2 Cipher Suites	168
		5.4.3 Certificate Management	173
		5.4.4 Alert Messages	173
		5.4.5 Other Differences	174
	5.5	Traffic Analysis of a TLS Session	174
	5.6	Security Analysis	178

	5.7	Final Remarks	178
		References	179
Chapter 6	DTLS Protocol		183
	6.1	Introduction	183
	6.2	DTLS 1.0	186
		6.2.1 Record Protocol	187
		6.2.2 Handshake Protocol	190
	6.3	DTLS 1.2	194
	6.4	Security Analysis	195
	6.5	Final Remarks	195
		References	196
Chapter 7	Firewall Traversal		199
	7.1	Introduction	199
	7.2	SSL/TLS Tunneling	202
	7.3	SSL/TLS Proxying	205
	7.4	Final Remarks	206
		References	207
Chapter 8	Public Key Certificates and PKIs		209
	8.1	Introduction	209
		8.1.1 PGP Certificates	213
		8.1.2 X.509 Certificates	215
	8.2	Server Certificates	218
		8.2.1 Wildcard Certificates	220
		8.2.2 International Step-Up and SGC Certificates	220
		8.2.3 Extended Validation Certificates	221
	8.3	Client Certificates	222
	8.4	Final Remarks	223
		References	224
Chapter 9	Conclusions and Outlook		227
	9.1	Deployment	227
	9.2	Research Challenges	230
		9.2.1 Performance Optimization	230
		9.2.2 Protection Against MITM Attacks	232
		9.2.3 Trust Management	235
	9.3	Future Developments	235
		References	236

Appendix Standardized TLS Cipher Suites	239
Abbreviations and Acronyms	243
About the Author	249
Index	251

Foreword

Over the last 15 years, the shift in the world economy and transaction activity to the online medium has perhaps been the fastest big shift in the society ever. It is quite common today for multiple people from several countries to electronically "talk" about participating in an online game. Imagine what that conversation would have been like just a short 20 years ago.

Since the early days of the Web, we have realized that commercial applications start to grow and become popular, and that securing traffic on the open Internet is a key requirement. It goes hand in hand with the requirement that end users do not have to perform any task in order for the secure connection to be established. Today, the success of SSL as an Internet and e-commerce security standard is perhaps the most visible achievement of the information security industry. There are many lessons to be learned from this experience.

The technology was developed by a world-class team in security and networking, but not within a security company. The fact that the protocol was embedded in the browsers from their first incarnations made SSL part of a new infrastructure that the Web accepted. When the first e-commerce applications were being considered, it was clear that the most vulnerable area was that everyone could have access to any information on the Internet—after all the Internet was designed to be an open network to provide information and serve as a collaboration medium for all concerned. SSL was designed from the beginning to prevent unauthorized access to secured data on the open wire. SSL has withstood the test of more than a billion users over 15 years, and has been the underpinning of the Web security for all e-commerce applications.

I joined Netscape as a chief scientist in early 1995, after the first version of SSL had been released. When it became apparent that SSL may in fact become the defacto standard for e-commerce, it was recognized that a redesign is necessary to make sure that transactions are safe. I had the opportunity to put together a great team of the best designers. Paul Kocher was contacted to be the security specialist for the team, Alan Freier was the networking specialist, and Phil Karlton was the overall architect. The team worked over a couple of months to put together a design that can support all the requirements, not the least of which is the overall security level of the protocol. It is noteworthy here to mention that Netscape recognized early on that security was one of the cornerstones of the success of the Web as a medium for conducting commerce and the company invested a lot in the security space. Jim Clark had contacted RSA Security at the very beginning of the company, when it was still called Mosaic Communications to make sure that he had the right security components in place. This was quite different from what most other companies did; security had always been an after the fact issue, but here security was in the middle of everything.

After the completion of the first incarnations of what was later called SSL 3.0, we thought that we needed the security industry to "bless" the protocol. So we did something that was quite new in the Internet industry: we contacted many security experts from other organizations, both academic and industrial and invited them to sessions at Netscape to work through the new protocol. These sessions proved to be very beneficial, not just because of the expertise level in that room, but also because this was the key for us to promote the protocol as an industry standard. The expert team soon became part of the Netscape team and SSL 3.0 became the industry standard for Web security.

There were two other important factors to making SSL succeed:

- The first factor was protecting the intellectual property. Often, companies file patents to protect their intellectual property against others who may be working on the same space. Netscape decided to file for patents to protect SSL in order to prevent others from moving into the same space, not to get others to obtain licenses. The patents were in fact awarded in 1997 and soon after given away to the community for everyone to use for free.

- The second factor was to get the standards communities to adopt and own the follow on work for SSL. We chose the Internet Engineering Task Force (IETF) for this task because of their involvement in other Internet and security standard work. The IETF did in fact adopt SSL 3.0 as the initial Web security standard and called it Transport Layer Security (TLS). It was perhaps the proper name for the protocol, versus Secure Sockets Layer (SSL), as sockets are not actually a layer in the Internet network stack and the protocol did actually apply at the transport layer.

The final, and perhaps most difficult, step to get SSL to be the Web security standard was to get competitors to adopt it. At the time, Microsoft was the primary competitor in the space, with independent effort in the same area. The effort to "give" the protocol to the IETF served also as the catalyst to bring Microsoft to the same table to adopt SSL as the one standard. Today, we use SSL for basically all e-commerce and other transactions on the Web, thanks to efforts from the Netscape team, the security experts we brought in, and the IETF for adopting SSL 3.0 as the first and basis protocol. The book you have in hand bears witness to the tremendous success of SSL and TLS.

Taher Elgamal
Axway and independent security expert
Redwood City, California
September 2009

Preface

Terms like electronic commerce (*e-commerce*), electronic business (*e-business*), and electronic government (*e-government*) are omnipresent today. When people use these terms, they often refer to stringent security requirements that must be met. If they want to show that they are tech-savvy, they bring in acronyms like SSL or TLS. Since SSL stands for *secure* sockets layer and TLS stands for transport layer *security*, people think that adding SSL or TLS to applications makes them inherently secure and magically solves all security-related problems. This is arguably not the case and largely overestimates the role SSL/TLS can play in the security arena. Nevertheless, SSL/TLS is still the most widely used and most important technology to secure e-∗ applications or certain aspects thereof. This is certainly true for applications for the World Wide Web (WWW) based on the Hypertext Transfer Protocol (HTTP), but it is also true for many other Internet applications, such as e-mail, instant messaging, file transfer, terminal access, or any other form of collaboration. As mentioned by Taher Elgamal in the foreword, it is even true for online games. Many of these applications are nowadays layered on top of SSL/TLS to provide basic security services.

Considering the large deployment of SSL/TLS, it is important to teach e-∗ application designers and developers the fundamental principles and the rationale behind the design of the SSL/TLS protocols. Simply invoking secure libraries and function calls is not enough to design and develop secure applications. In fact, it is fairly common today to invoke such libraries and function calls from exploitable code. The resulting application is not going to be secure—whether SSL/TLS is in place or not. Against this background, secure programming techniques are important to build secure applications. Also, a thorough understanding of a security technology is required to correctly apply it and to properly complement it with other security technologies. This rule of thumb also applies to SSL/TLS; it is necessary to fully understand what the SSL/TLS protocols can do and what they cannot do in order to properly apply them.

The SSL/TLS protocols are not a panacea. They enable applications to be only as secure as the underlying infrastructural components, both in terms of computer networks and hosts (i.e., clients and servers). In the case of SSL/TLS, things are even more involved than they could be due to the fact that the protocol specifications use a terminology and notation of their own. This makes it unnecessarily difficult for nonsecurity-minded readers to get in touch with the specifications (and specifics) of the SSL/TLS protocols. This is unfortunate (to say the least).

When I started to compile a teaching module on SSL/TLS some time ago, I was surprised to learn that the few books that were available either addressed the technology only superficially or—maybe worse—were out of date. This was particularly true for the two reference books used in the field [1, 2]. They both appeared in 2000—which, at the time of this writing, is almost 10 years ago. Against this background, I decided to take my lecture notes and compile a new book that would not only address the fundamental principles of the SSL/TLS protocols, but would also try to explain the rationale behind their current design. The resulting book is intended for anyone who wants to get a deep understanding of the SSL/TLS protocols and their proper use—be it a theorist or practitioner. The major focus of the book is SSL/TLS, but it also addresses related topics, such as TLS extensions, datagram TLS (DTLS), firewall traversal, as well as public key certificates and public key infrastructures (PKIs). Its claim is to provide a comprehensive overview and discussion of the SSL/TLS protocols, and to put them into perspective.

Implementation issues are intentionally not addressed (or only addressed in a very superficial way). There are so many implementations of the SSL/TLS protocols, both freely and commercially available, that it literally makes no sense to address them in a book like the one you have in hand. If you want to practically use the SSL/TLS protocols (e.g., to secure an e-∗ application), then you have to delve into the documentation and technical specification of the development environment you are using anyway. This book is only aimed at providing the basic knowledge to understand these documents—you still have to capture and read them. In the case of OpenSSL, you may use [3] as a reference book. In the case of another library or development environment, you may be be confined to use the original documentation. Apart from implementation issues, I hope that the book is reasonably complete. If I have missed important topics, then I am the one to blame and I hope to have the opportunity to improve the book in the future.

This book assumes basic familiarity with the TCP/IP protocols and their working principles. This assumption is reasonable, because anybody not familar with TCP/IP is well advised to first get in touch and try to comprehend TCP/IP networking, before he or she moves on to the SSL/TLS protocols. Only trying to understand SSL/TLS is not likely to be fruitful. Readers who are unfamilar with TCP/IP networking can consult one of the many books describing TCP/IP. Among these books, I particularly recommend the classic books of Richard Stevens [4] and Douglas Comer [5], but there are many other (or rather complementary) books available in the shelves of the bookstores.

To properly understand the contents of this book, it is also necessary to have a working knowledge of the Internet standardization process. Again, this process is likely to be explained in a book on TCP/IP networking. It is also explained in RFC 2026 [6] and Section 2.3 of [7]. For each protocol specified in an RFC document, we are going to say whether it is submitted to the Internet Standards Track or specified for experimental or informational purposes. This distinction is important and relevant in practice.

When we discuss the practical use of the SSL/TLS protocols, it is highly recommended to visualize things with a network protocol analyzer, such as *Wireshark* (http://www.wireshark.org) or another software tool that provides similar functionalities. Wireshark is a freely available open source software tool released under the GNU General Public License. With regard to SSL/TLS, it is sufficiently complete, meaning that it can be used to analyze SSL/TLS-based data exchanges. We don't reproduce screenshots in this book, mainly because the graphical user interfaces (GUIs) of tools like Wireshark are highly nonlinear and the corresponding screenshots are difficult to read and interpret. When we use Wireshark output, we provide it in textual form. This is visually less stimulating, but more useful in practice.

Because the SSL/TLS protocols are cryptographic in nature, properly understanding them requires at least some basic familiarity with cryptography. I try to introduce and overview the basic principles of cryptography in a short primer in Chapter 2, but I am well aware of the fact that—due to space limitations—the treatment is fairly superficial and incomplete. Anyone who wants to get a more complete picture is advised to additionally consult a book on cryptography. I certainly recommend my own book entitled *Contemporary Cryptography* [8], but there are many other books that can be used instead (many of them are referenced in [8] and Chapter 2 of this book).

SSL/TLS: Theory and Practice is organized and structured in the following nine chapters:

- Chapter 1, *Introduction*, provides some fundamentals and basic principles that are necessary for a serious and deep treatment of network security protocols, such as the SSL/TLS protocols.

- Chapter 2, *Cryptography Primer*, provides a cryptography primer, meaning that it introduces, overviews, and puts into perspective the basic principles of cryptography as far as they are relevant for the SSL/TLS protocols.

- Chapter 3, *Transport Layer Security*, briefly overviews, explains, and puts into perspective the various technologies and protocols that can be used to provide basic security services at the transport layer of the TCP/IP protocol stack.

- Chapter 4, *SSL Protocol*, introduces, overviews, puts into perspective, and thoroughly discusses the first main transport layer security protocol (i.e., the SSL protocol).

- Chapter 5, *TLS Protocol*, does the same with the second main transport layer security protocol (i.e., the TLS protocol). Unlike Chapter 4, it does not start from scratch, but focuses on the main differences between the SSL and TLS protocols.

- Chapter 6, *DTLS Protocol*, elaborates on the DTLS protocol, which is basically a UDP version of the TLS protocol. Again, the chapter mainly focuses on the differences between the SSL/TLS protocols and the DTLS protocol.

- Chapter 7, *Firewall Traversal*, addresses the practically relevant and nontrivial problem of how the SSL/TLS protocols can (securely) traverse a firewall. This is a relevant topic for the practical deployment of the SSL/TLS protocols.

- Chapter 8, *Public Key Certificates and PKIs*, elaborates on the management of public key certificates used for the SSL/TLS protocols, for example, as part of a PKI. Again, this chapter is kept as short as possible and only addresses the issues that are relevant for the understanding of the SSL/TLS protocols and their proper use.

- Chapter 9, *Conclusions and Outlook*, also introduces and discusses a few research challenges for the future.

Last but not least, the book also includes an appendix summarizing the standardized TLS cipher suites, a list of abbreviations and acronyms, a page about me (as an author), and an index.

I hope that *SSL/TLS: Theory and Practice* serves your needs. Also, I would like to take the opportunity to invite you as a reader to let me know your opinions and thoughts. If you have something to correct or add, please let me know. If I have not expressed myself clearly, please let me know, too. I appreciate and sincerely welcome any comment or suggestion in order to update the book in future editions and turn it into a reference book that can be used for educational purposes. The best way to reach me is to send a message to rolf.oppliger@esecurity.ch. You can also visit the book's home page at http://books.esecurity.ch/ssltls.html. I use this page to periodically post errata lists, additional information, and complementary material. I am looking forward to hearing from you.

References

[1] Rescorla, E., *SSL and TLS: Designing and Building Secure Systems*. Addison-Wesley, Reading, MA, 2000.

[2] Thomas, S.A., *SSL and TLS Essentials: Securing the Web*. John Wiley & Sons, New York, NY, 2000.

[3] Viega, J., Messier, M., and P. Chandra, *Network Security with OpenSSL*. O'Reilly, Sebastopol, CA, 2002.

[4] Stevens, W.R., *TCP/IP Illustrated, Volume 1: The Protocols*. Addison-Wesley Professional, New York, NY, 1994.

[5] Comer, D.E., *Internetworking with TCP/IP Volume 1: Principles, Protocols, and Architecture*, 4th edition. Prentice Hall, Upper Saddle River, NJ, 2000.

[6] Bradner, S., "The Internet Standards Process—Revision 3," Request for Comments 2026 (BCP 9), October 1996.

[7] Oppliger, R., *Internet and Intranet Security*, 2nd edition. Artech House Publishers, Norwood, MA, 2002.

[8] Oppliger, R., *Contemporary Cryptography*. Artech House Publishers, Norwood, MA, 2005.

Acknowledgments

Many people have contributed to the writing and publication of this book. First of all, I thank the designers and developers of the SSL/TLS protocols. With their work, they have provided the basis for many network security solutions in use today. More specifically related to this book, I thank my brother, Hans Oppliger, and Ruedi Rytz for answering specific questions, reading parts of the manuscript, and discussing some interesting issues with me; David M. Piscitello for reviewing the entire manuscript and providing valuable feedback; and Taher Elgamal for contributing the foreword. Once again, the staff at Artech House has been enormously helpful in producing and promoting the book. Among these people, I am particularly grateful to Wayne Yuhasz, Penelope Comans, Rebecca Allendorf, and Erin Donahue. Last but not least, I am indebted to my family—my wife, Isabelle, and our beloved children, Lara and Marc. They have supported the book project, and without their encouragement, patience, and love, this book would not have come into existence. The book is dedicated to my parents. They raised me and formed my way of thinking in a very gentle, supporting, and exemplary way. It is my challenge to pass on this spirit and achieve something similar with our children.

Chapter 1

Introduction

In this introductory chapter, we start slowly and gradually work towards the topic of the book. More specifically, we provide the fundamentals and basic principles that are necessary for a serious and deep treatment of network security protocols in general, and the SSL/TLS protocols in particular. We start with a generic network security architecture or terminology framework known as the OSI security architecture in Section 1.1, introduce a security definition and elaborate on how the SSL/TLS protocols attempt to meet this definition in Section 1.2, and conclude with some final remarks in Section 1.3.

1.1 OSI SECURITY ARCHITECTURE

According to the IETF Internet Security Glossary published in RFC 2828 [1], a *security architecture* refers to "a plan and set of principles that describe (a) the security services that a system is required to provide to meet the needs of its users, (b) the system elements required to implement the services, and (c) the performance levels required in the elements to deal with the threat environment." As such, a security architecture is always the result of applying principles of systems engineering and addresses issues related to physical security, computer security, communication security, organizational security (e.g., administrative and personnel security), and legal security. This integral approach to security is important; too many systems and applications are built and deployed without having an appropriate security architecture in mind.

Following the line of argumentation introduced in [2], it is worthwhile to have a look at the real world to illustrate the importance of having (implemented) an appropriate security architecture. If, for example, we want to build a house, then the first—and often most important—person to talk to is the architect. We hardly know anything about architecture and the art or science of designing and building a house, so we feel comfortable having a professional deal with these issues on our behalves. One of the first things an architect does—either explicitly or implicitly—is a threat and risk analysis. For example, given the fact that most burglars enter a house through the front door, he or she makes sure that the house has a front door with a lock, and that entering the house always requires breaking either the door's lock or a windowpane. In general, the architect does not design the house with unbreakable windowpanes; unbreakable windowpanes are simply too expensive and impractical for normal houses. If, however, the house were to host a branch bank, then broken windows would be more likely to occur, and the architect would probably suggest to install unbreakable windowpanes (or no windows at all). Also, he or she would consult a security specialist to get a burglar alarm system and a vault. The bottom line is that the threat and risk analysis leads to an architecture that is reasonably secure for a given environment. This type of analysis is omnipresent in daily life; often we don't even realize that it is going on in the back of our heads.

Contrary to the real world, the importance of doing a threat and risk analysis and coming up with an appropriate security architecture is less common and hardly understood in the digital world. Too many companies and organizations try to avoid security architectures and directly go to ad hoc testing (also known as ethical hacking[1]). They hire external forces that attack and try to break into their systems, networks, or applications. If the forces do not suceed, then the customers assume (or rather hope) that they are secure. If, however, the forces suceed, then the customers assume (or rather know) that they are insecure. In this case, they patch the found vulnerabilities and security holes, and then they hope that they are done, meaning that they have found and eliminated all relevant vulnerabilities and security holes. Against this background, the decision whether a customer is secure or not looks arbitrary and mainly depends on the capabilities of the external forces and the tools they are aware of and have at hand.

An interesting point to note is that the real-world analogy of an "ethical hacker" would be an "ethical burglar," and that we don't see this profession in the real world. In fact, ex-burglars are seldom hired to break windowpanes or rob houses simply to show that the initiator is vulnerable. We know that we are vulnerable, and hence there is no market for ex-burglars to ethically break into houses. In the real world, we neither trust them nor do we believe in the value of such investigations (if this statement were wrong, then there would be a market for such services in the first place). Why should the digital world be different? In fact, it does not seem to be different, and breaking into computer systems and networks is always possible—it

---

1   One commonly cited difference between an ethical hacker and an adversary is that the former operates with the knowledge, authorization, and consent obtained in advance, whereas the latter operates without these features.

is just a question of time, talent, and expenditure. Another point to keep in mind and consider with care when it comes to ethical hacking is that such investigations mainly address threats from the outside. This is not particularly useful, as most statistics reveal the fact that many IT systems and networks are routinely attacked from the inside. This means that insiders should also be considered to be part of the threats model.

In the digital world, we need a clear understanding of what we are going to design and implement, what adversaries we should keep in mind and protect against, what resources (in terms of time and computational power) these adversaries typically have, what attack strategies are most likely to occur, what the implications are if an adversary succeeds, what reactions are planned, and so on. All of these considerations should be made in a comprehensive threat and risk analysis that is backed with a security audit. Based on this analysis and audit, a comprehensive security architecture must be defined and documented. Keep in mind that the security architecture is specific and situational, and that there is no such thing as a universally applicable security architecture.

In an attempt to extend the field of application of the Open Systems Interconnection (OSI) basic reference model, the Joint Technical Committee 1 (JTC1) of the International Organization for Standardization (ISO) and the International Electrotechnical Commission (IEC) appended a security architecture as part two of ISO/IEC 7498 in 1989 [3]. Since its publication, the OSI security architecture has turned out to be a primary reference for network security professionals working in the field. In 1991, the Telecommunication Standardization Sector of the International Telecommunication Union (ITU), also known as ITU-T, adopted the OSI security architecture in recommendation X.800 [4]. Also in the early 1990s, the Privacy and Security Research Group (PSRG) of the Internet Research Task Force (IRTF[2]) preliminarly adapted the OSI security architecture in a corresponding Internet security architecture published as an Internet-Draft.[3] In essence, ISO/IEC 7498-2, ITU-T X.800, and the Internet security architecture draft all describe the same security architecture, and in this book we use the term *OSI security architecture* to refer to all of them. Contrary to the OSI basic reference model, the OSI security architecture is in widespread use today—at least for referential purposes.

In essence, the OSI security architecture provides a general description of security services and related security mechanisms and discusses their interrelationships. It also shows how the security services map onto a given network architecture

---

2 The IRTF is a sister group to the Internet Engineering Task Force (IETF). Its stated mission is "To promote research of importance to the evolution of the future Internet by creating focused, long-term and small Research Groups working on topics related to Internet protocols, applications, architecture and technology."
3 This work has been abandoned.

and briefly discusses their appropriate placement within the OSI reference model. Having the definition of a security architecture according to [1] in mind, it is quite obvious that the OSI security architecture as specified in [3] and [4] does not conform to it. In fact, the OSI security architecture rather refers to a terminological framework and a general description of security services and related security mechanisms than a full-fledged security architecture. For convenience, we still use the term OSI security architecture in this book. But keep in mind that an e-∗ application usually requires a security architecture that is more comprehensive and situational. It may use the OSI security architecture as a starting point, but it normally has to go beyond it and be more specific.

Table 1.1
Classes of OSI Security Services

1	Peer entity authentication service
	Data origin authentication service
2	Access control service
3	Connection confidentiality service
	Connectionless confidentiality service
	Selected field confidentiality service
	Traffic flow confidentiality service
4	Connection integrity service with recovery
	Connection integrity service without recovery
	Selected field connection integrity service
	Connectionless integrity service
	Selected field connectionless integrity service
5	Nonrepudiation with proof of origin
	Nonrepudiation with proof of delivery

1.1.1 Security Services

As shown in Table 1.1, the OSI security architecture distinguishes between five classes of security services (i.e., authentication, access control, data confidentiality, data integrity, and nonrepudiation[4] services). Just as layers define functionality in the OSI reference model, so do services in the OSI security architecture. These services may be placed at appropriate layers in the OSI reference model.

---

4   There is some controversy in the community regarding the correct spelling of the term "nonrepudiation." In fact, the OSI security architecture uses "non-repudiation" instead of "nonrepudiation," and there are many people still using this spelling. In this book, however, we use the more modern spelling of the term without a hyphen.

1.1.1.1 Authentication Services

As its name suggests, an *authentication service* is to provide for the authentication of a communicating peer entity or data origin. The corresponding services are slightly different:

- A *peer entity authentication service* provides each entity in an association with the ability to verify that the peer entity is what it claims to be. In particular, a peer entity authentication service provides assurance that an entity is not attempting to masquerade or performing an unauthorized replay. Peer entity authentication is typically performed either during a connection establishment phase or, occasionally, during a data transfer phase.
- A *data origin authentication service* allows the source of data received to be verified to be as claimed. A data origin authentication service is typically provided during a data transfer phase. It cannot provide protection against the duplication or modification of data units. To achieve this, the data origin authentication service must be complemented with a data integrity service.

Authentication services are important and a prerequisite for the provision of authorization, access control, and accountability services. Authorization refers to the process of granting rights, which includes the granting of access based on access rights. Access control refers to the process of enforcing access rights, and accountability refers to the property that actions of an entity can be traced uniquely to this particular entity.

1.1.1.2 Access Control Services

Access control services are to protect system resources against unauthorized use. The use of a system resource is unauthorized, if the entity that seeks to use the resource does not have the privileges or permissions necessary to do so. As such, access control services are typically the most commonly thought of services in computer and network security. But as mentioned above, access control services are closely tied to authentication services: a user or process acting on the user's behalf must usually be authenticated before an access control service can be invoked. Authentication and access control services therefore usually go hand in hand—this is why people sometimes use the term *authentication and authorization infrastructure* (AAI) to refer to an infrastructure that provides support for both authentication and authorization in terms of access control.

1.1.1.3 Data Confidentiality Services

In general parlance, data confidentiality refers to the property that data is not made available or disclosed to unauthorized individuals, entities, or processes, and hence *data confidentiality services* protect data from unauthorized disclosure. There are several forms of such services:

- A *connection confidentiality service* provides confidentiality for all data transferred over a connection.
- A *connectionless confidentiality service* provides confidentiality for individual data units.
- A *selective field confidentiality service* provides confidentiality for certain fields within individual data units or data transmitted in a connection.
- A *traffic flow confidentiality service* provides confidentiality for traffic flows, meaning that it attempts to protect all data that is associated with and communicated in a traffic flow from further analysis. Traffic analysis, in turn, can be defined as the "inference of information from observable characteristics of data flow(s), even when the data is encrypted or otherwise not directly available. Such characteristics include the identities and locations of the source(s) and destination(s), and the presence, amount, frequency, and duration of occurrence" [1].

The first three confidentiality services can be implemented in a simple and straightforward way by using standard cryptographic techniques. This is not necessarily the case for traffic flow confidentiality services. In fact, the provision of traffic flow confidentiality services is inherently more involved; it is certainly beyond the scope of SSL/TLS.

1.1.1.4 Data Integrity Services

Data integrity refers to the property that data is not altered or destroyed in some unauthorized way, and hence *data integrity services* are to protect data from unauthorized modification. Again, there are several forms of such services:

- A *connection integrity service with recovery* provides integrity for all data transmitted in a connection. If possible, the loss of integrity is recovered.
- A *connection integrity service without recovery* is similar to a connection integrity service with recovery, except that the loss of integrity is not recovered.

- A *selected field connection integrity service* provides integrity for specific fields within the data transmitted in a connection.
- A *connectionless integrity service* provides integrity for indiviual data units.
- A *selected field connectionless integrity service* provides integrity for specific fields within indiviual data units.

The use of a peer entity authentication service at the start of a connection and a connection integrity service during the connection can jointly provide for the corroboration of the source of all data units transferred on the connection, the integrity of those data units, and may additionally detect data units that are duplicated.

1.1.1.5 Nonrepudiation Services

Nonrepudiation services are implemented to prevent an entity involved in a communication from later denying having participated in all or part of the communication. In a messaging environment, for example, such services protect against an originator denying that he or she has originated the message, or a recipient denying that he or she has received the message. Consequently, there are at least two nonrepudiation services that are relevant in practice:

- A *nonrepudiation service with proof of origin* provides the recipient of a message with a proof of origin.
- A *nonrepudiation service with proof of delivery* provides the sender of a message with a proof of delivery.

Nonrepudiation services are increasingly important for many Internet-based e-commerce (e.g., [5]). Consider, for example, the situation in which an investor communicates with his or her stockbroker over the Internet. If the investor decides to sell a large number of stocks, then he or she sends a corresponding request to the stockbroker. If the prices are about to change only moderately, then everything works fine. But if the stock price raises sharply, then the investor may deny ever sending the order to sell the stocks. Conversely, it is possible that under reverse circumstances the stockbroker may deny receiving the order to sell the stocks. In situations like these, the provision of nonrepudiation services ought to be mandatory.

1.1.2 Security Mechanisms

In addition to the security services mentioned above, the OSI security architecture also itemizes security mechanisms that may be used to implement the services. A distinction is made between specific security mechanisms and pervasive ones.

Table 1.2
OSI Specific Security Mechanisms

1	Encipherment
2	Digital signature mechanisms
3	Access control mechanisms
4	Data integrity mechanisms
5	Authentication exchange mechanisms
6	Traffic padding mechanisms
7	Routing control mechanisms
8	Notarization mechanisms

1.1.2.1 Specific Security Mechanisms

Specific security mechanisms may be incorporated into an appropriate layer to provide some of the security services mentioned in Section 1.1.1. As shown in Table 1.2, the OSI security architecture enumerates eight specific security mechanisms that can be characterized as follows:

1. *Encipherment* can be used to protect the confidentiality of data units or to support or complement other security mechanisms. The cryptographic techniques used for encipherment are introduced in Chapter 2.

2. *Digital signature mechanisms* can be used to provide an electronic analog of handwritten signatures for electronic documents. Like handwritten signatures, digital signatures must not be forgeable, a recipient must be able to verify it, and the signatory must not be able to repudiate it later. But unlike handwritten signatures, digital signatures incorporate the data (or a hash value of the data) that is signed. Different data therefore results in different signatures even if the signatory remains the same. Again, we postpone the discussion of digital signature mechanisms to Chapter 2.

3. *Access control mechanisms* can be used to control access to system resources. Traditionally, a distinction is made between a discretionary access control (DAC) and a mandatory access control (MAC) [6]. In either case, the access control is described in terms of subjects, objects, and access rights:

- A subject is an entity that attempts to access objects. This can be a host, a user, or an application.
- An object is a resource to which access needs to be controlled. This can range from an individual data field in a file to a large program.
- Access rights specify the level of authority for a subject to access an object, so access rights are defined for each subject-object-pair. Examples of UNIX-style access rights are read, write, and execute.

More recently, people have introduced the notion of a role and have developed role-based access controls (RBACs) to make the assignment of access rights to subjects more dynamic and flexible (e.g., [7, 8]).

4. *Data integrity mechanisms* can be used to protect the integrity of data—be it individual data units or fields within them or sequences of data units or fields within them. Note that data integrity mechanisms, in general, do not protect against replay attacks that work by recording and replaying previously sent valid messages. Also, protecting the integrity of a sequence of data units and fields within these data units generally requires some form of explicit ordering, such as sequence numbering, time-stamping, or cryptographic chaining.

5. *Authentication exchange mechanisms* can be used to verify the claimed identities of entities. It is common to use the term *strong* to refer to an authentication exchange mechanism that uses cryptographic techniques to protect the messages that are exchanged, and *weak* to refer to an authentication exchange mechanism that does not do so. It goes without saying that weak authentication exchange mechanisms are vulnerable to passive wiretapping and replay attacks.

6. *Traffic padding mechanisms* can be used to protect against traffic analysis. It works by having the data originator generate and transmit randomly composed data hand in hand with the actual data. Only the data originator and intended recipient(s) know how these data are transmitted; thus, an unauthorized party who captures and attempts to replay the data cannot distinguish the randomly generated data from meaningful data.

7. *Routing control mechanisms* can be used to choose—either dynamically or by prearrangement—specific routes for data transmission. Communicating systems may, on detection of persistent passive or active attacks, wish to instruct the network service provider to establish a connection via a different route. Similarly, data carrying certain security labels may be forbidden by

policy to pass through certain networks or links. Routing control mechanisms are not always available, but if they are they tend to be very effective.

8. *Notarization mechanisms* can be used to assure certain properties of the data communicated between two or more entities, such as its integrity, origin, time, or destination. The assurance is provided by a trusted party—sometimes also called trusted third party (TTP)—in a testifiable manner.

All specific security mechanisms except access control, traffic padding, and routing control mechanisms are employed by the SSL/TLS protocols. Access control mechanisms must be used above the transport layer (typically at the application layer), whereas traffic padding and routing control mechanisms are best invoked underneath the transport layer.

1.1.2.2 Pervasive Security Mechanisms

Contrary to specific security mechanisms, pervasive security mechanisms are generally not specific to a particular security service. Some of these mechanisms can even be regarded as aspects of security management. As shown in Table 1.3, the OSI security architecture enumerates the following five security mechanisms that are pervasive in this sense:

Table 1.3
OSI Pervasive Security Mechanisms

1	Trusted functionality
2	Security labels
3	Event detection
4	Security audit trail
5	Security recovery

1. As its name suggests, *trusted functionality* is about functionality that can be trusted to perform as intended. From a security perspective, any functionality (provided by a service and implemented by a mechanism) should be trusted, and hence trusted functionality is a pervasive security mechanism that is orthogonal to all specific security mechanisms itemized above.

2. System resources may have *security labels* associated with them, for example, to indicate a sensitivity level. This allows the resources to be treated in an appropriate way. For example, it allows data to be encrypted transparently (i.e., without user invocation) for transmission. In general, a security label may be additional data associated with the data or it may be implicit (e.g.,

implied by the use of a specific key to encipher data or implied by the context of the data such as the source address or route).

3. It is increasingly important to complement preventive security mechanisms with detective and even corrective ones. This basically means that security-related events must be detected in one way or another. This is where *event detection* as another pervasive security mechanism comes into play. Event detection basically depends on heuristics.

4. A security audit refers to an independent review and examination of system records and activities to test for adequacy of system controls, to ensure compliance with established policy and operational procedures, to detect breaches in security, and to recommend any indicated changes in control, policy, and procedures. Consequently, a *security audit trail* refers to data collected and potentially used to facilitate a security audit. Needless to say that this a very fundamental and important pervasive security mechanism.

5. As mentioned above, corrective security mechanisms are getting more and more important. *Security recovery* is about implementing corrective security mechanisms and putting them in appropriate places. Similar to event detection, security recovery largely depends on heuristics.

The SSL/TLS protocols do not prescribe any pervasive security mechanism. Instead, it is up to a particular implementation to support one or several pervasive security mechanisms. It goes without saying that SSL/TLS alert messages at least provide a basis for event detection, security audit trail, and security recovery.

Last but not least, we recapitulate the fact that the OSI security architecture has not been developed to solve a particular network security problem, but rather to provide the network security community with a terminology that can be used to consistently describe and discuss security-related problems and corresponding solutions. In this book, we use the OSI security architecture exactly for this purpose.

1.2 SECURITY DEFINITION

With the profileration of the Internet and WWW for e-∗ applications, security has become a major issue. But the term *security* has many facets, and it not always clear what people mean when they talk about security (sometimes it is not even clear that they mean anything in the first place). Instead of properly analyzing the security requirements of an e-∗ application, people sometimes just bring in terms like *SSL* or *TLS*. Since the SSL/TLS protocols are not known to be insecure, people are expected to get a good feeling about the security of the e-∗ application. It goes without saying that the reduction of security to SSL/TLS is inappropriate and overly simplified, and that a deeper security discussion is required most of the time. The statement "SSL/TLS equals security" is wrong and sometimes even dangerous (because it leads to an easygoing user behavior).

In order to make precise statements about the security of a system, such as an e-∗ application, one must understand the security requirements of the application and how these are satisfied through deployment and administration. Unfortunately, reality looks different, and the world is full of systems that claim to be secure without providing an appropriate definition for security. This is unfortunate, because anything can be claimed to be secure, unless its meaning is defined and precisely nailed down. In general, a security definition must answer (at least) the following two questions:

1. *What are the capabilities of the adversary one has in mind?* An answer to this question must specifiy, for example, the adversary's computing power, available memory, available time, types of feasible attacks, and access to a priori or side information. Properly answering this question culminates in a threats model.

2. *What is the task the adversary must solve in order to be successful (i.e., to break the security of the system)?* In a typical setting, the adversary's task is to find (i.e., compute, guess, or otherwise determine) one or several pieces of information he or she should not be able to know. For example, if the adversary is able to determine a secret key used for encryption, then he or she must certainly be considered to be successful. There are, however, also weaker forms of attacks that may still be considered to be successful. For example, the adversary may be able to determine only the first plaintext bit or byte of a given ciphertext. This task may be simpler to solve, but being able to solve it may still be devastating in a given situation. For example, if the adversary knows that the plaintext message is either "Yes" or "No," then being able to determine the first plaintext byte reveals the entire plaintext message.

Strong security definitions are obtained when the adversary is assumed to be as powerful as possible, whereas the task he or she must solve is assumed to be as simple as possible. Let us consider a real-world analogy to illustrate this point: if we play a soccer game, then we may consider two scenarios:

1. Our team is playing against the world's best players and they are not even able to make a single goal.

2. Our team is playing against a group of schoolboys and they are not able to win the game.

In this example, it is obvious that our team is better in the first case. The adversary is stronger (i.e., the world's best soccer players) and the task to solve is simpler (i.e., make a single goal). Consequently, if this overly strong adversary is not able to solve even this simple task, then we are really good. In computer security, the situation is comparable. We assume a strong adversary who must solve a simple task. If he or she does not succeed, then we can feel secure.

More generally, we capture the notion of a secure system in the following Definition 1.1.

Definition 1.1 (Secure system) *A system is secure if an adversary with specified capabilities is not able to break it, meaning that he or she is not able to solve the specified task.*

Following the line of argumentation given above, there are different degrees of security (depending on the adversary and the task to solve) that fulfill Definition 1.1. If we want to argue about the security of a particular system, then we must at least answer the two questions itemized above. This applies in all cases, and hence it also applies to the SSL/TLS protocols or any e-* application that employs them.

With regard to the first question, it is reasonable to make standard cryptographic assumptions, such as that the adversary is polynomially bounded in terms of computational power and time, meaning that he or she cannot factorize large integers, compute discrete logarithms, and so on, and that the standard *Dolev-Yao model* [9] applies. In this model, the adversary is yet able to control the communications network used to transmit messages, but he or she is not able to compromise the end systems. This basically means that the adversary can mount all kinds of (passive and active) attacks on the network. Roughly speaking, a passive attack "attempts to learn or make use of information from the system but does not affect system resources," whereas an active attack "attempts to alter system resources or affect their operation" [1]. Obviously, passive and active attacks can (and will) be combined to effectively invade a computing or networking environment. For example, a passive wiretapping attack can be used to eavesdrop on the authentication information that is transmitted in the clear (e.g., username and password), and this information can then be used to masquerade the user and to actively attack the system accordingly. The SSL/TLS protocols have been designed to be secure in the Dolev-Yao model, but the model has some limitations and shortcomings. For example, many contemporary attacks are either based on malware or employ sophisticated techniques to spoof the user interface of the client systen. These attacks are outside the scope of the Dolev-Yao model, and hence the model needs to be extended. This is a current topic in network security research.

With regard to the second question, things are even more involved. We already mentioned the case in which the adversary is able to determine the first plaintext bit or byte from a given ciphertext. Whether this poses a problem mainly depends on the application context. Again, if we know, for example, that a given message represents either "Yes" or "No," then the decryption of the very first byte is sufficient to reveal the entire plaintext message. Similar situations occur if only a few plaintext messages are possible in the first place. To be as application-independent as possible, one usually requires that even a very simple task is impossible or infeasible to solve for the adversary one has in mind. For example, theorists often assume an ideal system and require that an adversary cannot tell a real system apart form this ideal system with a probability significantly greater than guessing. Note that telling two systems apart is indeed the simplest task to solve for an adversary, because any difference between the systems can be exploited. So if the real system cannot be told apart from the ideal system, then the real system obviously behaves like the ideal system, and hence, for all practical purposes, the real system implements the ideal system. Using this line of argumentation, many cryptographic systems have been shown to be secure in the past—at least in theory. Because people are looking for tasks that are as simple to solve as possible, they usually get nervous when a vulnerability is found in a real system. It may not be obvious how to exploit the vulnerability, but its mere existence may still lead to corrective actions. For example, as further addressed in Section 5.3, when some original block ciphers in CBC mode were shown to leak information, the TLS protocol specification was immediately modified to deal with the defect. This pattern frequently occurs and presses ahead with research and development.

The bottom line is that properly defining security is not trivial, and that one has to be very careful about the security definition one uses and refers to in a particular environment. This obviously also applies to the SSL/TLS protocols and the e-∗ applications that employ them.

1.3 FINAL REMARKS

In this chapter, we provided the fundamentals and basic principles that are necessary for a serious and deep treatment of cryptographic network security protocols, such as the SSL/TLS protocols. More specifically, we introduced and overviewed the OSI security architecture and possibilities to define security. We will use both topics in this book: we use the OSI security architecture as a terminology framework and we use the possibilities to define security whenever we claim that something is secure. With regard to the second point, we want to be precise in this book. We avoid striking statements about the security of the SSL/TLS protocols; instead, we want to specifically say what security services the SSL/TLS protocols are able to provide and what (specific and/or pervasive) security mechanisms are employed to actually provide the services. Also, when we elaborate on security-related modifications of the SSL/TLS protocols, we want to be specific and explain the attacks the modifications are intended to protect against. If there is no attack a modification can protect against, then the modification is useless and can be discarded in the first place. Or, alternatively speaking, if an attack is not relevant in a given application context, then the modification need not be considered in the first place. These considerations are important to put things into perspective.

References

[1] Shirey, R., "Internet Security Glossary," Informational Request for Comments 2828 (FYI 36), May 2000.

[2] Oppliger, R., "IT Security: In Search of the Holy Grail," *Communications of the ACM*, Vol. 50, No. 2, February 2007, pp. 96–98.

[3] ISO/IEC 7498-2, Information Processing Systems—Open Systems Interconnection Reference Model—Part 2: Security Architecture, 1989.

[4] ITU X.800, Security Architecture for Open Systems Interconnection for CCITT Applications, 1991 (CCITT is the acronym of "Comité Consultatif International Téléphonique et Télégraphique," which is the former name of the ITU).

[5] Zhou, J., *Non-Repudiation in Electronic Commerce*. Artech House Publishers, Norwood, MA, 2001.

[6] Bishop, M., *Computer Security: Art and Science*. Addison-Wesley, Reading, MA, 2002.

[7] Ferraiolo, D.F., Kuhn, D.R., and R. Chandramouli, *Role-Based Access Controls*, 2nd edition. Artech House Publishers, Norwood, MA, 2007.

[8] Coyne, E.J., and J.M. Davis, *Role Engineering for Enterprise Security Management*. Artech House Publishers, Norwood, MA, 2008.

[9] Dolev, D., and A.C. Yao, "On the Security of Public Key Protocols," *Proceedings of the IEEE 22nd Annual Symposium on Foundations of Computer Science*, 1981, pp. 350–357.

Chapter 2

Cryptography Primer

Cryptography is an increasingly important and broad subject area that is covered in many books (e.g., [1–20] itemized in alphabetical order with regard to their respective authors). In this chapter, we provide a short cryptography primer, meaning that we introduce, overview, and put into perspective the basic principles of cryptography as far as they are relevant for a proper understanding of the SSL/TLS protocols. In Section 2.1, we introduce the topic, in Section 2.2, we overview and put into perspective the cryptosystems in use today, and in Section 2.3, we conclude with some final remarks. As already mentioned in the Preface, more information is available, for example, in [15].

2.1 INTRODUCTION

In this section, we introduce cryptography at a fairly high level of abstraction. We start with some preliminary remarks mainly regarding terminology, introduce cryptographic systems (cryptosystems), distinguish between three classes of cryptosystems, elaborate on secure cryptosystems, provide some historical background information, and briefly overview the legal situation.

2.1.1 Preliminary Remarks

The term *cryptology* is derived from the Greek words "kryptós," standing for "hidden," and "lógos," standing for "word." Consequently, the meaning of the term cryptology is best paraphrased as "hidden word." This paraphrase refers to the original intent of cryptology, namely to hide the meaning of specific words and to protect their confidentiality and secrecy accordingly. From today's perspective, this viewpoint is too narrow and the term cryptology is used for many other security-related purposes and applications (this point should become clear in the remaining part of this chapter).

Cryptology refers to the mathematical science and field of study that comprises both cryptography and cryptanalysis.

- The term *cryptography* is derived from the Greek words "kryptós" (see above) and "gráphein," standing for "write." Consequently, the meaning of the term cryptography is best paraphrased as "hidden writing." According to [21], cryptography refers to the "mathematical science that deals with transforming data to render its meaning unintelligible (i.e., to hide its semantic content), prevent its undetected alteration, or prevent its unauthorized use. If the transformation is reversible, cryptography also deals with restoring encrypted data to intelligible form." Consequently, cryptography refers to the process of protecting data in a very broad sense.

- The term *cryptanalysis* is derived from the Greek words "kryptós" (see above) and "analýein," standing for "to loosen." Consequently, the meaning of the term cryptanalysis can be paraphrased as "to loosen the hidden word." This paraphrase refers to the process of destroying the cryptographic protection, or—more generally—to study the security properties and possibilities to break cryptographic techniques and systems. Again referring to [21], the term cryptanalysis is used to refer to the "mathematical science that deals with analysis of a cryptographic system in order to gain knowledge needed to break or circumvent the protection that the system is designed to provide." As such, the cryptanalyst is the antagonist of the cryptographer, meaning that his or her job is to break or at least circumvent the protection the cryptographer has designed and implemented in the first place. Quite naturally, there is an arms race going on between cryptographers and cryptanalysts.

Many other definitions for the terms cryptology, cryptography, and cryptanalysis are available in the literature. For example, the term cryptography is sometimes said to refer to the study of mathematical techniques related to all aspects of information security (e.g., [12]). These aspects include (but are not restricted to) data confidentiality, data integrity, entity authentication, data origin authentication, and/or nonrepudiation. Again, this definition is broad and comprises anything that is directly or indirectly related to information security.

In some literature, the term cryptology is even said to include steganography (in addition to cryptography and cryptanalysis).

- The term *steganography* is derived from the Greek words "steganos," standing for "impenetrable," and "gráphein" (see above). Consequently, the meaning of the term steganography can be paraphrased as "impenetrable writing." According to [21], the term steganography refers to "methods of hiding the existence of a message or other data. This is different than cryptography, which hides the meaning of a message but does not hide the message itself." Let us consider an analogy to make this point more clear: if we have money to protect or safeguard, then we can either hide its existence (by putting it, for example, under a mattress), or we can put it in a safe that is assumed to be burglarproof. In the first case, we are referring to steganographic methods, whereas in the second case, we are referring to cryptographic methods. An example of a formerly used steganographic method is invisible ink. Contemporary methods are more sophisticated and try to hide additional information in electronic files. In general, this information is arbitrary. It may, however, also be used to name the owner of a file or its recipient(s). In the first case, one refers to *digital watermarking*, whereas in the second case, one refers to *digital fingerprinting*. Digital watermarking and fingerprinting are currently very active areas of research and development (e.g., [22, 23]).

It goes without saying that cryptographic and steganographic techniques are not mutually exclusive, and that they can be combined to complement each other. In fact, there are increasingly many products that combine cryptographic and steganographic techniques in innovative and ingenious ways. We only refer to TrueCrypt's hidden volumes that are to provide plausible deniability.

2.1.2 Cryptographic Systems

According to [21], the term *cryptographic system* (or *cryptosystem* in short) refers to "a set of cryptographic algorithms together with the key management processes that support use of the algorithms in some application context." Again, this definition is broad and comprises all kinds of cryptographic algorithms and protocols.[1] The term *algorithm*, in turn, is usually defined as a well-defined computational procedure that takes a variable input and generates a corresponding output. It is sometimes also required that an algorithm halts within a reasonable amount of time. Typically, one distinguishes between deterministic and probabilistic algorithms.

---

[1] In some literature, the term *cryptographic scheme* is used to refer to a cryptographic system. Unfortunately, it is seldom explained what the difference(s) between a (cryptographic) scheme and a system really is (are). So for the purpose of this book, we don't make a distinction, and we use the term cryptographic system to refer to either of them. We hope that this simplification is not too confusing. In the realm of digital signatures, for example, people frequently talk about digital signature schemes. In this book, however, we are consistently talking about digital signature systems and actually mean the same thing.

- An algorithm is *deterministic* if its behavior is completely determined by the input. Consequently, the algorithm always generates the same output for the same input (if executed multiple times).

- An algorithm is *probabilistic* (or *randomized*) if its behavior is not completely determined by the input, meaning that the algorithm internally uses and takes advantage of randomly or pseudorandomly generated values. Consequently, a probabilistic algorithm may generate a different output each time it is executed with the same input.

If more than one entity takes part in the execution of an algorithm (or the computational procedure it defines, respectively), then one is in the realm of *protocols*. Consequently, a protocol can be viewed as a distributed algorithm in which two or more entities take part. Alternatively, one can also define a protocol as a distributed algorithm in which a set of entities (instead of two or more entities) takes part. In this case, it becomes immediately clear that an algorithm also represents a protocol, namely one that is degenerated in a specific sense (i.e., the set consists of only one entity). Hence, an algorithm can always be viewed as a special case of a protocol. The major distinction between an algorithm and a protocol is that only one entity is involved in the former, whereas typically two or more entities are involved in the latter. This distinguishing fact is important and must be kept in mind when one talks about algorithms and protocols (not only cryptographic ones). For example, it becomes immediately clear that protocols are typically more involved than algorithms. Similar to an algorithm, a protocol may be deterministic or probabilistic—depending on whether the protocol internally uses random values.

In cryptography, one is typically interested in *cryptographic algorithms* and *cryptographic protocols* (i.e., algorithms and protocols that employ and make use of cryptographic techniques and mechanisms). Remember the definition for a cryptographic system (or cryptosystem) given above. According to this definition, a cryptosystem may comprise more than one algorithm, and the algorithms need not necessarily be executed by the same entity (i.e., they may be executed by multiple entities in a distributed way). Consequently, this notion of a cryptosystem comprises the notion of a cryptographic protocol as suggested above. Hence, another way to look at cryptographic algorithms and protocols is to say that a cryptographic algorithm is a *single-entity cryptosystem*, whereas a cryptographic protocol is a *multientity* or *multiple entities cryptosystem*. These terms, however, are not really used in the literature.

It is important to note that cryptographic applications may consist of multiple (sub)protocols, that these (sub)protocols and their concurrent executions may interact in some subtle ways, and that these interactions and interdependencies may be exploited by chosen-protocol attacks (see, for example, [24]). As of this writing, we are just at the beginning of properly understanding chosen-protocol attacks and how they can be used in practice.

In the cryptographic literature, it is quite common to use human names to refer to the entities that take part and participate in a cryptographic protocol. For example, in a two-party protocol the participating entities are usually called *Alice* and *Bob*. This is a convenient way of making things unambiguous with relatively few words, since the pronoun *she* can then be used for Alice, and *he* can be used for Bob. The disadvantage of this naming scheme is that people assume that the names are referring to people. This need not be the case, and Alice, Bob, and all other entities may be computer systems, cryptographic devices, or anything else. In this book, we don't follow the tradition of using Alice, Bob, and the rest of the gang. Instead, we use single-letter characters, such as A, B, C, ..., to refer to the entities that take part and participate in a cryptographic protocol. This is less fun (we guess), but more appropriate (we hope). At least it gives us the opportunity to distinguish between the devices that implement cryptographic techniques and mechanisms and the human users of these devices.

2.1.3 Classes of Cryptographic Systems

Cryptographic systems may or may not use secret parameters (e.g., cryptographic keys). If secret parameters are used, then they may or may not be shared between the participating entities. Consequently, there are three classes of cryptographic systems (see Definitions 2.1–2.3).

Definition 2.1 (Unkeyed cryptosystem) *An unkeyed cryptosystem is a cryptographic system that uses no secret parameter.*

Representatives of unkeyed cryptosystems are one-way functions, cryptographic hash functions, and random bit generators as outlined in Section 2.2.1.

Definition 2.2 (Secret key cryptosystem) *A secret key cryptosystem is a cryptographic system that uses secret parameters that are shared between the participating entities.*

Representatives of secret key cryptosystems are symmetric encryption systems, message authentication codes, and pseudorandom bit generators (PRBGs) as outlined in Section 2.2.2.

Definition 2.3 (Public key cryptosystem) *A public key cryptosystem is a cryptographic system that uses secret parameters that are not shared between the participating entities.*

Representatives of public key cryptosystems are asymmetric encryption systems, digital signature systems, and key agreement protocols as outlined in Section 2.2.3.

More concrete examples of unkeyed, secret key, and public key cryptosystems are given in the sections referenced above. Let us now focus on the notion of a "secure" cryptosystem.

2.1.4 Secure Cryptosystems

The goal of cryptography is to design, implement, deploy, and make use of cryptographic systems that are secure in some meaningful way. In order to make precise statements about the security of a cryptosystem, one must formally define the term security. According to Section 1.2, one must answer at least two questions:

- What are the capabilities of the adversary?
- What is the task the adversary must solve in order to be successful (i.e., to break the security of the system)?

Referring to Definition 1.1, a cryptographic system is *secure* if an adversary with specified capabilities is not able to break it, meaning that he or she is not able to solve the specified task. Consequently, there are several notions of security that can be considered for a cryptographic system (one for every adversary and every possible task to solve). Depending on the adversary's capabilities, for example, there are two notions of security usually distinguished in the literature.

Unconditional security: If the adversary is not able to solve the task even with infinite computing power, then we talk about *unconditional* or *information-theoretic security*. The mathematical theories behind this type of security are probability theory and information theory.

Conditional security: If the adversary is theoretically able to solve the task, but it is computationally infeasible for him or her (meaning that he or she is not able to solve the task given his or her resources, capabilities, and access to a priori or side information), then we talk about *conditional* or *computational security*. The mathematical theory behind this type of security is computational complexity theory.

In some literature, *provable security* is mentioned as yet another notion of security. The idea of provable security goes back to the early days of public key cryptography, when Whitfield Diffie and Martin E. Hellman proposed a complexity-based proof (for the security of a public key cryptosystem) [25]. The idea is to show that breaking a cryptosystem is computationally equivalent to solving a hard mathematical problem. This means that one must prove the following two statements:

- If the hard problem can be solved, then the cryptosystem can be broken.
- If the cryptosystem can be broken, then the hard problem can be solved.

Diffie and Hellman proved only the first statement for their key exchange protocol. This is unfortunate, because the second statement is also important for the security of a system. If we can prove that an adversary who is able to break a cryptosystem is also able to solve the hard problem, then we can argue that it is very unlikely that such an adversary really exists and hence that the cryptosystem in question is likely to be secure. The notion of provable security has fueled a lot of research and there are many public key cryptosystems shown to be provably secure in this sense. It is, however, also important to note that a complexity-based proof is not absolute and that it is only relative to the assumed intractability of the underlying mathematical problem(s).

Provable security is difficult to achieve for complex cryptographic systems, such as security protocols. More recently, people have therefore come up with a methodology to design systems that are not really provably secure, but for which one can at least have a "good feeling" about their security properties [26]. The basic idea is to design an *ideal system* that employs one (or several) random function(s)—also known as random oracle(s)—and to prove the security of this system mathematically. The ideal system is then implemented in a *real system* by replacing each random oracle with a "good" and "appropriately chosen" publicly known pseudorandom function—typically a cryptographic hash function, such as MD5 or SHA-1. This way, one obtains an implementation of the ideal system in the real world (where random oracles do not exist). If the pseudorandom functions in use have good properties, then one can hope that the security proof of the ideal system is inherited to the real system. It is not a proof anymore, but it may still provide evidence for the security of the real system. Due to the use of random oracles, this design methodology is known as *random oracle methodology*; it yields cryptographic systems that are provably secure in the so-called *random oracle model*. Unfortunately, it has been shown that it is possible to craft cryptographic systems that are provably secure in the random oracle model, but become totally insecure whenever a cryptographic hash function is specified and nailed down [27]. This theoretical result is worrisome, and since its publication many researchers have started to think controversially about the usefulness of the random oracle methodology. In fact, most researchers prefer security proofs that do not require random oracles.

In the past, we have seen many examples in which people have tried to improve the security of a cryptographic system by keeping secret its design and internal working principles. This approach is sometimes referred to as "security through obscurity." Many of these systems do not work and can be broken trivially.[2] This insight has a long tradition in cryptography, and there is a well-known cryptographic principle—the *Kerckhoffs' principle*[3]—that basically states that a cryptographic system should be designed so as to be secure even when the adversary knows all details of the system, except for the values explicitly declared to be secret, such as cryptographic keys [28]. Kerckhoffs' principle is certainly something to keep in mind when one designs cryptographic systems.

Last but not least, it is important to note that a theoretically secure cryptosystem may not remain secure when implemented in practice, and that there are usually many possibilities to mount attacks against a concrete implementation of such a system (e.g., [29]). For example, there are many attacks that take advantage of and try to exploit side channel information an implementation may leak. Side channel information, in turn, is information that can be retrieved from the execution of the cryptosystem that is neither the specified input nor the specified output. In the case of an encryption system, for example, the specified input refers to the plaintext message and the key, whereas the specified output refers to the ciphertext. Hence, side channel information is information an implementation of the encryption system may leak except for the plaintext message, the key, or the ciphertext. This includes, for example, timing information, power consumption, as well as radiation of all sorts. Attacks that try to exploit side channel information are called *side channel attacks*. Since about the middle of the 1990s, researchers have found and come up with many possibilities to mount side channel attacks. Examples include timing attacks [30], differential power analysis [31], and fault analysis [32, 33]. It is reasonable to say that every computation done on a real computer system leads to physical effects and phenomena that may be measured and exploited to reveal information about the keying material in use. This problem is inherent and cannot be avoided by cryptography—be it provably secure or not.

2.1.5 Historical Background Information

Cryptography has a long and thrilling history that is addressed in many books (e.g., [34–36]). Since the very beginning of the spoken and—even more important— written word, people have tried to transform data "to render its meaning unintelligible (i.e., to hide its semantic content), prevent its undetected alteration, or prevent its

---

2   Note that "security through obscurity" may work well outside the realm of cryptography.
3   The principle is named after Auguste Kerckhoffs who lived from 1835 to 1903.

unauthorized use" [21]. According to this definition, these people have always employed cryptography and cryptographic techniques. The mathematics behind these early systems may not have been very advanced, but they still employed cryptography and cryptographic techniques. For example, Gaius Julius Caesar[4] used an encryption system in which every letter in the Latin alphabet was substituted with the letter that is found three positions afterwards in the lexical order (i.e., "A" is substituted with "D," "B" is substituted with "E," and so on). This simple additive cipher is known as *Caesar cipher*. Later on, people employed encryption systems that use more involved mathematical transformations. The encryption systems in use today are very different.

Until World War II, cryptography was considered to be an art (rather than a science) that was primarily used in military and diplomacy. The following two developments and scientific achievements turned cryptography from an art into a science:

- During World War II, Claude E. Shannon[5] developed a mathematical theory of communication [37] and a related communication theory of secrecy systems [38] when he was working at AT&T Laboratories.[6] After their publication, the two theories started a new branch of research that is commonly referred to as *information theory*.

- As mentioned earlier, Diffie and Hellman developed and proposed the idea of public key cryptography at Stanford University in the 1970s.[7] Their vision was to employ trapdoor functions to encrypt and digitally sign electronic documents. Informally speaking, a trapdoor function is a function that is easy to compute but hard to invert, unless one knows and has access to some specific trapdoor information. This information represents the private key that must be held by only one person. Diffie and Hellman's work culminated in a key agreement protocol that allows two parties that share no prior secret

---

4   Gaius Julius Caesar was a Roman emperor who lived from 102 BC to 44 BC.
5   Claude E. Shannon was a mathematician who lived from 1916 to 2001.
6   Similar studies were done by Norbert Wiener who lived from 1894 to 1964.
7   Similar ideas were pursued by Ralph C. Merkle at the University of California at Berkeley [39]. More recently, the British government announced that public key cryptography, including the Diffie-Hellman key agreement protocol and the RSA public key cryptosystem, was invented at the Government Communications Headquarters (GCHQ) in Cheltenham in the early 1970s by James H. Ellis, Clifford Cocks, and Malcolm J. Williamson under the name *non-secret encryption* (NSE). You may refer to the note "The Story of Non-Secret Encryption" written by Ellis in 1997 (available at http://citeseer.ist.psu.edu/ellis97story.html) to get the story. Being part of the world of secret services and intelligence agencies, Ellis, Cocks, and Williamson were not allowed to openly talk about their discovery.

to exchange a few messages over a public channel and to establish a shared (secret) key. This key can then be used as a session key.

After Diffie and Hellman published their discovery [25], a number of public key cryptosystems were developed and proposed. Some of these systems are still in use today, such as the RSA [40] and Elgamal[8] [41] public key cryptosystems. Other systems, such as a number of public key cryptosystems based on the knapsack problem, have been broken and are no longer in use.

Since around the early 1990s, we have seen a wide deployment and massive commercialization of cryptography. Today, many companies develop, market, and sell all kinds of cryptographic techniques, mechanisms, services, and products (implemented in hardware or software) on a global scale. Furthermore, there are many cryptography-related conferences and trade shows to learn more about particular products.

2.1.6 Legal Situation

The legal situation regarding cryptography is involved and tricky. This is particularly true on the international level. There are many regulations on the import, export, and use of cryptography and cryptographic products, and these regulations differ from country to country (see, for example, Bert-Jaap Koops' Crypto Law Survey[9] for a corresponding overview). In some countries, the use of cryptography is regulated and strictly controlled, whereas in other countries, it is encouraged or even mandatory to use cryptography to secure specific applications, such as, for example, applications in health care.

In many countries, the export of cryptographic products is regulated, whereas the import and use is not. This applies, for example, to the United States. Until the end of the 1990s, the United States had strong export controls on cryptographic products in place, and these controls were administered by the Department of Defense (DoD). These controls made it prohibitively difficult or next to impossible for U.S. companies to sell products that implement strong cryptography abroad. This led to a situation in which U.S. companies had to sell domestic and international versions of their cryptographic products, such as Web browsers. The domestic versions of these browsers were able to support SSL cipher suites with encryption algorithms of sufficiently long key lengths (e.g., 128 bits), whereas the international versions of the same browsers could only employ 40-bit keys. Later on, the companies added

---

8   The Elgamal public key cryptosystem was developed and proposed by Taher Elgamal—the author of this book's foreword—in the 1980s.
9   http://rechten.uvt.nl/koops/cryptolaw.

features to dynamically handle variable key lengths. For example, Netscape Communications added a feature named *International Step-Up* and Microsoft added a similar feature named *Server Gated Cryptography* (SGC). Both features allowed an international browser to switch to strong cryptography, if and only if the Web server was able to provide a specific certificate. So the browser-side use of cryptography was effectively controlled by the server and the certificate(s) it was able to provide. Because old browsers are still in use today, International Step-Up and SGC are still with us.

In 1999, the Clinton administration announced a new framework for U.S. export controls on cryptographic products. This was in response to the changing global market, advances in technology, and the need to give U.S. industry better access to these markets, while continuing to provide essential protections for national security. In January 2000, the administration published a regulation implementing this new framework. It included several items. For example, export controls were now administered by the Bureau of Industry and Security (BIS) of the Department of Commerce (DoC) instead of the DoD. More specifically, rules governing exports and reexports of cryptographic products were now found in the Export Administration Regulations (EAR). If a U.S. company wanted to sell a cryptographic product abroad, then it would still have to have export approval according to the EAR. These regulations, however, enlarge the use of license exceptions, implement the changes agreed to at the Wassenaar Arrangement[10] on export controls for conventional arms and dual-use goods and technologies in December 1998, and eliminate the deemed export rule for encryption technology. In addition, new license exception provisions were created for certain types of encryption, such as source code and toolkits. Some countries are exempted from the regulation (i.e., Cuba, Iran, Iraq, Libya, North Korea, Sudan, and Syria). Overall, the legal situation for U.S. companies regarding export controls are now comparable to their international competitors. Nevertheless, there are still a couple of remains of the former U.S. export controls.

---

10 The Wassenaar Arrangement is a treaty originally negotiated in July 1996 and signed by 31 countries to restrict the export of dual-use goods and technologies to specific countries considered to be dangerous. The countries that have signed the Wassenaar Arrangement include the former Coordinating Committee for Multilateral Export Controls (COCOM) member and cooperating countries, as well as some new countries such as Russia. The COCOM was an international munitions control organization that also restricted the export of cryptography as a dual-use technology. It was formally dissolved in March 1994. More recently, the Wassenaar Arrangement was updated. The participating countries of the Wassenaar Arrangement are Argentina, Australia, Austria, Belgium, Bulgaria, Canada, Czech Republic, Denmark, Finland, France, Germany, Greece, Hungary, Ireland, Italy, Japan, Luxembourg, The Netherlands, New Zealand, Norway, Poland, Portugal, Republic of Korea, Romania, Russian Federation, Slovakia, Spain, Sweden, Switzerland, Turkey, Ukraine, the United Kingdom, and the United States. Further information on the Wassenaar Arrangement can be found at http://www.wassenaar.org.

For the purpose of this book, we do not further address legal issues regarding the import, export, or use of cryptographic products. It is a topic of its own, and whenever you want to come in touch with cryptographic products you should be careful and talk to a lawyer (or any other legally savvy person) first. This is particularly true for the import and export of such products—there are many pitfalls to avoid.

2.2 CRYPTOSYSTEMS OVERVIEW

In this section, we overview and put into perspective the most important cryptosystems in use today. We follow the classification introduced above, meaning that we distinguish between unkeyed, secret key, and public key cryptosystems.

2.2.1 Unkeyed Cryptosystems

According to Definition 2.1, unkeyed cryptosystems use no secret parameter. The most important representatives of unkeyed cryptosystems are one-way functions, cryptographic hash functions, and random bit generators.

2.2.1.1 One-Way Functions

The notion of a one-way function plays a central role in modern cryptography. Informally speaking, a function $f : X \to Y$ is one way if it is easy to compute but hard to invert. The term *easy* means that the computation can be done efficiently, whereas the term *hard* means that the computation is not known to be feasible in an efficient way (i.e., no efficient algorithm is known to exist). Consequently, one can define a *one-way function* as suggested in Definition 2.4 and illustrated in Figure 2.1.

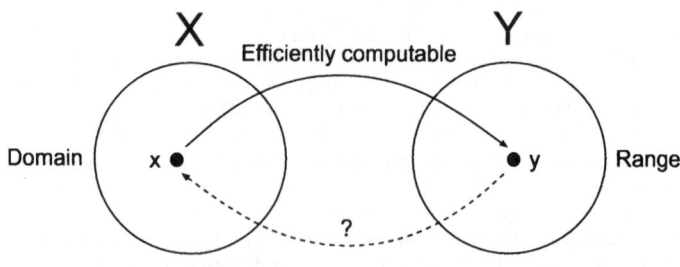

Figure 2.1 A one-way function.

Definition 2.4 (One-way function) *A function $f : X \to Y$ is one way if $f(x)$ can be computed efficiently for all $x \in X$, but $f^{-1}(y)$ cannot be computed efficiently for any randomly chosen $y \in Y$.*

To be more precise, one must say that it may be possible to compute $f^{-1}(y)$, but that the entity that wants to do the computation does not know how to do it. Also, Definition 2.4 is not mathematically precise, because we have not defined what an efficient computation really is. To do so requires complexity-theoretic arguments. We simplify things a little bit by saying that a computation is efficient, if the (expected) running time of the algorithm that does the computation is bounded by a polynomial in the length of the input. The algorithm itself may be probabilistic. Otherwise, for example, if the expected running time is not bounded by a polynomial, then the algorithm requires super-polynomial (e.g., exponential) time and is said to be inefficient.

A real-world example of a one-way function is a telephone book. Using such a book, the function that assigns a telephone number to a name is easy to compute (because the names are sorted alphabetically) but hard to invert (because the telephone numbers are not sorted numerically). Also, many physical processes are inherently one way. If, for example, we smash a bottle into pieces, then it is prohibitively difficult to put the pieces together and reconstruct the bottle. Similarly, if we drop a bottle from a bridge, it falls down. The reverse process does not frequently occur in real life. Last but not least, time is one way, and it is (currently) not known how to travel back in time. In fact, we continuously age and have no possibility to make ourselves young again.

In contrast to the real world, the idealized world of mathematics is less rich with one-way functions. In fact, there are only a few functions conjectured to be one way. Examples include the discrete exponentiation function, the modular power function, and the modular square function. These functions are frequently used in public key cryptography. But note that none of these functions has been shown to be one way, and that it is theoretically not even known whether one-way functions really exist. These facts should be kept in mind when people discuss the use (and usefulness) of one-way functions in contemporary cryptography.

Assuming the existence of one-way functions, there is a class of such functions that can be inverted efficiently if and—as it is hoped—only if some extra information is known. This brings us to the notion of a *trapdoor (one-way) function* as suggested in Definition 2.5.

Definition 2.5 (Trapdoor function) *A one-way function $f : X \to Y$ is a trapdoor function (or a trapdoor one-way function, respectively) if there exists some extra information (i.e., the* trapdoor*) with which f can be inverted efficiently, that is, $f^{-1}(y)$ can be computed efficiently for any randomly chosen $y \in Y$.*

The mechanical analog of a trapdoor (one-way) function is a padlock. It can be closed by everybody (if it is in an unlocked state), but it can be opened only by somebody who holds or has access to the proper key. In this analogy, a padlock without a keyhole represents a one-way function without trapdoor. In the real world, this is not a particularly useful construct, but in the digital world, there are many interesting applications for it. Consequently, one-way functions and trapdoor functions yield all kinds of public key cryptosystems, such as asymmetric encryption systems, digital signature systems, or key agreement protocols.

2.2.1.2 Cryptographic Hash Functions

Hash functions are frequently used and have many applications in computer science. Informally speaking, a hash function is an efficiently computable function that takes an arbitrarily sized input (string) and generates an output (string) of fixed size. This idea is captured in Defintion 2.6.

Definition 2.6 (Hash function) *Let Σ_{in} be an input alphabet and Σ_{out} be an output alphabet. Any function $h : \Sigma_{in}^* \to \Sigma_{out}^n$ that can be computed efficiently is said to be a* hash function. *It generates hash values of length n.*

In this definition, the domain of the hash function is Σ_{in}^*. This means that it consists of all strings over the input alphabet Σ_{in}. In theory, these strings can be infinitely long. In practice, however, one usually has to assume a maximum string length n_{max} for technical reasons. In this case, a hash function can be formally expressed as

$$h : \Sigma_{in}^{n_{max}} \to \Sigma_{out}^n.$$

Note that the hash function must be efficiently computable in complexity-theoretic terminology. Also, note that the two alphabets Σ_{in} and Σ_{out} can be (and typically are) the same. In this case, Σ is used to refer to either of them. In a typical (cryptographic) setting, Σ is the binary alphabet (i.e., $\Sigma = \{0, 1\}$) and n is 128 or 160 bits. In such a setting, a hash function h generates binary strings of 128 or 160 bits.

In cryptography, we are interested in hash functions with the following properties:

- A hash function h is *one-way* or *preimage resistant* if it is computationally infeasible to find an input word $x \in \Sigma_{in}^*$ with $h(x) = y$ for any given (and randomly chosen) output word $y \in \Sigma_{out}^n$.

- A hash function h is *second-preimage resistant* or *weak collision resistant* if it is computationally infeasible to find a second input word $x' \in \Sigma_{in}^*$ with $x' \neq x$ and $h(x') = h(x)$ for any given (and randomly chosen) input word $x \in \Sigma_{in}^*$.

- A hash function h is *collision resistant* or *strong collision resistant* if it is computationally infeasible to find two input words $x, x' \in \Sigma_{in}^*$ with $x' \neq x$ and $h(x') = h(x)$.

The third property is a stronger version of the second property. The first property, however, is independent from the other two properties. Consequently, the first property can be combined with either the second or the third property.

- A *one-way hash function* is a hash function that is preimage resistant and second-preimage resistant (or weak collision resistant);

- A *collision resistant hash function* is a hash function that is preimage resistant and collision resistant (or strong collision resistant).

As suggested in Definition 2.7, either of these functions is called *cryptographic* and can be used for cryptographic purposes (e.g., for data integrity protection, message authentication, and digital signatures).

Definition 2.7 (Cryptographic hash function) *A hash function $h : \Sigma_{in}^* \to \Sigma_{out}^n$ is cryptographic if it is one way or collision resistant.*

A cryptographic hash function h is typically used to hash arbitrarily long messages to binary strings of fixed size. This is illustrated in Figure 2.2, where the ASCII-encoded message "This is a file that includes some important but long statements. Consequently, we may need a short representation of this file." is hashed to 0xE423AB7D1767D13EF6EAEA69805FF6E0 (in hexadecimal notation). The resulting hash value represents a *fingerprint* or *digest* that is characteristic for the message and—in some sense—uniquely identifies it. The collision resistance property implies that it is difficult or computationally intractable to find another message that hashes to the same fingerprint or digest.

Examples of cryptographic hash functions in widespread use are MD5 (as used in Figure 2.2) and SHA-1. Both functions represent interated hash functions that follow the Merkle-Damgård construction [42, 43]. This basically means that a collision-resistant compression function is applied iteratively on subsequent message blocks, and that the resulting hash function inherits the collision resistance-property of the underlying compression function.

```
This is a file that includes some important but long statements.
Consequently, we may need a short representation of this file.
```

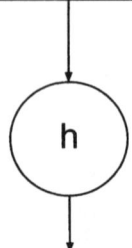

E4 23 AB 7D 17 67 D1 3E F6 EA EA 69 80 5F F6 E0

Figure 2.2 A cryptographic hash function.

MD5

MD5 is a cryptographic hash function that was originally designed by Ron Rivest in 1991. It is specified in RFC 1321 [44], and it generates hash values of 128 bits (independent from the input message length).

Since its publication, many people have tried to find collisions for MD5. Some of them have been successful for incomplete or simplified versions of MD5. With regard to the full version of MD5, collisions were found in 2004 [45]. Since then, it has been recommended to replace MD5 with stronger (i.e., more collision-resistant) cryptographic hash functions. More recently, this recommendation has become more severe, because a group of international researchers has been able to exploit MD5 collisions to generate a rogue CA certificate.[11]

SHA

Soon after Rivest released the specification of MD5, the U.S. NIST proposed the *Secure Hash Algorithm* (SHA) that is conceptually similar to MD5, but is a little bit stronger and slower. Probably after discovering a never-published weakness in the

---

11 http://www.win.tue.nl/hashclash/rogue-ca.

orginal SHA proposal,[12] the NIST revised it and called the revised version SHA-1. As such, SHA-1 was specified in the Federal Information Processing Standards Publication (FIPS) PUB 180-1 [47],[13] also known as *Secure Hash Standard* (SHS). In 2002, FIPS PUB 180 was revised a second time and the resulting FIPS PUB 180-2[14] superseded FIPS PUB 180-1 beginning February 1, 2003. In addition to superseding FIPS 180-1, FIPS 180-2 added three new algorithms that produce and output larger hash values. The SHA-1 algorithm specified in FIPS 180-2 is the same algorithm as specified in FIPS 180-1, although some of the notation has been modified to be consistent with the notation used for SHA-256, SHA-384, and SHA-512—collectively referred to as SHA-2. As summarized in Table 2.1, SHA-1, SHA-256, SHA-384, and SHA-512 produce and output hash values of different sizes (160, 256, 384, and 512 bits), and their maximal message sizes, block sizes, and word sizes also vary considerably.

In February 2004, the NIST published a change notice for FIPS 180-2 to include SHA-224.[15] SHA-224 is identical to SHA-256, but uses different initial hash values and truncates the final hash value to the leftmost 224 bits. All SHA-2 algorithms can be implemented efficiently. A long hash value does not necessarily mean that the corresponding implementation is inefficient; it only means that the resulting output is longer. This is advantageous from a collision resistance point of view, but it is disadvantageous from a space requirements point of view.

Table 2.1
Secure Hash Algorithms as Specified in FIPS 180-2

Algorithm	Message Size	Block Size	Word Size	Hash Value Size
SHA-1	$< 2^{64}$ bits	512 bits	32 bits	160 bits
SHA-224	$< 2^{64}$ bits	512 bits	32 bits	224 bits
SHA-256	$< 2^{64}$ bits	512 bits	32 bits	256 bits
SHA-384	$< 2^{128}$ bits	1,024 bits	64 bits	384 bits
SHA-512	$< 2^{128}$ bits	1,024 bits	64 bits	512 bits

Like MD5, many people have tried to find collisions for SHA-1. It was not until 2005 that Wang et al. found an attack that finds collisions for the full version of SHA-1 requiring fewer than 2^{69} operations (note that a brute-force search would require 2^{80} operations). This result was later improved to 2^{63} [50], and it is currently a research topic to lower this bound. The bottom line is that the collision resistance

---

12 At CRYPTO '98, Florent Chabaud and Antoine Joux published a weakness of SHA-0 [46]. This weakness was fixed by SHA-1, so it is reasonable to assume that they found the original weakness.
13 SHA-1 is also specified in informational RFC 4634 [48].
14 http://csrc.nist.gov/publications/fips/fips180-2/fips180-2.pdf.
15 SHA-224 is also specified in informational RFC 3874 [49].

of SHA-1 is in question (to say the least), and that people are looking for viable alternatives. Certainly, SHA-2 provides such an alternative. But in addition to SHA-2, people are also looking for alternative paradigms for the design of cryptographic hash functions. The U.S. NIST holds a competiton to find a successor of SHA-2—preliminarily termed SHA-3. The official release of SHA-3 is scheduled for 2012. It is possible and likely that SHA-3 will be widely deployed in practice.

2.2.1.3 Random Bit Generators

Randomness is one of the most fundamental ingredients of and prerequisites for the security of cryptographic systems. In fact, the generation of secret and unpredictable random quantities (i.e., random bits or random numbers) is at the heart of most practically relevant cryptographic systems. The frequency and volume of these quantities vary from system to system. If, for example, we consider secret key cryptography, then we must have random quantities that can be used as secret keys. In the most extreme case, we must have a random bit for every bit that we want to encrypt in a perfectly secure way. If we consider public key cryptography, then we must have random quantities to generate public key pairs. In either case, a cryptographic system may be probabilistic, meaning that random quantities must be generated for every use of the system. The required quantities must then be random in the sense that the probability of any particular value being selected must be sufficiently small to preclude an adversary from gaining advantage through optimizing a search strategy based on such probability. This is where the notion of a *random bit generator* as introduced in Definition 2.8 and illustrated in Figure 2.3 comes into play.

Definition 2.8 (Random bit generator) *A random bit generator is a device or algorithm that outputs a sequence of statistically independent and unbiased bits.*

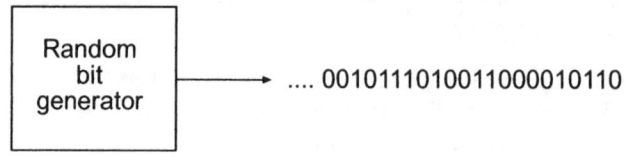

Figure 2.3 A random bit generator.

Alternatively, a random bit generator is sometimes also defined as an idealized model of a device that generates and outputs a sequence of statistically independent and unbiased bits. In either case, it is important to note that a random bit generator has no input (i.e., it only generates an output), and that because the output of the random bit generator is a sequence of statistically independent and unbiased bits, the bits occur with the same probability (i.e., $\Pr[0] = \Pr[1] = 1/2$), or—more generally—all 2^k different k-tuples occur approximately equally often for all $k \in \mathbb{N}$. There are many statistical tests that can be used to verify the (randomness) properties of a given random bit generator.

There is no known deterministic (i.e., computational) realization or implementation of a random bit generator. There are, however, many nondeterministic realizations and implementations thereof. Many of these realizations and implementations make use of physical events and phenomena. In fact, it is fair to say that a (true) random bit generator requires a naturally occuring source of randomness. Designing and implementing a device or algorithm that exploits this source of randomness to generate binary sequences that are free of biases and correlations is a challenging engineering task.

2.2.2 Secret Key Cryptosystems

According to Definition 2.2, secret key cryptosystems use secret parameters that are shared between the participating entities. The most important representatives of secret key cryptosystems are symmetric encryption systems, MACs, and PRBGs.

2.2.2.1 Symmetric Encryption Systems

If one talks about cryptography, then one often implicitly refers to confidentiality protection using symmetric encryption (i.e., to encrypt and decrypt data). *Encryption* is the process that turns a *plaintext message* (or *plaintext* in short) into a *ciphertext*, and *decryption* is the reverse process (i.e., the process that turns a ciphertext into a plaintext message). As suggested in Definition 2.9, a *symmetric encryption system* consists of a set of possible plaintext messages (i.e., the plaintext message space), a set of possible ciphertexts (i.e., the ciphertext space), and a set of possible keys (i.e., the key space), as well as two families of encryption and decryption functions (or algorithms) that are inverse to each other.

Definition 2.9 (Symmetric encryption system) *A symmetric encryption system or cipher consists of the following five components:*

- *A plaintext message space* $\mathcal{M}$;
- *A ciphertext space* $\mathcal{C}$;
- *A key space* $\mathcal{K}$;

- A family $E = \{E_k : k \in \mathcal{K}\}$ of (deterministic or probabilistic) encryption functions $E_k : \mathcal{M} \to \mathcal{C}$;
- A family $D = \{D_k : k \in \mathcal{K}\}$ of (deterministic) decryption functions $D_k : \mathcal{C} \to \mathcal{M}$.

For every key $k \in \mathcal{K}$ and every message $m \in \mathcal{M}$, the functions D_k and E_k must be inverse to each other, that is, $D_k(E_k(m)) = m$.

In most symmetric encryption systems, it does not matter whether one encrypts first and then decrypts or decrypts first and then encrypts; that is,

$$D_k(E_k(m)) = E_k(D_k(m)) = m.$$

Typically, $\mathcal{M} = \mathcal{C} = \{0,1\}^*$ (i.e., the set of binary strings of arbitrary but finite length), and $\mathcal{K} = \{0,1\}^l$ for some fixed key length l (e.g., $l = 128$).

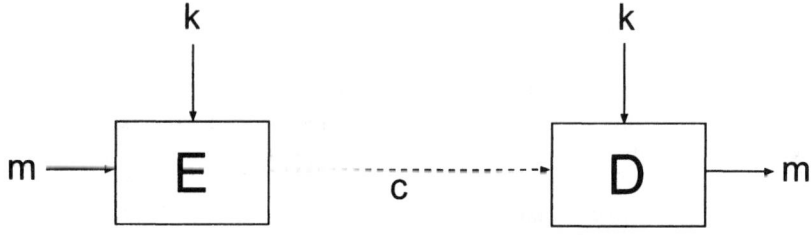

Figure 2.4 The working principle of a symmetric encryption system.

The working principle of a symmetric encryption system is illustrated in Figure 2.4. On the left side, the sender encrypts the plaintext message $m \in \mathcal{M}$ with his or her implementation of the encryption function E (parametrized with the secret key k). The resulting ciphertext $E_k(m) = c \in \mathcal{C}$ is sent to the recipient over a potentially unsecure channel (drawn as a dotted line in Figure 2.4). On the right side, the recipient decrypts c with his or her implementation of the decryption function D (again, parametrized with the secret key k). If the decryption is successful, then the recipient is able to recover the plaintext message m. The characteristic feature of a symmetric encryption system is that the k on the sender side and the k on the recipient side are equal or trivially computable from each other, meaning that k represents a bilateraly known (encryption and decryption) key.

On a high level of abstraction, people sometimes distinguish between block and stream ciphers.

- A *block cipher* operates on fixed-length groups of bits (i.e., blocks) with an unvarying transformation (determined by the key).

- A *stream cipher* operates on individual bits or bytes, and the actual transformation varies during the encryption process.

The distinction between block and stream ciphers is not as sharp as it may look like, and there are modes of operation that effectively turn a block cipher into a stream cipher. A block cipher can, for example, be operated in the electronic code book (ECB) or—more preferrably—cipherblock chaining (CBC) mode. Alternatively, a block cipher can also be turned into a stream cipher by operating it in the cipher feedback (CFB) or output feedback (OFB) mode [51]. Alternatively, the block cipher can also be operated in counter mode or one of the newer modes that provide message authentication (in addition to data encryption). We will revisit these modes when we address TLS 1.2 in Section 5.4.

Many examples of symmetric encryption systems are described in the literature. Some of these systems are relevant and used in practice, whereas others are not (i.e., they are only theoretically or historically interesting, or they are used only in small and typically closed environments). The *Data Encryption Standard* (DES) and *Advanced Encryption Standard* (AES) are the two most widely deployed block ciphers, whereas *RC4* is the most widely deployed stream cipher. Note that all practically relevant symmetric encryption systems are "only" conditionally or computationally secure. Unconditionally or information-theoretically secure symmetric encryption systems exist, but they require keys that are at least as long as the plaintext messages that are encrypted, and hence their key management is prohibitively expensive. Let us now have a brief look at DES, AES, RC4, and a few other symmetric encryption systems relevant for the SSL/TLS protocols, such as RC2, IDEA, Skipjack, and Camellia.

DES

The DES is a block cipher that was orginally designed at IBM (after an encryption algorithm named Lucifer) and standardized in FIPS PUB 46. It was reaffirmed as an official standard three times. The last reaffirmation took place in 1999 [52]. In some literature, a distinction is made between DES as a standard and DES as an encryption algorithm. In the latter case, the DES is also termed *Data Encryption Algorithm* (DEA). For the purpose of this book, however, we don't make a distinction and we use the terms DES and DEA synonymously and interchangeably.

Technically speaking, DES is a Feistel cipher that has a block size of 64 bits and operates in 16 rounds. The key length is 64 bits, but the last bit in every byte of the key represents a parity bit. Consequently, the effective key length is only 56 bits.

The overall security of DES seems to be good and the encryption algorithm has turned out to be surprisingly resistant against the most powerful cryptanalytical attacks (in particular, differential and linear crytanalysis). The major weakness and vulnerability of DES is its restricted key length of 56 bits. This means that an exhaustive key search can be done in 2^{56} operations in the worst case and 2^{55} operations on the average. People have built DES cracking machines and designed distributed algorithms to do an exhaustive search for DES keys. The bottom line is that breaking DES is perfectly feasible today, and that the use of DES cannot be recommended anymore. In many applications, DES is therefore replaced with a multiple-iteration version of it. Double DES is not particularly useful, because it is vulnerable to the meet-in-the-middle attack. But Triple DES (3DES) is useful and has a large acceptance rate in practice. The major disadvantage of 3DES is performance, since a 3DES implementation is roughly three times slower than a normal DES implementation.

AES

In the late 1990s, the U.S. NIST carried out a competition for a successor of DES. The competition was won by a block cipher named *Rijndael* that was originally developed by two Belgian cryptographers, Joan Daemen and Vincent Rijmen. Rijndael was chosen to become the AES and was published in FIPS PUB 197 [53].

Table 2.2
The Three Official Versions of the AES

	Block size	Key length	Number of rounds
AES-128	128	128	10
AES-192	128	192	12
AES-256	128	256	14

The AES is a block cipher with a fixed block size of 128 bits. As summarized in Table 2.2, there are three official versions of the AES: AES-128 takes a 128-bit key, AES-192 takes a 192-bit key, and AES-256 takes a 256-bit key. Like the key length, the number of rounds also increases from version to version (i.e., 10, 12, and 14 rounds).

Unlike DES, the AES has a clean mathematical structure. This allows a mathematical treatment of its security properties. Unfortunately, it also gives mathematical structure to the adversary who may try to exploit it. The bottom line is that mathematical structure is a double-edged sword that may speak in favor or against the security of a cipher. As of this writing, nobody has found a way to break the AES that is significantly more efficient than an exhaustive key search. So people have a good feeling when they use AES today. This is amplified by the fact that the NSA announced in June 2003 that the AES may be used for the encryption of classified information. This even applies to TOP SECRET information for 192- or 256-bit keys.

RC4

Most stream ciphers in use today are based on linear feedback shift registers (LFSRs). LFSRs can be efficiently implemented in hardware, but they are rather slow when implemented in software. Consequently, there is room for non-LFSR-based stream ciphers that can be efficiently implemented in hardware and software. The most widely deployed example is RC4 designed by Ron Rivest in 1987. While it is officially termed *Rivest Cipher 4*, the RC acronym is alternatively understood to stand for "Ron's Code." RC4 was initially a trade secret of RSA Security. But in September 1994, a description was anonymously posted to the Cypherpunks mailing list. The leaked code was confirmed to be genuine as its output was found to match that of proprietary software using licensed RC4. Because the algorithm is known, it is no longer a trade secret. But the name "RC4" is still trademarked, so it is often referred to as *ARCFOUR* or *ARC4*. This name stands for "alleged RC4," because RSA Security has never officially released the algorithm (mainly to avoid possible trademark problems).

RC4 is an additive stream cipher, meaning that it generates a stream of pseudorandom bits (a keystream) that, for encryption, is combined with the plaintext using the bitwise addition modulo 2 (i.e., XOR operaton). Decryption is performed the same way. To generate the keystream, the cipher makes use of a variable-length secret key. The ability to handle variable-length keys is one of the advantages of RC4. It was particularly important when U.S. companies had to implement and support domestic and international versions of their software. The domestic versions could use keys of arbitrary length, whereas the international versions could use keys of up to 40 bits. This flexibility in key lengths is one of the major reasons for RC4's success.

In spite of the fact that RC4 is more than 20 years old, no serious vulnerability has been found so far. The only known weakness is that the keystream generated by RC4 is biased in varying degrees towards certain bit sequences. This weakness was exploited in attacks against the way RC4 is used in the wired equivalent privacy (WEP) encryption used with 802.11 wireless local area networks (WLANs). The consequence is that the first 512 bytes of every keystream should be discarded. This is best practice. If RC4 is used this way, then it may provide a reasonable level of security.

RC2

RC2 is a block cipher also developed by Ron Rivest in 1987 for inclusion in Lotus Notes. After the NSA suggested a couple of changes and Rivest incorporated these changes, the cipher was approved for export in 1989. Along with RC4, RC2 with a 40-bit key size was treated favorably under the former U.S. export controls.

Initially, the details of RC2 were kept secret. But in January 1996, source code for RC2 was anonymously posted to the Internet (similar to the disclosure of RC4). It is unclear whether the poster had access to the specifications or whether it had been reverse engineered. Unlike RC4, the correctness of the posting was offically confirmed in 1998 [54, 55].

RC2 has a block length of 64 bits and can handle key lengths between 8 and 128 bits. The algorithm operates in 18 rounds. In 1997, RC2 was cryptanalyzed using 2^{34} chosen plaintexts [56]. Consequently, the security of RC2 is known to be weak and the symmetric encryption system should therefore not be used anymore (at least not for any security-critical application).

IDEA

The *International Data Encryption Algorithm* (IDEA) is a block cipher that was originally designed by Xuejia Lai and James Massey as a replacement for the DES [57]. In fact, IDEA is a minor revision of an earlier cipher, the Proposed Encryption Standard (PES), and was originally called Improved PES (IPES). The cipher is patented in Austria, France, Germany, Italy, Japan, Netherlands, Spain, Sweden, Switzerland, United Kingdom, and the United States, but most of these patents are about to expire soon. Note, however, that the name "IDEA" is also a trademark. IDEA is best known for its use in former versions of the *Pretty Good Privacy* (PGP) software.

IDEA is a block cipher with a block length of 64 bits and a key length of 128 bits. To encrypt a block, a series of eight identical transformations and an output transformation are performed. The processes for encryption and decryption are similar. IDEA derives much of its security by interleaving operations from different groups that are algebraically incompatible to some extent. The operations are addition modulo 2^{16}, multiplication modulo $2^{16}+1$, and bitwise addition modulo 2 (i.e., XOR).

The IDEA was designed to be resistant against differential cryptanalysis and related attacks. Concerning this matter, IDEA has been very successful; no successful linear or algebraic weaknesses have been reported so far. As of 2007, the best attack that applies to all keys can break IDEA reduced to 6 rounds (the full IDEA cipher uses 8 identical rounds and a different final round). In spite of its cryptanalytical strength, a successor of IDEA has been developed [58]. So far, however, this successor has not been particularly successful.

Skipjack

Skipjack is a block cipher developed by the NSA. Initially classified, it was intended for use in the controversial Clipper chip. The key escrow facility was achieved through the use of a complementary mechanism known as the law enforcement access field (LEAF). The Clipper chip was not successful, and it was later decided to implement Skipjack also in FORTEZZA[16] cards—in addition to a digital signature system, SHA-1, and a key exchange algorithm (KEA)—known as FORTEZZA KEA (see below). Probably to speed up the deployment rate of FORTEZZA cards, Skipjack was declassified in June 1998. Its specification is now publicly available and provides a unique insight into the cipher designs of a government intelligence agency.[17]

Skipjack has a block cipher with a block length of 64 bits and a key length of 80 bits. It operates in 32 rounds. Cryptanalysts have been able to find attacks against 31-round versions of Skipjack, but they have not been able to find attacks against the full version of Skipjack. In spite of its resistance against cryptanalytical attacks (at least in its full version), Skipjack is avoided in practice and this is probably due to its questionable role with regard to key escrow.

Camellia

Camellia is a block cipher that was jointly developed by Mitsubishi and NTT in 2000 [59, 60],[18] and that has been evaluated favorably by several organizations in Europe and Japan. Similar to DES, Camellia represents a Feistel cipher. It has a block size of 128 bits, and—similar to the AES—can use 128-bit, 192-bit, or 256-bit keys. The number of rounds is 18 (for 128-bit keys) or 24 (for 192-bit or 256-bit keys). Also, Camellia was designed to be suitable for both software and hardware implementations and to cover all possible encryption applications, from low-cost smart cards to high-speed network systems.

Camellia has been designed to be particularly resistant against known block cipher attacks. Similar to the AES, it can be completely defined by minimal systems of multivariate polynomials. But the number of free terms is approximately the same

---

16 FORTEZZA is derived from the Italian word for fortress or fort. It is a registered trademark of the NSA, and it refers to a family of security products and devices (e.g., PCMCIA cards, serial port devices, Ethernet cards, and modems) that were originally developed to create user-friendly, low-cost security solutions for the Defense Message System (DMS) of the DoD.
17 http://csrc.nist.gov/groups/ST/toolkit/documents/skipjack/skipjack.pdf.
18 http://info.isl.ntt.co.jp/crypt/eng/camellia/.

number as for AES. Theoretically, such properties might make it possible to break Camellia (and AES) using an algebraic attack, but as of this writing such an attack is not feasible.

Although patented, Camellia is available under a royalty-free license.[19] This has allowed Camellia cipher to become part of the OpenSSL project in 2006. More recently, Camellia has also become part of some TLS 1.2 cipher suites (see Section 5.4) that are supported by Mozilla Firefox 3 since June 2008. Camellia has also been submitted to other standardization bodies, such as ISO and the IETF S/MIME Mail Security (SMIME) WG.[20]

2.2.2.2 Message Authentication Codes

It is not always necessary to encrypt messages and to protect their confidentiality. Sometimes, it is sufficient to protect their authenticity and integrity, meaning that it must be possible for the recipient of a message to verify its authenticity and integrity (note that message authenticity and integrity always go hand in hand). In this case, one can add an *authentication tag* to a message and have the recipient verify the tag before he or she accepts the message as being genuine. A message and a tag computed from it (and appended to the message) are illustrated in Figure 2.5.

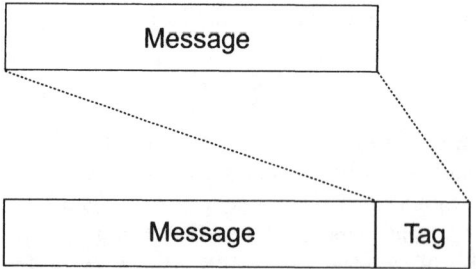

Figure 2.5 A message and a tag computed from it.

One possibility to compute and verify an authentication tag is to use public key cryptography and digital signatures. This is, however, neither necessary nor always desired, and sometimes more lightweight mechanisms based on secret key cryptography are preferred. This is where the notion of a MAC as suggested in Definition 2.10 comes into play.[21]

---
19 http://www.ntt.co.jp/news/news01e/0104/010417.html
20 http://www.ietf.org/html.charters/smime-charter.html
21 In some literature, the term *message integrity code* (MIC) is used synonymously and interchangeably with MAC.

Definition 2.10 (Message authentication code) *A MAC is an authentication tag that can be computed and verified with a secret parameter (e.g., secret cryptographic key).*

In the case of a message that is sent from one sender to a single recipient, the secret parameter must be shared between the two entities. If, however, a message is sent to multiple recipients, then the secret parameter must be shared between the sender and all receiving entities. In this case, the distribution and management of the secret parameter is a major issue (and probably one of the Achilles' heels of the entire system).

Similar to a symmetric encryption system, one can introduce and formally define a *message authentication system* to compute and verify MACs. As captured in Definition 2.11, such a system consists of a set of possible messages (i.e., the message space), a set of possible authentication tags (i.e., the tag space), a set of possible keys (i.e., the key space), as well as two families of related message authentication and verification functions.

Definition 2.11 (Message authentication system) *A message authentication system consists of the following five components:*

- *A message space $\mathcal{M}$;*
- *A tag space $\mathcal{T}$;*
- *A key space $\mathcal{K}$;*
- *A family $A = \{A_k : k \in \mathcal{K}\}$ of authentication functions $A_k : \mathcal{M} \to \mathcal{T}$;*
- *A family $V = \{V_k : K \in \mathcal{K}\}$ of verification functions $V_k : \mathcal{M} \times \mathcal{T} \to \{valid, invalid\}$. $V_k(m,t)$ must yield valid if t is a valid authentication tag for message m and key k (i.e., $t = A_k(m)$).*

For every key $k \in \mathcal{K}$ and every message $m \in \mathcal{M}$, $V_k(m, A_k(m))$ must yield valid.

Typically, $\mathcal{M} = \{0,1\}^*$, $\mathcal{T} = \{0,1\}^{l_{tag}}$ for some fixed tag length l_{tag}, and $\mathcal{K} = \{0,1\}^{l_{key}}$ for some fixed key length l_{key}. In a typical setting, $l_{tag} = l_{key} = 128$), meaning that tags and keys are both 128 bits long. There are many message authentication systems developed and proposed in the literature. Some of them are unconditionally (i.e., information-theoretically) secure, whereas others are conditionally (i.e., computationally) secure. In fact, most message authentication systems used in practice are conditionally secure and reuse a key to authenticate multiple messages.

For all practical purposes, there is is a MAC construction, known as *hashed MAC* (HMAC), that is omnipresent in network security protocols [61]. The HMAC construction works as follows:

$$HMAC_k(m) = h(k \oplus opad \parallel h(k \oplus ipad \parallel m))$$

In this construction, h denotes the cryptographic hash function in use (e.g., MD5, SHA-1, ...), k the secret key (used for message authentication), m the message to be authenticated, $ipad$ (standing for "inner pad") the byte 0x36 (i.e., 00110110) repeated 64 times, $opad$ (standing for "outer pad") the byte 0x5C (i.e., 01011100) repeated 64 times, $\oplus$ the bit-wise addition modulo 2, and $\parallel$ the concatenation operation. Note that $k \oplus ipad$ and $k \oplus opad$ are intermediate values that can be precomputed at the time of generation of the key k, or before its first use. This precomputation allows the HMAC construction to be implemented very efficiently. Also note the output of the HMAC construction may be truncated to a value that is shorter than the output of the hash value in use, typically 80 or 96 bits. The truncated HMAC construction is, for example, also supported by the most recent version of the TLS protocol (see Section 5.4.1.5).

2.2.2.3 PRBGs

As mentioned above, random bit generators are important building blocks for many cryptographic systems. There is no deterministic (computational) realization or implementation of such a generator, but that there are nondeterministic realizations and implementations making use of physical events and phenomena. Unfortunately, these realizations and implementations are not always appropriate, and there are situations in which one needs to deterministically generate binary sequences that appear to be random (e.g., if one needs a random bit generator but none is available, or if one must make statistical simulations or experiments that can be repeated as needed). Also, one may have a short random bit sequence that must be stretched into a long sequence. This is where the notion of a PRBG as illustrated in Figure 2.6 and introduced in Definition 2.12 comes into play.[22] Again, the definition is not precise in a mathematically strong sense, because we have neither defined the notion of an efficient algorithm nor have we specified what we really mean by saying that a binary sequence "appears to be random."

Definition 2.12 (Pseudorandom bit generator) *A PRBG is an efficient deterministic algorithm that takes as input a random binary sequence of length k (i.e., the seed) and generates as output another binary sequence (i.e., the pseudorandom bit sequence) of length $l \gg k$ that appears to be random.*

---

[22] Note the subtle difference between Figures 2.3 and 2.6. Both generators output a binary sequence. The random bit generator has no input, whereas the PRBG has a seed that serves as input.

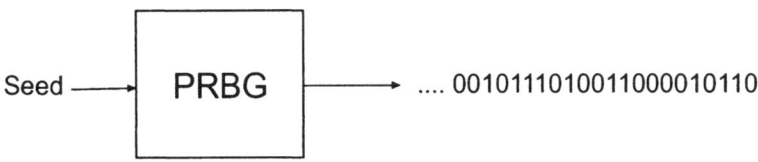

Figure 2.6 A PRBG.

Note that the pseudorandom bit sequence a PRBG outputs may be of infinite length (i.e., $l = \infty$). Also note that in contrast to a random bit generator, a PRBG represents a deterministic algorithm (i.e., an algorithm that can be implemented in a deterministic way). This suggests that a PRBG is implemented as a finite state machine and that the sequence of generated bits must be cyclic (with a potentially very large cycle). This is why we cannot require that the bits in a pseudorandom sequence be truly random, only that they appear to be so (for a computationally bounded adversary). Again, statistical tests can be used to verify the randomness properties of the output of a PRBG.

From a theoretical perspective, a PRBG is *cryptographically secure* if it is not possible for an adversary to predict the next output bit with a success probability that is significantly better than guessing. There are some constructions that employ a one-way function with a hard-core predicate to come up with a cryptographically secure PRBG. The most important example is the *BBS generator* originally developed by Lenore and Manuel Blum as well as Michael Shub (e.g., [62]).

2.2.3 Public Key Cryptosystems

According to Definition 2.3, public key cryptosystems use secret parameters that are not shared between the participating entities. Instead, each entity holds a set of secret parameters (collectively referred to as *private key* k^{-1}) and publishes another set of parameters (collectively referred to as *public key* k) that don't have to be secret and can be published at will.[23] A necessary (but usually not sufficient) condition for a public key cryptosystem to be secure is that it is computationally infeasible to compute the private key from the public key. This means that the public key can be published without running the risk of compromising the private key.

---

23 It depends on the cryptosystem, whether it matters which set of parameters is used to represent the private key and which set of parameters is used to represent the public key.

Because public key cryptography is computationally less efficient than secret key cryptography, public key cryptosystems are mainly used for authentication and key management. The resulting cryptosystems combine secret and public key cryptography and are often called *hybrid*. In fact, hybrid cryptosystems are very frequently used in practice—including, for example, the SSL/TLS protocols.

The fact that public key cryptosystems use secret parameters that are not shared between the participating entities implies that the corresponding algorithms must be executed by different entities. Consequently, such cryptosystems are typically defined as sets of algorithms (that may be executed by different entities). Examples include asymmetric encryption systems, digital signature systems, and key agreement protocols.

2.2.3.1 Asymmetric Encryption Systems

Similar to a symmetric encryption system, an asymmetric encryption system can be used to encrypt and decrypt plaintext messages. The major difference between a symmetric and an asymmetric encryption system is that the former employs secret key cryptography and corresponding techniques, whereas the latter employs public key cryptography and corresponding techniques.

As already mentioned above, an asymmetric encryption system requires a trapdoor function.[24] Each public key pair yields a public key that represents a one-way function and a private key that represents the trapdoor or inverse of the function. To send a secret message to a recipient, the sender must look up the recipient's public key, apply the corresponding one-way function to the plaintext message, and send the resulting ciphertext to the recipient. The recipient, in turn, is the only person who is supposed to know the trapdoor (information) necessary to invert the one-way function. Consequently, he or she is the only person who is able to properly decrypt the ciphertext and to recover the original (plaintext) message accordingly.

In the literature, the encryption (decryption) algorithm is often denoted as E (D), and subscripts are used to refer to the entities that hold the appropriate keys. For example, E_A refers to the encryption algorithm fed with the public key of A (i.e., k_A), whereas D_A refers to the decryption algorithm fed with the private key of A (i.e., k_A^{-1}). Consequently, it is implicitly assumed that the public key is used for encryption and the private key is used for decryption.

The working principle of an asymmetric encryption system is illustrated in Figure 2.7. On the left side, the sender applies the recipient B's one-way function (implemented by the encryption algorithm E parametrized with B's public key k_B)

---

[24] More specifically, an asymmetric encryption system requires a family of trapdoor functions.

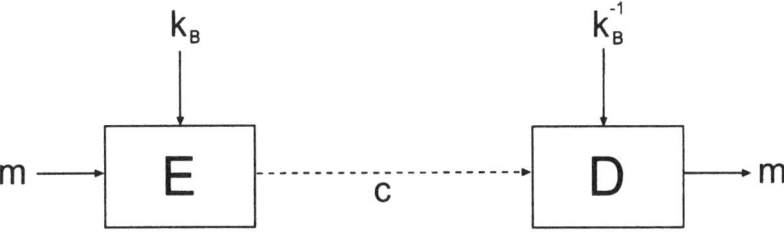

Figure 2.7 The working principle of an asymmetric encryption system.

to the plaintext message m, and sends the resulting ciphertext

$$c = E_B(m) = E_{k_B}(m)$$

to B. On the right side, B knows his or her private key k_B^{-1} (representing the trapdoor information) and can use this key to invert the one-way function and decrypt the original plaintext message

$$m = D_B(c) = D_{k_B^{-1}}(c).$$

According to Definition 2.13, an asymmetric encryption system is a public key cryptosystem that can be specified by a set of three algorithms.

Definition 2.13 (Asymmetric encryption system) *An asymmetric encryption system consists of the following three efficiently computable algorithms:*

- Generate(1^n) *is a probabilistic key generation algorithm that takes as input a security parameter 1^n and generates as output a public key pair (consisting of a public key k and a corresponding private key k^{-1}).*[25]

- Encrypt(k, m) *is a deterministic or probabilistic encryption algorithm that takes as input a public key k and a plaintext message m, and that generates as output a ciphertext c (i.e., $c =$ Encrypt(k, m)).*

- Decrypt(k^{-1}, c) *is a deterministic decryption algorithm that takes as input a private key k^{-1} and a ciphertext c, and that generates as output a plaintext message m (i.e., $m =$ Decrypt(k^{-1}, c)).*

---

25 In most literature, the security parameter is denoted by 1^k (i.e., k written in unary representation). Because this notation may provide confusion between k standing for the security parameter and k standing for the public key, we don't use it. Instead, we use 1^n to refer to the security parameter.

For every public key pair (k, k^{-1}) and every plaintext message m, the algorithms $\text{Encrypt}(k, \cdot)$ *and* $\text{Decrypt}(k^{-1}, \cdot)$ *must be inverse to each other, meaning that*

$$\text{Decrypt}(k^{-1}, \text{Encrypt}(k, m)) = m.$$

If k and k^{-1} do not correspond to each other, then the ciphertext must decrypt to gibberish.

An asymmetric encryption system can be fully specified by a triple of algorithms Generate, Encrypt, and Decrypt. Many such systems have been developed, proposed, and published in the literature. Still the most important example is RSA overviewed next.

RSA

The RSA public key cryptosystem was designed by Ron Rivest, Adi Shamir, and Len Adleman in 1977 [40]. It was the first viable implementation of the ideas developed by Diffie and Hellman in the preceding year. As such, the RSA public key cryptosystem yields both an asymmetric encryption system and a digital signature system. This means that the same set of algorithms can be used to encrypt and decrypt messages, as well as to digitally sign messages and verify digital signatures. The function provided depends on the cryptographic key in use:

- If the recipient's public key is used to encrypt a plaintext message, then the RSA public key cryptosystem yields an asymmetric encryption system. In this case, the recipient's private key is used to decrypt the ciphertext. Ideally, this can only be done by the recipient of the message.

- If the sender's private key is used to encrypt a plaintext message (or hash value thereof), then the RSA key cryptosystem yields a digital signature system. In this case, the sender's public key is used to verify the digital signature. This can be done by anybody.

The RSA public key cryptosystem is based on modular exponentiation and the RSA family of trapdoor functions (or permutations, respectively). Recognizing the relevance of their work, Rivest, Shamir, and Adleman were granted the prestigious ACM Turing Award in 2002.

Let us introduce the RSA asymmetric encryption system by elaborating on the three algorithms mentioned above.

- The RSA Generate algorithm first randomly selects two appropriately sized prime numbers p and q and computes the RSA modulus $n = pq$. It then randomly selects an integer $1 < e < \phi(n)$ with $gcd(e, \phi(n)) = 1$ and computes another integer $1 < d < \phi(n)$ with $de \equiv 1 \pmod{\phi(n)}$ using, for example, the extended Euclid algorithm. d then represents the multiplicative inverse of e modulo $\phi(n)$. The output of the algorithm is a public key pair that consists of a public key (n, e) and a corresponding private key d.

- The RSA Encrypt algorithm is deterministic. It takes as input a public key (n, e) and a plaintext message $m \in \mathbb{Z}_n$, and it generates as output the ciphertext $c = m^e \pmod{n}$.

- The RSA Decrypt algorithm is deterministic, too. It takes as input a private key d and a ciphertext c, and it generates as output the corresponding plaintext message $m = c^d \pmod{n}$.

Let us consider a toy example to illustrate the working principles of the RSA asymmetric encryption system. The RSA Generate algorithm randomly selects $p = 11$ and $q = 23$, and computes $n = 11 \cdot 23 = 253$ and $\phi(253) = 10 \cdot 22 = 220$. It then selects $e = 3$ and uses the extended Euclid algorithm to compute $d = 147$ modulo 220. Note that $3 \cdot 147 = 441 \equiv 1 \pmod{220}$, and hence $d = 147$ indeed is the multiplicative inverse element of $e = 3$ modulo 220. Consequently, $(253, 3)$ represents the public key, and 147 represents the private key. If somebody wants to encrypt the plaintext message $m = 26$, then he or she computes $c = 26^3 = 17,576 \pmod{253} \equiv 119$. This value represents the ciphertext transmitted to the recipient(s). On the recipient side, the RSA Decrypt algorithm decrypts 119 and recovers the original plaintext message $m = 119^{147} \pmod{253} \equiv 26$.

The security of the RSA public key cryptosystem is based on the assumed intractability of the integer factorization problem: it is not known how to efficiently (i.e., in polynomial time) factorize large integers. If somebody found an efficient integer factorization algorithm, then the RSA public key cryptosystem would be broken. More worrisome, it may even be possible to break the RSA public key cryptosystem without having to factorize integers, meaning that the computational equivalence of breaking RSA and factorizing large integers has not been shown so far.

2.2.3.2 Digital Signature Systems

Digital signatures can be used to protect the authenticity and integrity of data objects. According to RFC 2828, a *digital signature* refers to "a value computed with a cryptographic algorithm and appended to a data object in such a way that any recipient of the data can use the signature to verify the data's origin and integrity" [21]. This definition refers to the notion of a *digital signature with appendix*, because the signature is appended to the data object. There is also the notion of a *digital signature giving message recovery*, in which case the data unit is cryptographically transformed in a way that it represents both the data unit (or message) that is signed and the signature. This type of digital signatures is less common in practice, so we can ignore them for the purpose of this book.

A digital signature system is used to digitally sign messages and verify digital signatures. The entity that digitally signs a message is called *signer* or *signatory*, whereas the entity that verifies the signature is called *verifier*. With the proliferation of the Internet in general, and Internet-based electronic commerce in particular, digital signatures and the legislation thereof have become important and very timely topics.

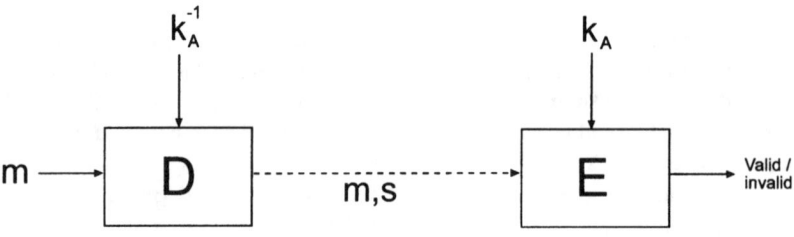

Figure 2.8   The working principle of a digital signature system.

The working principle of a digital signature system (with appendix) is illustrated in Figure 2.8. Having in mind the notion of a trapdoor function, it is simple and straightforward to explain what is going on. On the left side, the signatory A uses its private key k_A^{-1}—the trapdoor—to invert the one-way function for message m and to compute the signature s:

$$s = D_A(m) = D_{k_A^{-1}}(m)$$

The signatory then sends m and s to the verifier. On the right side, the verifier must use the signatory's public key (i.e., k_A) to compute the one-way function for s. The result is compared with m. If and only if the two values are equal is the signature valid. In practice, the message m can be very long, and it is therefore appropriate to hash it with a cryptographic hash function h before it is signed. In this case, the signature s is computed as

$$s = D_A(h(m)) = D_{k_A^{-1}}(h(m))$$

and this signature is valid if and only if s subjected to A's one-way function equals to the hash value of m. In either case, it is important to note that only A can compute s (because only A is assumed to know k_A^{-1}), whereas everybody can verify s (because everybody has access to k_A). In fact, public verifiability is a basic property of most digital signatures and corresponding digital signature systems in use today.

As outlined in Definition 2.14, a digital signature system can be defined as a set of three efficiently computable algorithms.

Definition 2.14 (Digital signature system with appendix) *A digital signature system with appendix consists of the following three efficiently computable algorithms:*

- Generate(1^n) *is a probabilistic key generation algorithm that takes as input a security parameter 1^n and generates as output a signing key k^{-1} and a corresponding verification key k. Both keys represent the public key pair (k, k^{-1}).*

- Sign(k^{-1}, m) *is a deterministic or probabilistic signature generation algorithm that takes as input a signing key k^{-1} and a message m (i.e., the message to be signed), and that generates as output a digital signature s for m.*[26]

- Verify(k, m, s) *is a deterministic signature verification algorithm that takes as input a verification key k, a message m, and a purported digital signature s for m, and that generates as output a binary decision (i.e., whether the digital signature is valid). In fact,* Verify(k, m, s) *must yield valid if and only if s is a valid digital signature for message m and verification key k.*

For every public key pair (k, k^{-1}) and message m, Verify($k, m,$ Sign(k^{-1}, m)) *must yield valid.*

The definition of a digital signature system giving message recovery is similar (the major difference is that the Verify algorithm is replaced with a Recover algorithm). With regard to the SSL/TLS protocols, the relevant digital signature systems are RSA and DSA.

RSA

As mentioned above, the RSA public key cryptosystem [40] also yields a digital signature system. If—instead of the recipient's public key—the signatory's private

---

26 Optionally, the signing algorithm may also output a new (i.e., updated) signing key. Note, however, that in a memoryless digital signature system, the signing key always remains the same.

key is used to encrypt a message (or its hash value), then an RSA signature is generated for that particular message. The signature, in turn, can be verified with the signatory's public key.

More specifically, the RSA Generate algorithm is the same as stated above (see Section 2.2.3.1). The RSA Sign algorithm takes as input a signing key (n, d) and a message $m \in \mathbb{Z}_n$, and it generates as output the digital signature

$$s = m^d \pmod{n} \quad or \quad s = h(m)^d \pmod{n}$$

The RSA Verify algorithm takes as input a verification key (n, e), a message m, and a digital signature s, and it generates as output one bit saying whether s is a valid signature for m with respect to (n, e). It therefore computes

$$m' = s^e \pmod{n}$$

and compares it either with m or $h(m)$. The signature is valid if and only if equality holds (i.e., $m' = m$ or $m' = h(m)$).

Again, we use the toy example with $p = 11$, $q = 23$, $n = 253$, $\phi(n) = (p-1)(q-1) = 10 \cdot 22 = 220$, $e = 3$, and $d = 147$ (generated by the RSA Generate algorithm). If the signatory wants to digitally sign the message $m = 26$ (or $h(m) = 26$, respectively) then the RSA Sign algorithm computes

$$d \equiv m^d \pmod{n} \equiv 26^{147} \pmod{253} = 104$$

and this value represents the digital signature for 26. Similarly, the RSA Verify algorithm computes

$$m' = \text{RSA}_{253,3}(104) \equiv 104^3 \pmod{253} = 26$$

and returns $valid$ (because $m' = 26$ matches the message $m = 26$ transmitted with the signature s).

DSA

In 1985, Taher Elgamal turned the Diffie-Hellman key exchange protocol into a public key cryptosystem that yields an asymmetric encryption system and a digital signature system [41]. The system also employs modular exponentiation and a large prime p that serves as modulus. The Elgamal digital signature system has the disadvantage that computation is done in $\mathbb{Z}_p^*$, and that the digital signatures are represented by two elements of this group. In the early 1990s, Claus-Peter Schnorr proposed (and patented) a modification of the Elgamal digital signature system that can be used to optimize the signature generation and signature verification algorithms considerably [63]. The idea is to do the modular arithmetic not in a group of order $p - 1$ (e.g., $\mathbb{Z}_p^*$), but in a much smaller subgroup of prime order q with $q \mid p - 1$. As a consequence, the computations can be done more efficiently and the resulting digital signatures can be made much shorter (as compared to the Elgamal digital signature system).

Based on the Elgamal digital signature system and the proposed modification of Schnorr, the NIST developed the *digital signature algorithm* (DSA) and specified a corresponding *digital signature standard* in FIPS PUB 186 [64]. Since its publication in 1994, FIPS PUB 186 has been revised twice.[27] Since 1993, the DSA has been covered by U.S. Patent 5,231,668 attributed to David W. Kravitz, a former NSA employee. The patent was given to "The United States of America as represented by the Secretary of Commerce, Washington, D.C." and the NIST has made the patent available worldwide without having to pay any royalty. Schnorr still claims that his patent covers DSA, but this claim has been disputed ever since.

The acronym ECDSA refers to the elliptic curve analog of the DSA. This basically means that, instead of working in a subgroup of $\mathbb{Z}_p^*$, one works in a group of points on an elliptic curve over a finite field. The mathematical formulae look more involved, but the actual computations are simpler and can be done with shorter keys (for the same level of security). Consequently, ECDSA is the preferred choice im many constrained environments. It is also supported in the more recent versions of the TLS protocol.

2.2.3.3 Key Agreement Protocols

If two or more entities want to employ and make use of secret key cryptography, then they must share a secret parameter or cryptographic key. Consequently, in a large system many secret keys must typically be generated, stored, managed, and destroyed in a highly secure way. If, for example, n entities want to securely communicate with each other, then there are

$$\binom{n}{2} = \frac{n(n-1)}{1 \cdot 2} = \frac{n^2 - n}{2}$$

secret keys that must be generated, stored, managed, and destroyed. This number grows in the order of n^2, and hence the establishment of secret keys is a major practical problem (and probably the Achilles' heel) for the large-scale deployment

---

[27] The first revision was made in December 1998 and led to the publication of FIPS PUB 186-1. The second revision was made in January 2000 and led to the publication of FIPS PUB 186-2. It is electronically available at http://csrc.nist.gov/publications/fips/fips186-2/fips186-2-change1.pdf. The third and latest revision was made in March 2006. The corresponding draft is FIPS PUB 186-3.

of secret key cryptography. For example, if $n = 1{,}000$ entities want to securely communicate with each other, then there are

$$\binom{1000}{2} = \frac{1000^2 - 1000}{2} = 499500$$

secret keys. Even for moderately large n, the generation, storage, and management of so many keys is prohibitively expensive, and the predistribution of the keys is infeasible.

Things get even more involved when one considers that keys are often used in dynamic environments, where new entities join and other entities leave at will, and that it is usually impossible, impractical, or simply too expensive to transmit keys over secure channels (e.g., by a trusted courier). Consequently, one typically faces a key establishment problem in computer networks and distributed systems. There are basically two approaches to address (and hopefully solve) the key establishment problem in computer networks and distributed systems:

- The use of a key distribution center (KDC);
- The use of a key establishment protocol.

A prominent and widely deployed example of a KDC is the Kerberos authentication and key distribution system. Unfortunately, KDCs have many disadvantages. The most important disadvantage is that each entity must unconditionally trust the KDC and share a secret master key with it. There are situations in which this level of trust is neither justified nor can be accepted by the communicating entities. Consequently, the use of key establishment protocols (that typically make use of public key cryptography in some way or another) provides a viable alternative in many situations. For example, a simple and straightforward key establishment protocol can be constructed by having one enitity (pseudo)randomly generate a session key, asymmetricly encrypt this key with the public key of the other entity, and send the encrypted key to this other entity. In this case, the RSA asymmetric encryption system (or any other asymmetric encryption system) can be used. From a security viewpoint, however, one may face the problem that the security of the session key is bound by the quality and the security of the key generation process (which is typically a PRBG). Consequently, it is advantageous to have a mechanism in place in which two or more entities can establish and agree on a commonly shared secret key. This is where the notion of a key agreement protocol comes into play (as opposed to a key distribution protocol). The most important key agreement protocol for two entities is introduced next.

Diffie-Hellman Key Exchange

As its name suggests and was mentioned above, the *Diffie-Hellman key exchange protocol* was developed by Diffie and Hellman [25]. It can be used by two entities that have no prior relationship to agree on a secret key by communicating over a public but authentic channel. As such, the mere existence of the Diffie-Hellman key exchange protocol sounds like a paradox.

Protocol 2.1 The Diffie-Hellman key exchange protocol using $\mathbb{Z}_p^*$.

A	B
(p, g)	(p, g)
$x_a \in_R \{0, \ldots, p-2\}$	$x_b \in_R \{0, \ldots, p-2\}$
$y_a \equiv g^{x_a} \pmod{p}$	$y_b \equiv g^{x_b} \pmod{p}$
$\xrightarrow{y_a}$	
	$\xleftarrow{y_b}$
$K_{ab} \equiv y_b^{x_a} \pmod{p}$	$K_{ba} \equiv y_a^{x_b} \pmod{p}$
(K_{ab})	(K_{ba})

The Diffie-Hellman key exchange protocol can be implemented in any cyclic group G in which the discrete logarithm problem (i.e., given a generator g of G and an arbirary element $y \in G$, find x so that $y = g^x$) is intractable. The simplest example of such a group is the multiplicative group of a finite field $\mathbb{Z}_p$ (i.e., $\mathbb{Z}_p^*$). The Diffie-Hellman key exchange protocol using this group is illustrated in Protocol 2.1. Let p be a large prime and g a generator of $\mathbb{Z}_p^*$. A and B know p and g, and want to use the Diffie-Hellman key exchange protocol to agree on a shared secret key K. A randomly selects a private exponent $x_a \in \{0, \ldots, p-2\}$, computes the corresponding public exponent $y_a \equiv g^{x_a} \pmod{p}$, and sends y_a to B. B, in turn, randomly selects a private exponent $x_b \in \{0, \ldots, p-2\}$, computes the corresponding public exponent $y_b \equiv g^{x_b} \pmod{p}$, and sends y_b to A. A then computes

$$K_{ab} \equiv y_b^{x_a} \equiv g^{x_b x_a} \pmod{p}$$

and B computes

$$K_{ba} \equiv y_a^{x_b} \equiv g^{x_a x_b} \pmod{p}.$$

Because the exponents commute, K_{ab} is equal to K_{ba}. It is the output of the Diffie-Hellman key exchange protocol and can be used as a secret key K.

Let us consider a toy example to illustrate the Diffie-Hellman key exchange protocol. Let $p = 17$ and $g = 3$ (i.e., $g = 3$ generates $\mathbb{Z}_{17}^*$). A randomly selects $x_a = 7$, computes $y_a \equiv 3^7 \pmod{17} = 11$, and sends the resulting value 11 to B. B, in turn, randomly selects $x_b = 4$, computes $y_b \equiv 3^4 \pmod{17} = 13$, and sends the resulting value 13 to A. A now computes $y_b^{x_a} \equiv 13^7 \pmod{17} = 4$, and B computes $y_a^{x_b} \equiv 11^4 \pmod{17} = 4$. Consequently, $K = 4$ is the shared secret that can be used as a session key.

Note that an adversary eavesdropping on the communication channel between A and B knows p, g, y_a, and y_b, but does not know x_a and x_b. The problem of determining $K \equiv g^{x_a x_b} \pmod{p}$ from y_a and y_b (without knowing x_a or x_b) is known as the *Diffie-Hellman problem*. It is known to be as difficult to solve as the discrete logarithm problem (see above), but it is still an open question whether it is always (i.e., in every group) necessary to compute a discrete logarithm to solve an instance of the Diffie-Hellman problem.

Also note that the Diffie-Hellman key exchange protocol can be transformed into a (probabilistic) asymmetric encryption system. For a plaintext message m (that represents an element of the cyclic group), A randomly selects an x_a, computes the common key K_{ab} (using B's public exponent and following the Diffie-Hellman key exchange protocol), and combines m with K_{ab} to obtain the ciphertext c. The special case where $c = mK_{ab}$ refers to the Elgamal asymmetric encryption system introduced in [41] and mentioned above.

Like any other protocol that employs public key cryptography, the Diffie-Hellman key exchange protocol is vulnerable to the *man-in-the-middle attack*. Note what happens if an adversary C is able to place himself or herself between A and B and provide both with messages of his or her choice. In this case, C can provide A and B with faked public exponents. More specifically, C can provide A with y_b' (of which he or she knows the private exponent x_b') and B with y_a' (of which he or she knows the private exponent x_a'). In this case, A computes $K_{ab'} \equiv y_b'^{x_a} \pmod{p}$ and thinks that he or she shares this key with B, and B computes $K_{b'a} \equiv y_a'^{x_b} \pmod{p}$ and thinks that he or she shares this key with A. In reality, they both don't share any key with each other, but they both share a key with C. If, for example, A wanted to send a secret message to B, A would use the key he or she thinks is being shared with B to encrypt the message, and send it to B accordingly. C would be sitting in the line and grab the message. Equipped with $K_{ab'}$, C would be able to decrypt the message, eventually modify it, reencrypt it with $K_{b'a}$, and forward it to B. B, in turn, would successfully decrypt the message using $K_{b'a}$ and think that the message is authentically coming from A. The only way to protect the communicating entities against this type of attack is to make sure that the public exponents are authentic. So, in practice, the native Diffie-Hellman key exchange protocol is usually combined with a mutual authentication protocol to come up with an authenticated key exchange protocol. In most of these protocols, the public exponents used in the Diffie-Hellman key exchange are authenticated using RSA signatures. Consequently, digital certificates and PKIs must be used to securely deploy authenticated key exchange protocols.

As mentioned earlier, the Diffie-Hellman key exchange protocol can be used in any group (other than $\mathbb{Z}_p^*$) in which the discrete logarithm problem is intractable. There are basically two reasons for using other groups.

- *Performance:* There may be groups in which the Diffie-Hellman key exchange protocol (or the modular exponentiation function) can be implemented more efficiently in hardware or software.

- *Security:* There may be groups in which the discrete logarithm problem is more difficult to solve.

The two reasons are not independent from each other. If, for example, one has a group in which the discrete logarithm problem is more difficult to solve, then one can work with much smaller keys (for a similar level of security). This is the major advantage of elliptic curve cryptography (ECC). The ECC-based version of a Diffie-Hellman key exchange is intuitively called elliptic curve Diffie-Hellman (ECDH) key exchange. Again, it works in a group of points on an elliptic curve over a finite field, and again it is supported by some of the more recent versions of the TLS protocol. Last but not least, we note that the acronym ECMQV stands for elliptic curve Menezes-Qu-Vanstone, which is a version of ECDH that provides an authenticated key exchange. Its original version was proposed by Alfred Menezes, Minghua Qu, and Scott Vanstone in 1995 [65], but it has been updated several times since then. Today, the security of ECMQV and its descendant is discussed contraversionally, but the term ECMQV still appears frequently in the cryptographic literature.

FORTEZZA KEA

As mentioned above, FORTEZZA cards implement a key exchange algorithm known as FORTEZZA KEA. It was originally designed by NSA in 1994. Its design, however, was kept secret until 1998 when it was declassified and became available to the public. It is conceptually similar to a protocol proposed in 1997 [66] and its security was throughly analyzed in 2006 [67].

The FORTEZZA KEA basically refers to a modified Diffie-Hellman key exchange protocol. In short, a long-term certificate-based Diffie-Hellman key exchange is combined with an ephemeral Diffie-Hellman key exchange. Furthermore, the block cipher Skipjack (see Section 2.2.2.1) is utilized to reduce the final values to a key that is 80 bits long. The FORTEZZA KEA protocol requires a 1,024-bit prime modulus p and a few related values that are generated according to the DSA specification. More specifically, the FORTEZZA KEA requires a 160-bit prime divisor q of $p-1$, a 1,024-bit base g for the exponentiation (referring to an element of order q in the multiplicative group modulo p), a 160-bit private value x_A and a 1,024-bit public value $Y_A \equiv g^{x_A} \pmod{p}$ for user A. It is assumed that the public values can be retrieved from a directory in some authenticated form. In addition, the FORTEZZA KEA also requires an 80-bit padding value pad and a 160-bit random number r.

Protocol 2.2 The FORTEZZA KEA.

A		B
(p, q, g)		(p, q, g)
$x_A \in_R (0, \ldots, q)$		$x_B \in_R (0, \ldots, q)$
$Y_A \equiv g^{x_A} \pmod{p}$		$Y_B \equiv g^{x_B} \pmod{p}$
	$\xrightarrow{Y_A}$	
	$\xleftarrow{Y_B}$	
$r_A \in_R (0, \ldots, q)$		$r_B \in_R (0, \ldots, q)$
$R_A \equiv g^{r_A} \pmod{p}$		$R_B \equiv g^{r_B} \pmod{p}$
	$\xrightarrow{R_A}$	
	$\xleftarrow{R_B}$	
$t_{AB} \equiv (Y_B)^{r_A} \pmod{p}$		$t_{BA} \equiv (R_A)^{x_B} \pmod{p}$
$u_{AB} \equiv (R_B)^{x_A} \pmod{p}$		$u_{BA} \equiv (Y_A)^{r_B} \pmod{p}$
$w \equiv (t_{AB} + u_{AB}) \pmod{p}$		$w \equiv (t_{BA} + u_{BA}) \pmod{p}$
(K)		(K)

The FORTEZZA KEA is illustrated in Protocol 2.2. The input parameters p, q, and g are common on either side. A randomly selects a 160-bit private value x_A, computes the corresponding 1,024-bit public value $Y_A \equiv g^{x_A} \pmod{p}$, and sends Y_A to B. B does the same thing with x_B and Y_B. Next, A randomly selects a 160-bit private value r_A, computes the corresponding 1024-bit public value $R_A \equiv g^{r_A} \pmod{p}$, and sends R_A to B. Again, B does the same thing with r_B and R_B. Now, A and B check all values received. If everything is fine, then A and B compute $t \equiv g^{r_A x_B} \pmod{p}$. More specifically, A computes $t_{AB} \equiv (Y_B)^{r_A} \pmod{p}$ and B computes $t_{BA} \equiv (R_A)^{x_B} \pmod{p}$. Both values refer to t. Similarly, A and B compute $u \equiv g^{x_A r_B} \pmod{p}$ (A computes $u_{AB} \equiv (R_B)^{x_A} \pmod{p}$ and B computes $u_{BA} \equiv (Y_A)^{r_B} \pmod{p}$). Both parties can then compute w and verify that $w \neq 0$. If this inequality holds, then A and B both extract v_1 and v_2 from w and form the session key K from v_1, v_2, and the pad. These steps are not included

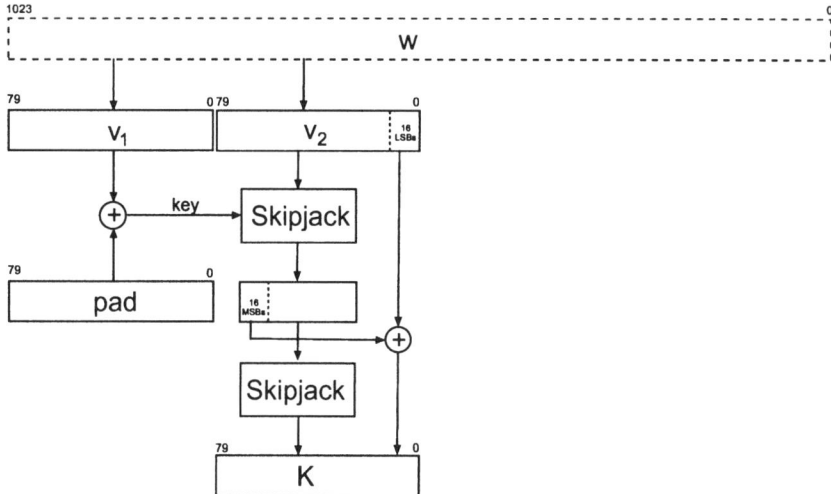

Figure 2.9 The formation of the TEK K according to the FORTEZZA KEA.

in Protocol 2.2, but they are illustrated in Figure 2.9. Note that the block cipher Skipjack is used here. In the terminology of the FORTEZZA KEA, K represents the *token encryption key* (TEK).

2.3 FINAL REMARKS

In this chapter, we provided a cryptography primer, meaning that we introduced, overviewed, and put into perspective the basic principles of cryptography as far as they are relevant for a proper understandig of the SSL/TLS protocols. This is particularly true for a few cryptographic hash functions, symmetric encryption systems (also known as ciphers), and key exchange algorithms. The examples given in the text are exactly the ones that we will see when we go through the SSL/TLS protocols. If your thirst for knowledge is not yet satisfied, then you may refer to [15] or any other books referenced at the beginning of this chapter to get more and advanced information about the current state of the art in cryptography. But keep in mind that cryptography is a very broad and conceptually rich (and hence very involved) field of study. So one of the biggest dangers is not to see the forest for the trees. We hope that this primer helps you still see the forest.

References

[1] Buchmann, J.A., *Introduction to Cryptography*, 2nd edition. Springer-Verlag, New York, 2004.

[2] Delfs, H., and H. Knebl, *Introduction to Cryptography: Principles and Applications*, 2nd edition. Springer-Verlag, New York, 2007.

[3] Dent, A.W., and C.J. Mitchell, *User's Guide to Cryptography and Standards*. Artech House Publishers, Norwood, MA, 2004.

[4] Ferguson, N., and B. Schneier, *Practical Cryptography*. John Wiley & Sons, New York, 2003.

[5] Garrett, P.B., *Making, Breaking Codes: Introduction to Cryptology*. Prentice Hall PTR, Upper Saddle River, NJ, 2001.

[6] Goldreich, O., *Foundations of Cryptography: Volume 1, Basic Tools*. Cambridge University Press, Cambridge, UK, 2001.

[7] Goldreich, O., *Foundations of Cryptography: Volume 2, Basic Applications*. Cambridge University Press, Cambridge, UK, 2004.

[8] Katz, J., and Y. Lindell, *An Introduction to Modern Cryptography*. Chapman & Hall/CRC, Boca Raton, FL, 2007.

[9] Koblitz, N.I., *A Course in Number Theory and Cryptography*, 2nd edition. Springer-Verlag, New York, 1994.

[10] Luby, M., *Pseudorandomness and Cryptographic Applications*. Princeton Computer Science Notes, Princeton, NJ, 1996.

[11] Mao, W., *Modern Cryptography: Theory and Practice*. Prentice Hall PTR, Upper Saddle River, NJ, 2003.

[12] Menezes, A., P. van Oorschot, and S. Vanstone, *Handbook of Applied Cryptography*. CRC Press, Boca Raton, FL, 1996.

[13] Mollin, R.A., *RSA and Public-Key Cryptography*. Chapman & Hall/CRC, Boca Raton, FL, 2002.

[14] Mollin, R.A., *An Introduction to Cryptography*, 2nd edition. Chapman & Hall/CRC, Boca Raton, FL, 2006.

[15] Oppliger, R., *Contemporary Cryptography*. Artech House Publishers, Norwood, MA, 2005.

[16] Schneier, B., *Applied Cryptography: Protocols, Algorithms, and Source Code in C*, 2nd edition. John Wiley & Sons, New York, 1996.

[17] Smart, N., *Cryptography, An Introduction*. McGraw-Hill, Berkshire, UK, 2003, freely available on the Internet (http://www.cs.bris.ac.uk/~nigel/Crypto_Book/).

[18] Stinson, D., *Cryptography: Theory and Practice*, 3rd edition. Chapman & Hall/CRC, Boca Raton, FL, 2005.

[19] van Tilborg, H.C.A. (Ed.), *A Encyclopedia of Cryptography and Security*. Springer-Verlag, New York, 2005.

[20] Vaudenay, S., *A Classical Introduction to Cryptography: Applications for Communications Security*. Springer-Verlag, New York, 2005.

[21] Shirey, R., "Internet Security Glossary," Informational Request for Comments 2828 (FYI 36), May 2000.

[22] Katzenbeisser, S., and F. Petitcolas (Eds.), *Information Hiding Techniques for Steganography and Digital Watermarking*. Artech House Publishers, Norwood, MA, 2000.

[23] Arnold, M., Schmucker, M., and S.D. Wolthusen, *Digital Watermarking and Content Protection: Techniques and Applications*. Artech House Publishers, Norwood, MA, 2003.

[24] Kelsey, J., B. Schneier, and D. Wagner, "Protocol Interactions and the Chosen Protocol Attack," *Proceedings of the 5th International Workshop on Security Protocols*, Springer-Verlag, 1997, pp. 91–104.

[25] Diffie, W., and M.E. Hellman, "New Directions in Cryptography," *IEEE Transactions on Information Theory*, IT-22(6), 1976, pp. 644–654.

[26] Bellare, M., and P. Rogaway, "Random Oracles Are Practical: A Paradigm for Designing Efficient Protocols," *Proceedings of First Annual Conference on Computer and Communications Security*, ACM Press, New York, 1993, pp. 62–73.

[27] Canetti, R., O. Goldreich, and S. Halevi, "The Random Oracles Methodology, Revisited," *Proceedings of 30th STOC*, ACM Press, New York, 1998, pp. 209–218.

[28] Kerckhoffs, A., "La Cryptographie Militaire," *Journal des Sciences Militaires*, Vol. IX, January 1883, pp. 5–38, February 1883, pp. 161–191.

[29] Anderson, R., "Why Cryptosystems Fail," *Communications of the ACM*, Vol. 37, No. 11, November 1994, pp. 32–40.

[30] Kocher, P., "Timing Attacks on Implementations of Diffie-Hellman, RSA, DSS, and other Systems," *Proceedings of CRYPTO '96*, Springer-Verlag, LNCS 1109, 1996, pp. 104–113.

[31] Kocher, P., J. Jaffe, and B. Jun, "Differential Power Analysis," *Proceedings of CRYPTO '99*, Springer-Verlag, LNCS 1666, 1999, pp. 388–397.

[32] Boneh, D., R. DeMillo, and R. Lipton, "On the Importance of Checking Cryptographic Protocols for Faults," *Proceedings of EUROCRYPT '97*, Springer-Verlag, LNCS 1233, 1997, pp. 37–51.

[33] Biham, E., and A. Shamir, "Differential Fault Analysis of Secret Key Cryptosystems," *Proceedings of CRYPTO '97*, Springer-Verlag, LNCS 1294, 1997, pp. 513–525.

[34] Kahn, D., *The Codebreakers: The Comprehensive History of Secret Communication from Ancient Times to the Internet*. Scribner, New York, 1996.

[35] Bauer, F.L., *Decrypted Secrets: Methods and Maxims of Cryptology*, 2nd edition. Springer-Verlag, New York, 2000.

[36] Levy, S., *Crypto: How the Code Rebels Beat the Government—Saving Privacy in the Digital Age*. Viking Penguin, New York, 2001.

[37] Shannon, C.E., "A Mathematical Theory of Communication," *Bell System Technical Journal*, Vol. 27, No. 3/4, July/October 1948, pp. 379–423/623–656.

[38] Shannon, C.E., "Communication Theory of Secrecy Systems," *Bell System Technical Journal*, Vol. 28, No. 4, October 1949, pp. 656–715.

[39] Merkle, R.C., "Secure Communication over Insecure Channels," *Communications of the ACM*, 21(4), April 1978 (submitted in 1975), pp. 294–299.

[40] Rivest, R.L., A. Shamir, and L. Adleman, "A Method for Obtaining Digital Signatures and Public-Key Cryptosystems," *Communications of the ACM*, 21(2), February 1978, pp. 120–126.

[41] Elgamal, T., "A Public Key Cryptosystem and a Signature Scheme Based on Discrete Logarithm," *IEEE Transactions on Information Theory*, IT-31(4), 1985, pp. 469–472.

[42] Merkle, R.C., "One Way Hash Functions and DES," *Proceedings of CRYPTO '89*, Springer-Verlag, LNCS 435, 1989, pp. 428–446.

[43] Damgård, I.B., "A Design Principle for Hash Functions," *Proceedings of CRYPTO '89*, Springer-Verlag, LNCS 435, 1989, pp. 416–427.

[44] Rivest, R.L., *The MD5 Message-Digest Algorithm*, Request for Comments 1321, April 1992.

[45] Wang, X., and H. Yu, "How to Break MD5 and Other Hash Functions," *Proceedings of EUROCRYPT '05*, Springer-Verlag, LNCS 3494, 2005, pp. 19–35.

[46] Chabaud, F., and A. Joux, "Differential Collisions in SHA-0," *Proceedings of CRYPTO '98*, Springer-Verlag, LNCS 1462, 1998, pp. 56–71.

[47] U.S. Department of Commerce, National Institute of Standards and Technology, *Secure Hash Standard*, FIPS PUB 180-1, April 1995.

[48] Eastlake 3rd, D., and T. Hansen, *US Secure Hash Algorithms (SHA and HMAC-SHA)*, Informational Request for Comments 4634, July 2006.

[49] Housley, R., *A 224-Bit One-Way Hash Function: SHA-224*, Request for Comments 3874, September 2004.

[50] Wang, X., Yin, Y., and R. Chen, "Finding Collisions in the Full SHA-1," *Proceedings of CRYPTO 2005*, Springer-Verlag, LNCS, 2005.

[51] U.S. Department of Commerce, National Institute of Standards and Technology, *DES Modes of Operation*, FIPS PUB 81, December 1980.

[52] U.S. Department of Commerce, National Institute of Standards and Technology, *Data Encryption Standard (DES)*, FIPS PUB 46-3, October 1999.

[53] U.S. Department of Commerce, National Institute of Standards and Technology, *Specification for the Advanced Encryption Standard (AES)*, FIPS PUB 197, November 2001.

[54] Rivest, R., *A Description of the RC2(r) Encryption Algorithm*, Request for Comments 2268, March 1998.

[55] Knudsen, L.R., Rijmen, V., Rivest, R.L., and M.J.B. Robshaw, "On the Design and Security of RC2," *Proceedings of the Fifth International Workshop on Fast Software Encryption*, Springer-Verlag, LNCS 1372, 1998, pp. 206–221.

[56] Kelsey, J., Schneier, B., and D. Wagner, "Related-Key Cryptanalysis of 3-WAY, Biham-DES, CAST, DES-X, NewDES, RC2, and TEA," *Proceedings of the First International Conference on Information and Communication Security*, Springer-Verlag, LNCS 1334, 1997, pp. 233–246.

[57] Lai, X., and J.L. Massey, "A Proposal for a New Block Encryption Standard," *Proceedings of EUROCRYPT '90*, Springer-Verlag, LNCS 473, 1991, pp. 389–404.

[58] Junod, P., and S. Vaudenay, "FOX: A New Family of Block Ciphers," *Proceedings of the Eleventh Annual Workshop on Selected Areas in Cryptography (SAC 2004)*, Springer-Verlag, LNCS 3357, 2004, pp. 114–129.

[59] Aoki, P., et al., "Camellia: A 128-Bit Block Cipher Suitable for Multiple Platforms—Design and Analysis," *Proceedings of the Seventh Annual Workshop on Selected Areas in Cryptography (SAC 2000)*, Springer-Verlag, LNCS 2012, 2000, pp. 39–56.

[60] Matsui, M., Nakajima, J., and S. Moriai, *A Description of the Camellia Encryption Algorithm*, Informational Request for Comments 3713, April 2004.

[61] Krawczyk, H., Bellare, M., and R. Canetti, *HMAC: Keyed-Hashing for Message Authentication*, Request for Comments 2104, February 1997.

[62] Blum, L., M. Blum, and M. Shub, "A Simple Unpredictable Pseudo-Random Number Generator," *SIAM Journal of Computing*, Vol. 15, May 1986, pp. 364–383.

[63] Schnorr, C.P., "Efficient Signature Generation by Smart Cards," *Journal of Cryptology*, Vol. 4, 1991, pp. 161–174.

[64] U.S. National Institute of Standards and Technology (NIST), *Digital Signature Standard (DSS)*, FIPS PUB 186, May 1994.

[65] Menezes, A., Qu, M., and S. Vanstone, "Some New Key Agreement Protocols Providing Mutual Implicit Authentication," *Proceedings of the Workshop on Selected Areas in Cryptography (SAC '95)*, Springer-Verlag, 1995, pp. 22–32.

[66] Blake-Wilson, S., Johnson, D., and A. Menezes, "Key Agreement Protocols and their Security Analysis," *Proceedings of the 6th IMA International Conference on Cryptography and Coding*, Springer-Verlag, LNCS 1355, 1997, pp. 30–45.

[67] Lauter, K., and A. Mityagin, "Security Analysis of KEA Authenticated Key Exchange Protocol," *Proceedings of PKC 2006*, Springer-Verlag, LNCS 3958, 2006, pp. 378–394.

Chapter 3

Transport Layer Security

After having introduced the fundamentals and basic principles of cryptography, we are now ready to approach the real topic of the book. To set the stage, we use this chapter to overview and put into perspective the various technologies and protocols that can be used to provide basic security services at the transport layer of the TCP/IP protocol stack. More specifically, we give an introduction in Section 3.1, overview the evolution of the transport layer security protocols in Section 3.2, and conclude with some final remarks in Section 3.3.

3.1 INTRODUCTION

When the WWW started its triumphal procession in the first half of the 1990s, people started to purchase items electronically. Among the electronic payment systems available at this time, credit card transactions were the most widely deployed ones. Because people had reservations about the transmission of credit card information as part of Web transactions, many companies and researchers were looking into possibilities to provide Web transaction security and corresponding services. The greatest common denominator of all these possibilities was the use of cryptographic techniques to provide some basic security services. Except for this fact, there was hardly any consensus about what cryptographic techniques to use and at what layer to apply them.

The bird's-eye view reveals that there are many possibilities to invoke cryptographic techniques at various layers of the TCP/IP protocol stack. In principle, all Internet security protocols overviewed in [1] or Chapter 5 of [2] can be used to secure Web transactions:

- On the network access layer, IEEE 802.1AE elaborates on media access control MAC security and specifies ways to provide data origin authentication, connectionless confidentiality, and connectionless integrity services to MAC frames. Also, there are several virtual private networking technologies and protocols, such as the point-to-point tunneling protocol (PPTP) or the layer 2 tunneling protocol (L2TP) when combined with IPsec/IKE (see next bullet). All of these network access layer security protocols can also be used to securely transmit Web transactions (among other things).

- On the Internet layer, there are the IP security (IPsec) and Internet Key Exchange (IKE) protocols [3] that can be used to establish a secure connection between two IP entities. Again, the secure connections can then be used to securely transmit Web transactions. The nice thing about IPsec/IKE is that it coresides with IP, and hence all Internet applications are layered on top of them. This means that it can be used to secure all Internet applications. The less nice thing about IPsec/IKE is that the protocols are overly complex; this makes the deployment and operation of IPsec/IKE involved and tricky.

- On the transport layer, the Transmission Control Protocol (TCP)—on which HTTP is layered—can be enhanced to invoke cryptographic techniques and to provide basic security services for Web transactions. This is basically the approach of the SSL/TLS protocols.

- On the application layer, either HTTP can be enhanced to invoke cryptographic techniques and to provide Web transaction security, or an authentication and key distribution system, such as Kerberos, can be employed to basically achieve the same thing. In the second case, the use of a standardized application programming interface (API) is an important requirement.

Last but not least, there is also the possibility to layer Web transaction security above the application layer, meaning that the Web transactions are protected in a way that is independent from the transmission technologies in use. This is conceptually similar to secure messaging approaches, like PGP, OpenPGP, or Secure MIME (S/MIME) [4].

The Internet security protocols and their placement in the TCP/IP protocol stack is illustrated in Figure 3.1. All possibilities have advantages and disadvantages. Roughly speaking, providing Web transaction security at a low layer has the advantage that applications don't have to care (and needn't be modified accordingly), whereas providing Web transaction security at a high layer has the advantage that it has no impact on the networking infrastructure, and hence the infrastructure can be left as it is.

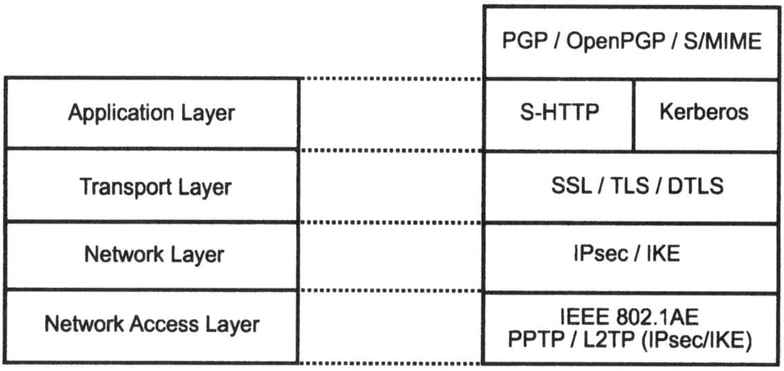

Transport Layer Security

		PGP / OpenPGP / S/MIME
Application Layer		S-HTTP / Kerberos
Transport Layer		SSL / TLS / DTLS
Network Layer		IPsec / IKE
Network Access Layer		IEEE 802.1AE / PPTP / L2TP (IPsec/IKE)

Figure 3.1 The Internet security protocols and their placement in the TCP/IP protocol stack.

There is a famous *end-to-end argument* in system design [5] that strongly speaks in favor of providing security services at a high layer. The argument basically says

- That any nontrivial communications system involves intermediaries, such as network devices, relay stations, computer systems, and software modules that are, in principle, unaware of the context of the communication being involved.
- That these intermediaries are incapable of ensuring that the data is processed correctly.

The bottom line is that, whenever possible, communications protocol operations should be defined to occur at the end points of a communications system, or as close as possible to the resource being controlled. The end-to-end argument applies generally (i.e., for any type of functionality). As pointed out in [6], it particularly applies to the provision of network security services.

Following the end-to-end argument and design principle, the IETF chartered a Web Transaction Security (WTS) WG in the early 1990s.[1] The goal of the WG was to develop requirements and a specification for the provision of security services to Web transaction (e.g., transactions using the HTTP). The outcome of the WG is documented in [7–9]. A group of researchers at Enterprise Integration Technologies (EIT) was particularly active. They developed and came up with a proposal to enhance HTTP with a possibility to encrypt and/or digitally sign documents or specific parts thereof. The proposal was named *Secure Hypertext Transfer Protocol* (S-HTTP or SHTTP), and it was later officially specified in an experimental RFC

---

1 http://www.ietf.org/html.charters/OLD/wts-charter.html.

[9]. S-HTTP is conceptually similar to today's specifications of the World Wide Web Consortium (W3C) related to eXtensible Markup Language (XML) encryption and XML signatures. It was submitted to the Web transaction discussion in 1994, and due to its strong initial support in the software industry it seemed to be only a question of time until it would become the dominant key player in the field.

But things evolved differently. Independent from the end-to-end argument and the S-HTTP proposal, the developers at Netscape Communications prosecuted the claim that transport layer security provides an interesting compromise between low-layer and high-layer security. In fact, they took the viewpoint of the application developer and wanted to enable him or her to establish secure connections (instead of "normal" connections) in a way that is as simple as possible. To achieve this goal, they inserted an intermediate layer between the transport layer and the application layer. This layer was named *Secure Sockets Layer* (SSL) and its job was to handle security, meaning that it had to establish secure connections and to transmit data over these secure connections. As such, its functionality is deeply interwinded with the one of a transport layer protocol like TCP, and hence we technically assign the SSL protocol to the transport layer. More specifically, the SSL protocol is layered on top of connection-oriented and reliable transport layer protocol like TCP. The connectionless best effort datagram delivery protocol that operates at the transport layer protocol is named User Datagram Protocol (UDP),[2] and it has only been recently that the TLS protocol has been adapted to be used on top of UDP, as well. This is the realm of the DTLS protocol further addressed in Chapter 6. The SSL protocol was so successful that it became the starting point of a whole evolution of similar but still slightly different transport layer security protocols. This evolution is sketched next.

3.2 PROTOCOL EVOLUTION

Netscape Communications started to develop the SSL protocol soon after the National Center for Supercomputing Applications (NCSA) released Mosaic 1.0—the first popular Web browser—in 1993. Eight months later, in the middle of 1994,

---

2   It is sometimes argued that TCP is connection-oriented and reliable, whereas UDP is connectionless and unreliable. This characterization is imprecise, mainly because the term "unreliable" suggests that UDP was intentionally designed to lose packets. This was clearly not the case. Instead, a best-effort delivery protocol has no built-in functions to detect or correct for packet loss but relies on underlying protocols to provide this service. Over a modern LAN, for example, loss is nearly zero, and hence a best-effort delivery protocol is sufficient for many applications. A key benefit from providing no loss detection is that the resulting protocol is efficient to process and introduces no latency to the delivery. The bottom line is that it is more appropriate to say that UDP is a best-effort datagram delivery protocol than an unreliable one.

Netscape Communications already completed the design for SSL version 1 (SSL 1.0). This version circulated only internally (i.e., inside Netscape Communications), since it had several shortcomings and flaws. For example, it didn't provide data integrity protection. In combination with the use of the stream cipher RC4 for data encryption, this allowed an adversary to make predictable changes to the plaintext messages. Also, SSL 1.0 did not use sequence numbers, so it was vulnerable to replay attacks. Later on, the designers of SSL 1.0 added sequence numbers and checksums, but still used an overly simple cyclic redundancy check (CRC) instead of a cryptographically strong hash function that is one-way and collision-resistant.

This and a few other problems had to be resolved, and at the end of 1994 Netscape Communications came up with SSL version 2 (SSL 2.0).[3] Among other changes, the CRC was replaced with MD5 that was still assumed to be secure at this time. Netscape Communications then released the Netscape Navigator that implemented SSL 2.0 together with a few other products that also supported SSL 2.0. The official SSL 2.0 protocol specification was written by Kipp E.B. Hickman from Netscape Communications, and it was submitted as an Internet-Draft entitled "The SSL Protocol" in April 1995.[4] In August 1995, Netscape Communications also filed a patent application entitled "Secure Socket Layer Application Program Apparatus and Method" that basically referred to the SSL protocol (hence the patent is also called the *SSL patent*). The SSL patent was granted in August 1997 (U.S. Patent No. 5,657,390) and was assigned to Netscape Communications. Remember from the foreword that Netscape Communications filed for patents to protect SSL in order to prevent others from moving into the same space, and that the SSL patent was given away to the community for everyone to use for free.

With the release of the Netscape Navigator (supporting the newly specified SSL 2.0 protocol), the Internet and WWW started to take off. This made some other companies nervous about the potential and the lost opportunities of not getting involved. Most importantly, Microsoft decided to become active and came up with the Internet Explorer in the second half of 1995. Microsoft also published a protocol—named *Private Communication Technology* (PCT)—that is conceptually and technically very similar to SSL 2.0.[5] In fact, the PCT protocol's record format is compatible with that of SSL. Servers implementing both protocols can distinguish between PCT and SSL clients because the version number field occurs in the same position in the first handshake message in both protocols, and in the case of PCT, the most significant bit of the protocol version number is set to one (instead of zero as with SSL). From today's perspective, the PCT protocol is only historically relevant. Some Microsoft products still support it, but outside the world of Microsoft products

3   http://tools.ietf.org/html/draft-hickman-netscape-ssl-00.
4   draft-hickman-netscape-ssl-00.txt.
5   http://graphcomp.com/info/specs/ms/pct.htm.

the PCT protocol has never been supported and probably will never be supported. So we can safely ignore it for the purpose of this book. All you need to know is the acronym and what is actually stands for (roughly speaking, PCT is the Microsoft version of SSL).

In addition to a few minor changes (mainly regarding the handshake phase), the PCT protocol improved some weaknesses and vulnerabilities of SSL 2.0. The ideas were also incorporated in SSL version 3 (SSL 3.0) that was released soon after the publication of PCT (still before the end of 1995). The SSL 3.0 protocol was specified by Alan O. Freier and Philip Karlton from Netscape Communications with the support of an independent consultant named Paul C. Kocher (Kocher later founded Cryptography Research[6]). Also, around this time, Netscape Communications employed several security professionals, including, for example, Taher Elgamal—the inventor of the Elgamal public key cryptosystem [10] and the provider of this book's foreword. These distinguished security professionals helped making SSL 3.0 more robust and secure. The specification of SSL 3.0 was finally published as an Internet-Draft entitled "The SSL Protocol Version 3.0" in November 1996.[7] Even today this document serves as a primary reference for the SSL protocol.

From todays perspective, SSL 2.0 is known to have several shortcomings and security problems that are corrected in SSL 3.0:

- SSL 2.0 permits the client and server to send only one public key certificate each. Thus, this certificate has to be directly signed by a trusted root CA. Contrary to that, SSL 3.0 allows clients and servers to have arbitrary-length certificate chains.

- SSL 2.0 uses the same keys for message authentication and encryption, which may lead to problems for certain ciphers. Also, if SSL 2.0 is used with RC4 in export mode, then the message authentication and encryption keys are both based on 40 bits of secret data. This is in contrast to the fact that the message authentication keys can be longer (export restrictions typically apply only to encryption keys). In SSL 3.0, different keys are used, and hence even if weak ciphers are used, mounting attacks against message authenticity and integrity can still be made intractable (by using long keys for message authentication).

- SSL 2.0 exclusively uses the cryptographic hash function MD5 to generate MACs. In SSL 3.0, MD5 is complemented with SHA-1, and the MAC construction is more sophisticated.

Because of these shortcomings and security problems, it is generally recommended to avoid the use of SSL 2.0, and to consistantly replace it with SSL 3.0.

6 http://www.cryptography.com
7 draft-freier-ssl-version3-02.txt.

After the publication of SSL 3.0 and PCT, there was quite a lot of confusion in the security community. On the one hand, there was Netscape Communications and a large part of the Internet and Web security community pushing SSL 3.0. On the other hand, there was Microsoft with its huge installed base pushing PCT (they also had to support SSL for interoperability reasons). To make things worse, Microsoft had even came up with yet another protocol proposal, named *Secure Transport Layer Protocol* (STLP), that was basically a modification of SSL 3.0, providing additionl features which Microsoft considered to be critical, such as support for UDP, client authentication based on shared secrets, and some performance optimizations (many of these features are discussed today for inclusion in the TLS protocol). In this situation, an IETF Transport Layer Security (TLS) Working Group[8] was formed in 1996 to resolve the issue and to standardize a unified TLS protocol. This task was technically simple (because the protocols to begin with—SSL 3.0 and PCT/STLP— were already technically very close), but still difficult for at least three reasons:

- First, the Internet standards process [11] requests that a statement be obtained from a patent holder indicating that a license will be made available to applicants under reasonable terms and conditions. This also applied to the SSL patent (such a statement was not included in the original specification of SSL 3.0).

- Second, at the April 1995 IETF meeting in Danvers, Massachusetts, the IESG adopted the *Danvers Doctrine*, which basically said that the IETF should design protocols that embodied good engineering principles, regardless of exportability issues. This doctrine implied support for DES at a minimum and over time it came to mean 3DES.

- Third, the IETF had a longstanding preference for unencumbered algorithms when possible. So when the Merkle-Hellman patent (covering many public key cryptosystems) expired in 1998, but RSA was still patented, the IESG began pressuring working groups to adopt the use of unpatented public key cryptosystems.

When the IETF TLS WG finished its work in late 1997, it sent the first version of the TLS protocol specification off to the IESG. The IESG, in turn, returned the specification with a few instructions to add other cryptosystems, namely DSA for authentication, Diffie-Hellman for key exchange (note that the Merkle-Hellman patent was about to expire), and 3DES for encryption, mainly to solve the two last issues mentioned above (the first issue could be solved by adding a corresponding statement in the TLS protocol specification). Much discussion

---

8 http://www.ietf.org/html.charters/tls-charter.html

on the mailing list ensued, with Netscape Communications in particular resisting mandatory cryptographic systems in general and 3DES in particular. After some heated discussions between the IESG and the IETF TLS WG, grudging consensus was reached and the protocol specification was resubmitted with the appropriate changes in place.

Unfortunately, in the meantime, another problem appeared: the IETF Public Key Infrastructure (PKIX) WG had been tasked to standardize a profile for X.509 certificates in the Internet, and this WG was just winding up its work. For reasons discussed later in this book, the TLS protocol depended on X.509 certificates and hence on the outcome of the IETF PKIX WG. In the meantime, the rules of the IETF forbid protocols advancing ahead of other protocols on which they depend. PKIX finalization took rather longer than expected and added another delay. The bottom line is that it took almost three years until the IETF TLS WG could officially release its resulting security protocol of the same name.[9] In fact, the first version of the TLS protocol (i.e., TLS 1.0), was specified in RFC 2246 [12] and was released in January 1999. The required patent statement was included in appendix G of this document. Despite the change of names, TLS 1.0 is nothing more than a new version of SSL 3.0. In fact, there are fewer differences between TLS 1.0 and SSL 3.0 than there are differences between SSL 3.0 and SSL 2.0 (the latter is not addressed in this book). TLS 1.0 is therefore sometimes also referred to as SSL 3.1. In addition to the TLS 1.0 specification, the IETF TLS WG also completed a series of extensions to the TLS protocol that are documented elsewhere.

After the 1999 release of TLS 1.0, work on the TLS protocol continued in the IETF TLS WG. In April 2006, the TLS protocol version 1.1 (TLS 1.1) was specified in Standards Track RFC 4346 [13], making RFC 2246 obsolete. As discussed later, there were some cryptographic problems resolved in TLS 1.1. After another two-years' revision period, in August 2008, the TLS protocol version 1.2 (TLS 1.2) was specified in Standards Track RFC 5246 [14]. This document not only made RFC 4346 obsolete, but also RFC 3268 (that specified the use of the AES in TLS) [15] and RFC 4366 (that specified extensions for TLS) [16]. Furthermore, RFC 5246 also updated informational RFC 4492 [17] that elaborates on the use of ECC-based cipher suites for TLS. Most of these extensions have been incorportaed in TLS 1.2. They represent the most substantial progress of TLS 1.2. The bottom line is that the standardization of the TLS protocol and its extensions has become highly involved and subtle. We will more thoroughly address the topic in Chapter 5. Also, the TLS protocol has been adapted to be used to secure UDP-based applications. The corresponding DTLS protocol is addressed in Chapter 6.

---

9   The name had to be changed from SSL to TLS to avoid the appearance of bias toward any particular company.

3.3 FINAL REMARKS

In this chapter, we overviewed and put into perspective the technologies and protocols that can be used to provide basic security services on the transport layer of the TCP/IP protocol stack. Most importantly, the SSL/TLS protocols represent transport layer security protocols that are omnipresent and in widespread use. In fact, for the last few years, support for SSL/TLS has been built into nearly every Web browser and server software. This even applies to Microsoft (as mentioned above, Microsoft originally came up with protocol proposals of its own acronymed PCT and STLP, but these proposals very rapidly sank into oblivion).

There are two major advantages of transport layer security technologies and protocols:

- On the one hand, they can be used to secure any application layer protocol that is layered on top of them. This means that any TCP-based application can potentially be secured with the SSL/TLS protocols. Also, there is the possibility to secure any UDP-based application with the DTLS protocol.

- On the other hand, they can operate nearly transparently for users, meaning that users need not be aware of the fact that the SSL/TLS protocols are in place.[10] This simplifies the deployment of the protocols considerably.

All transport layer security protocols mentioned so far employ public key cryptography and public key certificates. This is almost always true for the servers that support the SSL/TLS protocols, but it is optionally also true for the clients. The corresponding protocol specifications assume the existence of certificates, but they do not address the proper management of these certificates. In fact, the management of public key certificates is assumed to take place outside the scope of the SSL/TLS protocols. We postpone the discussion of digital certificates and PKIs to Chapter 8.

References

[1] Oppliger, R., *Internet and Intranet Security*, 2nd edition. Artech House Publishers, Norwood, MA, 2002.

[2] Oppliger, R., *Security Technologies for the World Wide Web*, 2nd edition. Artech House Publishers, Norwood, MA, 2003.

[3] Frankel, S., *Demystifying the IPsec Puzzle*, Artech House Publishers, Norwood, MA, 2001.

[4] Oppliger, R., *Secure Messaging with PGP and S/MIME*, Artech House Publishers, Norwood, MA, 2001.

---

10 The only place where user involvement is ultimately required is when the user must verify the server certificate. This is actually also the Achilles' heel of SSL/TLS.

[5] Saltzer, J.H., Reed, D.P., and D.D. Clark, "End-to-End Arguments in System Design," *ACM Transactions on Computer Systems*, Vol. 2, No. 4, November 1984, pp. 277–288.

[6] Voydock, V., and S.T. Kent, "Security Mechanisms in High-Level Network Protocols," *ACM Computing Surveys*, Vol. 15, 1983, pp. 135–171.

[7] Bossert, G., Cooper, S., and W. Drummond, "Considerations for Web Transaction Security," Informational Request for Comments 2084, January 1997.

[8] Rescorla, E., and A. Schiffman, "Security Extensions For HTML," Experimental Request for Comments 2659, August 1999.

[9] Rescorla, E., and A. Schiffman, "The Secure HyperText Transfer Protocol," Experimental Request for Comments 2660, August 1999.

[10] Elgamal, T., "A Public Key Cryptosystem and a Signature Scheme Based on Discrete Logarithm," *IEEE Transactions on Information Theory*, IT-31(4), 1985, pp. 469–472.

[11] Bradner, S., "The Internet Standards Process—Revision 3," Request for Comments 2026 (BCP 9), October 1996.

[12] Dierks, T., and C. Allen, "The TLS Protocol Version 1.0," Standards Track Request for Comments 2246, January 1999.

[13] Dierks, T., and E. Rescorla, "The Transport Layer Security (TLS) Protocol Version 1.1," Standards Track Request for Comments 4346, April 2006.

[14] Dierks, T., and E. Rescorla, "The Transport Layer Security (TLS) Protocol Version 1.2," Standards Track Request for Comments 5246, August 2008.

[15] Chown, P., "Transport Layer Security (TLS) Extensions," Standards Track Request for Comments 3268, June 2002.

[16] Blake-Wilson, S., Nystrom, M., Hopwood, D., Mikkelsen, J., and T. Wright, "Advanced Encryption Standard (AES) Ciphersuites for Transport Layer Security (TLS)," Standards Track Request for Comments 4366, April 2006.

[17] Blake-Wilson, S., Bolyard, N., Gupta, V., Hawk, C., and B. Moeller, "Elliptic Curve Cryptography (ECC) Cipher Suites for Transport Layer Security (TLS)," Informational Request for Comments 4492, May 2006.

Chapter 4

SSL Protocol

After having introduced the notion of a transport layer security, we now delve more deeply into the SSL protocol. More specifically, we introduce the topic in Section 4.1, overview the protocols SSL consists of in Section 4.2, provide a traffic analysis of an SSL session in Section 4.3, analyze the security of the SSL protocol in Section 4.4, and conclude with some final remarks in Section 4.5. This chapter represents one of the main parts of the book; as such, it is a little bit more voluminous than most other chapters.

4.1 INTRODUCTION

In Section 3.2, we looked back into the 1990s and explained why Netscape Communications proposed SSL and how the SSL protocol evolved in three versions—SSL 1.0, SSL 2.0, and SSL 3.0—to finally become the protocol we know as TLS today. Referring to the terminology introduced in Section 1.1, the SSL protocol is a client/server protocol that provides the following basic security services to the communicating peers:

- Authentication (both peer entity and data origin authentication) services;
- Connection confidentiality services;
- Connection integrity services (without recovery).

In spite of the fact that the SSL protocol uses public key cryptography, it does not provide nonrepudiation services—neither nonrepudiation with proof of origin nor nonrepudiation with proof of delivery. This is in sharp contrast to S-HTTP and XML signatures that are able (and have been specifically designed) to provide such services. As its name suggests, the SSL protocol is sockets-oriented, meaning that all or none of the data that is sent to or received from a socket are cryptographically protected in exactly the same way (i.e., there is no way to digitally sign individual pieces of the data).

The term SSL refers to a layer that is best viewed as an intermediate layer between the transport and the application layer. Its scope of functions is twofold:

- On the one hand, it is to establish a secure (i.e., authentic and confidential) connection between the communicating peers.

- On the other hand, it is to use this connection to securely transmit higher-layer protocol data from the sender to the recipient. It therefore fragments the data into manageable pieces (called fragments), and processes each fragment individually. More specifically, each fragment is optionally compressed, authenticated with a MAC, encrypted, prepended with a header, and transmitted to the recipient. Each fragment that is treated and prepared this way is called an *SSL record*.[1] On the recipient's side, the SSL records must be decrypted, verified (with regard to their MACs), decompressed, and reassembled, before the data can be delivered to the respective higher-layer—typically the application layer—protocol.

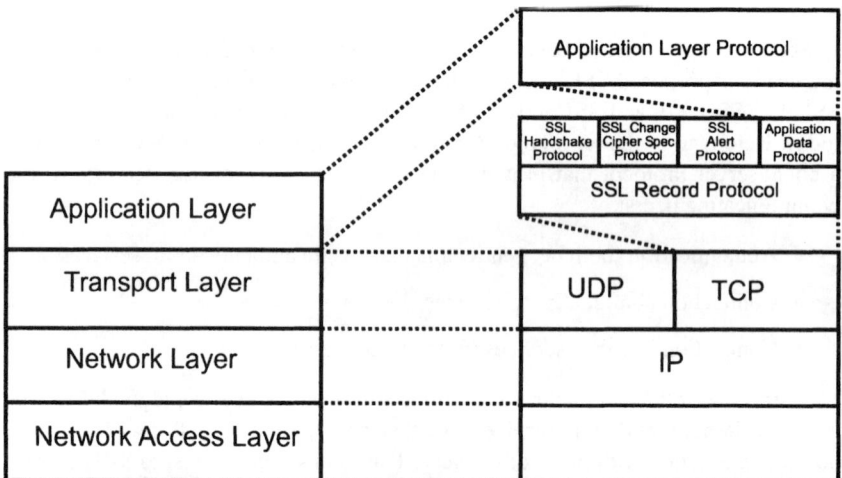

Figure 4.1 The SSL with its (sub)layers and (sub)protocols.

---

1 To be precise, an SSL record consists of four fields: a type field, a version field, a length field, and a fragment field. The fragment field, in turn, comprises the higher-layer protocol data.

The placement of the SSL layer is illustrated in Figure 4.1. It consists of two sublayers and a few subprotocols:

- The lower layer is stacked on top of some connection-oriented and reliable transport layer protocol, such as TCP in the case of the TCP/IP protocol stack.[2] This layer basically comprises the *SSL Record Protocol* that is used for the first function mentioned above (i.e., the encapsulation of higher-layer protocol data).
- The higher layer is stacked on top of the SSL Record Protocol and comprises four protocols:
    - The *SSL Handshake Protocol* is the core protocol of SSL. It allows the communicating peers to authenticate each other and to negotiate a cipher suite and a compression method used for the communications. As its name suggests, the cipher suite is used to cryptographically protect data in terms of authenticity, integrity, and confidentiality, whereas the compression method is to optionally compress data.
    - The *SSL Change Cipher Spec Protocol* allows the communicating peers to signal a cipher spec change (i.e., a change in the ciphering strategy and the way data is cryptographically protected). While the SSL Handshake Protocol is used to negotiate security parameters, the SSL Change Cipher Spec Protocol is used to put these parameters in place and make them effective.
    - The *SSL Alert Protocol* allows the communicating peers to signal indicators of potential problems and to exchange corresponding alert messages.
    - The *SSL Application Data Protocol* is used for the second function mentioned above (i.e., the secure transmission of application data). This protocol is the actual workhorse of SSL: it takes higher-layer—typically application layer—data and feeds it into the SSL Record Protocol for cryptographic protection and secure transmission.

In spite of the fact that SSL consists of several subprotocols, we use the term *SSL protocol* to refer to all of them. This may be oversimplified, but we think it is more appropriate to carry the main messages and to make the points. When we refer to a specific subprotocol, we usually employ its full name.

---

2 This is in contrast to the DTLS protocol that is stacked on top of UDP. The DTLS protocol is addressed in Chapter 6.

Like most protocols based on TCP, the SSL protocol is self-delimiting, meaning that it can autonomously determine the beginning and ending of an SSL message inside an SSL record or TCP segment (i.e., without the assistance of TCP). The SSL protocol therefore employs various length fields. In fact, each SSL record is tagged with a length field that refers to the length of the entire record. In addition, each SSL message carried inside an SSL record is also tagged with a respective length field. As explained later, multiple SSL messages of the same type can in fact be carried inside a single SSL record.

One major advantage of the SSL protocol is that it is application layer protocol independent, meaning that any TCP-based application protocol can be layered on top of SSL to provide the basic security services mentioned above. In order to accomodate connections from clients that do not employ SSL, servers must typically be prepared to accept both secure and nonsecure versions of a given application layer protocol. There are usually two strategies to achieve this goal: separate ports and upward negotiation.

- In a *separate port strategy*, a different port number is assigned to the secure version of the application layer protocol. This suggests that the server has to listen both on the original port and the new (secure) port. For any connection that arrives on the secure port, SSL is invoked automatically.

- In contrast, in an *upward negotiation strategy*, a single port is used for both versions of the application layer protocol. This protocol, in turn, must be extended to support a message indicating that one side would like to upgrade to SSL. If the other side agrees, SSL is invoked and a secure channel is established to be used by the application layer protocol.

Both strategies have advantages and disadvantages, and hence, in principle, both strategies can be pursued. For example, in the case of HTTP, the upward negotiation strategy is employed in the standards track RFC 2817 [1],[3] whereas the separate port strategy is employed in the informational RFC 2818 [2].

- RFC 2817 explains how to use the upgrade mechanism in HTTP/1.1 to initiate SSL/TLS over an existing TCP connection. This mechanism can be invoked by either the client or server, and upgrading can be optional or mandatory. In either case, the HTTP/1.1 Upgrade header must be employed. This is a hop-by-hop header, and hence care must be taken to upgrade across (possibly multiple) proxy servers. The bottom line is that the upgrade mechanism in HTTP/1.1 allows unsecured and secured HTTP traffic to share the same port (typically 80). It also enables virtual hosting, so a single HTTPS server can

---

3 Note that this RFC is written for the TLS protocol, but the same mechanism also applies to the SSL protocol.

Table 4.1
Port Numbers Reserved for Applicaton Protocols Layered over SSL/TLS

Protocol	Description	Port #
nsiiops	IIOP Name Service over SSL/TLS	261
https	HTTP over SSL/TLS	443
nntps	NNTP over SSL/TLS	563
ldaps	LDAP over SSL/TLS	636
ftps-data	FTP Data over SSL/TLS	989
ftps	FTP Control over SSL/TLS	990
telnets	Telnet over SSL/TLS	992
imaps	IMAP4 over SSL/TLS	993
ircs	IRC over SSL/TLS	994
pop3s	POP3 over SSL/TLS	995
tftps	TFTP over SSL/TLS	3713
sip-tls	SIP over SSL/TLS	5061
...	...	...

differentiate between traffic intended for several hostnames at a single IP address.

- RFC 2818 elaborates on using a different server port for the secured HTTP traffic. This is comparably simple and straightforward.

In general, it is up to the designer of the application layer protocol to make a choice between the separate port and upward negotiation strategy. Historically, most protocol designers have made a choice in favor of the separate port strategy. For example, until the SSL 3.0 protocol specification was officially released in 1996, the Internet Assigned Numbers Authority (IANA) had already reserved the port number 443 for use by HTTP over SSL (https), and was about to reserve the port numbers 465 for use by the Simple Mail Transfer Protocol (SMTP) over SSL (ssmtp) and 563 for the Network News Transfer Protocol (NNTP) over SSL (snntp). Later on, the IANA decided to consistently append the letter "s" after the protocol name, so snntp effectively became nntps. Today, there are several port numbers reserved by the IANA for application layer protocols stacked on top of SSL/TLS.[4] The most important examples are summarized in Table 4.1. Among these examples, ldaps, ftps (and ftps-data), imaps and pop3s are particularly important and most widely used in practice. In contrast, there are only a few application layer protocols that implement an upward negotiation strategy. We mentioned the HTTP/1.1 upgrade mechanism above. But by far the most prominent example is SMTP with its STARTTLS feature specified in RFC 2487 [3] that invokes SSL for

---

[4] http://www.iana.org/assignments/port-numbers.

the secure transmission of data between two mail servers. STARTTLS is based on the SMTP extensions mechansism specified in RFC 1869 [4].

The separate port strategy has the disadvantage that it effectively halves the number of available ports on the server side (because two ports must be reserved for each application protocol and service). During an IETF meeting in 1997, the Applications Area Directors and the IESG therefore affirmed that the upward negotiation strategy would be the way to go, and that the separate port strategy should therefore be deprecated. In reality, however, we see a distinct development: in spite of the fact that RFC 2817 (specifying an upgrade mechanism for HTTP/1.1) has been available for almost a decade and is even representing a standards track RFC, there has hardly been any interest in implementing alternatives to port 443. This may change for future application protocols. But for HTTP, implementing the separate port strategy and using port 443 is still the most widely deployed option. This is not likely to change in the foreseeable future.

The SSL protocol was designed with interoperability in mind. This means that the protocol is intended to make the probability that two independent SSL implementations interoperate as large as possible. As such, the design of the SSL protocol is simpler and more straightforward than the design of many other security protocols, including, for example, the IPsec/IKE protocols. But the simple and straightforward design of the SSL protocol is also slightly stashed away by the fact that the Internet-Draft that specifies SSL 3.0 as well as the RFC documents that specify the various versions of the TLS protocol all use a specific presentation language. For the purpose of this book, we neither introduce this language nor do we actually use it. Instead, we use plain English text to describe the protocols with as few bit-level details as necessary.

The SSL protocol and its successors are block-oriented with a block size of one byte (i.e., eight bits). Against this background, multiple-byte values are just concatenations of bytes. The concatenations are written from left to right and from top to bottom, but keep in mind that the resulting strings are just byte strings transmitted over the wire. The byte ordering—also known as *endianness*—for muliple-byte values is the usual *network byte order* or *big endian* format. So the sequence of the hexadecimal bytes 0x01, 0x02, 0x03, and 0x04 is equivalent to the decimal value

$$\begin{aligned} 1 \cdot 16^6 + 2 \cdot 16^4 + 3 \cdot 16^2 + 4 \cdot 16^0 &= 16,777,216 + 131,072 + 768 + 4 \\ &= 16,909,060. \end{aligned}$$

The aim of the SSL protocol is to securely transmit application data between communicating peers. The SSL protocol therefore establishes and employs SSL connections and SSL sessions. Both terms are required to properly understand the functioning of SSL.

- An *SSL connection* is used to actually transmit data between two communicating peers, typically a client and a server, in some cryptographically protected and optionally compressed form. Hence, there are some cryptographic (and other) parameters that must be put in place and applied to the data transmitted over the SSL connection. One or several SSL connections may then be associated with an SSL session.

- Similar to an IPsec/IKE security association,[5] an *SSL session* refers to an association between two communicating peers that is created by the SSL Handshake Protocol. The SSL session defines a set of cryptographic (and other) parameters that are commonly used by the SSL connections associated with the session to cryptographically protect and optionally compress the data in transmission. Hence, an SSL session can be shared among multiple SSL connections, and SSL sessions are primarily used to avoid the expensive negotiation of new parameters for each SSL connection.

Between a pair of entities, there may be multiple SSL connections in place. In theory, there may also coexist multiple simultaneous SSL sessions, but this possibility is seldom used in the field.

SSL sessions and connections are stateful, meaning that the client and server must keep some state information. It is in the responsibility of the SSL Handshake Protocol to establish and coordinate (as well as possibly synchronize) this state on the client and server side, thereby allowing the SSL protocol state machines on either side to operate consistently. Logically, the state is represented twice, once as the *current state*, and once as the *pending state*. Also, separate *read* and *write* states are maintained. So there is a total of four states that need to be managed. The transition from a pending to a current state occurs when a CHANGECIPHERSPEC message is sent or received during an SSL handshake negotiaton (as further explained below). The rules are as follows:

- If an entity (i.e., client or server) sends a CHANGECIPHERSPEC message, then it copies the pending write state into the current write state. The read states remain unchanged.

---

5 There are still a few conceptual and subtle differences between an IPsec/IKE security association and an SSL session: (1) An IPsec/IKE security association is unidirectional, whereas an SSL session is bidirectional. (2) An IPsec/IKE security association identifier—also known as *security parameter index* (SPI)—is intentionally kept as short as 32 bits (as it is being transmitted in each IP packet), whereas the length of an SSL session identifier does not really matter and need not be minimized. (3) IPsec/IKE do not really represent client/server protocols, mainly because clients and servers do not really exist at the Internet layer (instead the terms *initiator* and *responder* are used in this context). In contrast, the SSL protocol in general, and the SSL Handshake Protocol in particular represent real client/server protocols.

- If an entity receives a CHANGECIPHERSPEC message, then it copies the pending read state into the current read state. In this case, the write states remain unchanged.

When the SSL handshake negotiaton is complete, the client and server have exchanged CHANGECIPHERSPEC messages, and hence they can communicate using the newly agreed-upon cryptographic (and other) parameters. As discussed below, the FINISHED message is the first SSL handshake message that is protected according to these new parameters.

For each SSL session and connection, the SSL protocol state machine must hold some information elements. The corresponding session state and connection state elements are summarized in Tables 4.2 and 4.3. We revisit some of these elements when we go through the SSL protocol in detail (later in this chapter).

Table 4.2
SSL Session State Elements

session identifier	Arbitrary byte sequence chosen by the server to identify an active or resumable session state (maximum length is 32 bytes)
peer certificate	X.509v3 certificate of the peer (if available)
compression method	Data compression algorithm used (prior to encryption)
cipher spec	Data encryption and MAC algorithms used (together with cryptographic parameters, such as the length of the hash values)
master secret	48-byte secret that is shared between the client and the server
is resumable	Flag indicating whether the SSL session is resumable, meaning that it can be used to initiate new connections

The SSL protocol is a cryptographic protocol, meaning that it employs cryptography and cryptographic technques. More specifically, the SSL protocol employs secret key cryptography for message authentication and bulk data encryption, and it uses public key cryptography for peer entity authentication and key establishment. Before secret key cryptographic techniques can be invoked, some keying material must be established. There are basically three key exchange algorithms that can be used to establish a 48-byte premaster secret, termed pre_master_secret in the SSL protocol specification: RSA, Diffie-Hellman, and FORTEZZA.[6] Some of these algorithms combine a key exchange with peer entity authentication, and hence actually refer to authenticated key exchange algorithms. To make this distinction explicit, a key exchange without peer entity authentication can also be called an anonymous

---

6   Remember from Section 2.2.2.1 that the Skipjack cipher and the FORTEZZA KEA were declassified in 1998. Because the SSL 3.0 specification was released in 1996, the details of the FORTEZZA KEA could not be included. Instead, the FORTEZZA KEA was treated as a black box in the specification of SSL 3.0.

Table 4.3
SSL Connection State Elements

server and client random	Byte sequences that are chosen by the server and client for each connection
server write MAC key	Secret used in MAC operations on data written by the server
client write MAC key	Secret used in MAC operations on data written by the client
server write key	Key used for data encrypted by the server and decrypted by the client
client write key	Key used for data encrypted by the client and decrypted by the server
initialization vectors	If a block cipher in CBC mode is used for data encryption, then an IV must be maintained for each key. This field is first initialized by the SSL Handshake Protocol. Afterwards, the final ciphertext block from each SSL record is preserved to serve as IV for the next record.
sequence numbers	SSL message authentication employs sequence numbers. This basically means that the client and server must maintain a sequence number for the messages that are transmitted or received on a particular connection. Each sequence number is 64 bits long and ranges from 0 to $2^{64} - 1$. It is set to zero whenever a CHANGECIPHERSPEC message is sent or receved.

key exchange. To keep things simple, the SSL protocol specification only speaks about key exchange algorithms and does not distinguish between authenticated and anonymous ones. Let us now briefly explore the possibilities the SSL provides to exchange cryptographic keys.

- If RSA is used for key exchange, then the client generates a premaster secret, encrypts it under the server's public key, and sends the resulting ciphertext to the server. The server's public key, in turn, can either be long-termed and retrieved from a public key certificate, or short-termed and provided for a particular key exchange. In either case, the server uses the corresponding private key to decrypt the premaster secret.
- If Diffie-Hellman is used for key exchange, then a Diffie-Hellman key exchange is performed and the resulting Diffie-Hellman value (without leading zero bytes) represents the premaster secret. The SSL protocol provides support for three versions of the Diffie-Hellman key exchange:

- In a *fixed Diffie-Hellman key exchange* (abbreviated DH), some Diffie-Hellman parameters are fixed and part of the respective public key certificates. This applies to the server, but and it may also apply to the client. This means that the client's Diffie-Hellman parameters can either be fixed and part of the client certificate, if client authentication is required, or they may be dynamically generated and provided in corresponding SSL handshake messages.
- In an *ephemeral Diffie-Hellman key exchange* (abbreviated DHE), the Diffie-Hellman parameters are not fixed and are not part of public key certificates. Instead, a Diffie-Hellman key exchange is performed to generate an ephemeral key. The corresponding Diffie-Hellman parameters are dynamically generated and must be authenticated in some way. Usually, the parameters are digitally signed with the sender's private (RSA or DSS) signing key. The recipient can then use the sender's public key to verify the signature. Authenticity of the public key is guaranteed, if it is retrieved from a valid public key certificate.
- In an *anonymous Diffie-Hellman key exchange* (abbreviated DH_anon), a Diffie-Hellman key exchange is performed, but the Diffie-Hellman parameters that are exchanged are not authenticated. This means that the resulting key exchange is susceptible to a man-in-the-middle attack.

The ephemeral Diffie-Hellman key exchange appears to be the most secure version of the Diffie-Hellman key exchange, because it yields temporary but authenticated keys. The fixed Diffie-Hellman key exchange has the problem that the keying material generated is always the same for two participating entities, and the anonymous Diffie-Hellman key exchange has the problem that it is vulnerable to man-in-the-middle attacks. Anyway, if the same Diffie-Hellman keypair is to be used for multiple handshakes, either because the client or server has a certificate containing a fixed Diffie-Hellman key or because the server is reusing keying material, care must be taken to prevent small subgroup attacks. Such attacks are most easily avoided by using an ephemeral key exchange and generating a fresh Diffie-Hellman key for each handshake. This has the additional advantage that it provides perfect forward secrecy (PFS). This basically means that the compromise of long-term keying material does not necessarily compromise each and every session key.

- In the case of FORTEZZA, the key exchange process yields a TEK that can then be used to securely transmit a randomly chosen premaster secret together with some additional keys and cryptographic parameters to the server. Note that FORTEZZA encryption keys are generated by the token and not derived from the premaster or master secret.

In the past, RSA has been the predominant SSL key exchange method. This is in spite of the fact that the ephemeral Diffie-Hellman key exchange method has some security advantages (mainly because both parties participate in the generation of the keying material).

Once a premaster secret is established, it can be used to construct a master secret that is called `master_secret` in the SSL protocol specification. According to Table 4.2, the master secret represents an SSL session state element. It is constructed as follows:

```
master_secret =
   MD5(pre_master_secret + SHA('A' + pre_master_secret
      + ClientHello.random + ServerHello.random)) +
   MD5(pre_master_secret + SHA('BB' + pre_master_secret
      + ClientHello.random + ServerHello.random)) +
   MD5(pre_master_secret + SHA('CCC' + pre_master_secret
      + ClientHello.random + ServerHello.random))
```

In this notation, SHA refers to SHA-1, `'A'`, `'BB'`, and `'CCC'` refer to the respective byte strings 0x41, 0x4242, and 0x434343, `ClientHello.random` and `ServerHello.random` refer to a pair of values that are randomly chosen by the client and server and exchanged in SSL Handshake Protocol messages (see below), and + refers to the string concatenation operator. Interestingly, the construction does not use either MD5 or SHA-1, but combines the two cryptographic hash functions (probably to compensate any potential deficiency).

An MD5 hash value is 16 bytes long, so the total length of the master secret is $3 \cdot 16 = 48$ bytes. Its construction is the same for the RSA, Diffie-Hellman, or FORTEZZA key exchange algorithms (but in the case of FORTEZZA, the master secret is not used to derive encryption keys). As illustrated in Table 4.2, the master secret is part of the session state and is treated accordingly. It serves as a source of entropy for the generation of the cryptographic parameters (e.g., cryptographic keys and IVs) that are used to secure the communications. Note that the premaster secret can be safely deleted from memory once the master secret has been constructed.

Equipped with the master secret, a handcrafted PRF can be employed to generate an arbitrarily long key block, termed `key_block` in the SSL protocol specification. In this PRF construction, the master secret serves as a seed, and the client and server random values represent salt values (to make cryptanalysis more difficult). The key block is iteratively constructed in the following way:

```
key_block =
```

```
MD5(master_secret + SHA('A' + master_secret +
    ServerHello.random + ClientHello.random)) +
MD5(master_secret + SHA('BB' + master_secret +
    ServerHello.random + ClientHello.random)) +
MD5(master_secret + SHA('CCC' + master_secret +
    ServerHello.random + ClientHello.random)) +
[...]
```

Every iteration adds 16 bytes (i.e., the length of the MD5 hash value), and hence the construction is continued until the key block is sufficiently long to form the cryptographic SSL connection state elements of Table 4.3 that are still missing:

```
client_write_MAC_secret
server_write_MAC_secret
client_write_key
server_write_key
client_write_IV
server_write_IV
```

The first two values represent message authentication keys, the second two values represent encryption keys, and the third two values represent IVs that are needed if a block cipher in CBC mode is used (so these values are optional). Any additional material in the key block is discarded. The construction equally applies to RSA and Diffie-Hellman, as well as for the MAC key contruction of FORTEZZA. It does not apply to the construction of encryption keys and IVs for FORTEZZA—these values are generated inside the FORTEZZA token of the client and securely transmitted in a corresponding key exchange message.

If the encryption algorithm in use is exportable, then some additional processing is required to derive the final encryption keys and IVs:

```
final_client_write_key =
   MD5(client_write_key + ClientHello.random +
       ServerHello.random);
final_server_write_key =
   MD5(server_write_key + ServerHello.random +
       ClientHello.random);
client_write_IV =
   MD5(ClientHello.random + ServerHello.random);
server_write_IV =
   MD5(ServerHello.random + ClientHello.random);
```

The output of MD5 is always trimmed to the appropriate size by discarding the least-significant bytes.

The SSL protocol partly conforms to standards. For example, RSA digital signatures are always performed using public key cryptography standard (PKCS) #1 block type 1,[7] whereas RSA public key encryption employs PKCS #1 block type 2. The PKCS #1 version that was relevant when the SSL protocol was specified in 1996 was 1.5 [5]. As discussed later in this chapter, PKCS #1 version 1.5 turned out to be susceptible to adaptive chosen ciphertext attacks, and hence it was replaced with a more secure version 2.0 in 1998 [6]. Later on, some subtle vulnerabilities led to another revision of PKCS #1, so that the current version is 2.1 [7].

4.2 PROTOCOLS

As mentioned above, the SSL protocols comprise the SSL Record Protocol, the SSL Handshake Protocol, the SSL Change Cipher Spec Protocol, the SSL Alert Protocol, and the SSL Application Data Protocol. We overview and discuss these protocols in this order.

4.2.1 SSL Record Protocol

We already said that the SSL Record Protocol is used for the encapsulation of higher-layer protocol data, and that it therefore fragments the data into manageable pieces (called fragments), and processes each fragment individually. More specifically, each fragment is optionally compressed and cryptographically protected according to the compression method and cipher spec of the SSL session state and the cryptographic parameters of the SSL connection state. The result represents the fragment of the SSL record sent to the recipient.

The SSL record processing is overviewed in Figure 4.2. Fragmentation, compression, and cryptographic protection lead to data structures that are called SSLPlaintext, SSLCompressed, and SSLCiphertext in the SSL protocol specification. At the end, an SSL record header is appended to the SSLCiphertext structure to form an SSL record. Each structure comprises four fields: a type field, a version field, a length field, and a fragment field. The four steps are more thoroughly addressed next.

---

7 There is another block type 0 specified in PKCS #1. This type, however, is not used in the SSL protocol specification.

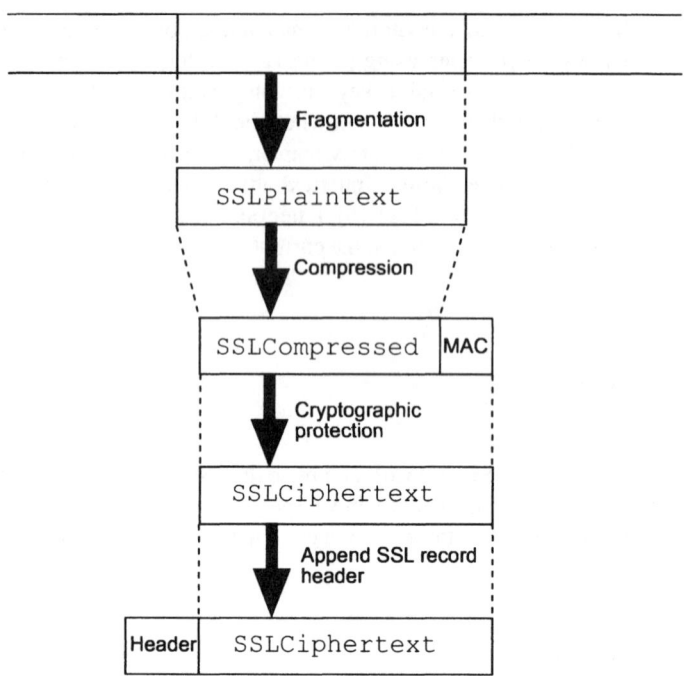

Figure 4.2 The SSL record processing (overview).

4.2.1.1 Fragmentation

In the first step, the SSL Record Protocol fragments the higher-layer protocol data into blocks of 2^{14} bytes or less. Each block is packed into an `SSLPlaintext` structure. Client message boundaries are not preserved, meaning that multiple messages of the same type may be coalesced into a single `SSLPlaintext` structure.

4.2.1.2 Compression

In the second step, the SSL Record Protocol compresses the `SSLPlaintext` structure according to the compression method specified in the SSL session state. This method is initially set to null, so compression is optional by default. In spite of the fact that compression is seldom used in practice, providing the possibility for compression before encryption is still an important feature. This is because data cannot be significantly compressed anymore once it is encrypted (i.e., encrypted data cannot be distinguished from random data, and hence there is hardly any redundancy that can be removed with data compression).

The SSL specification mandates that the compression is lossless and that it should not increase the length of the fragment by more than 1,024 bytes.[8] As a practical matter, no compression method other than null compression has been defined for SSL 3.0. Anyway, compression turns an SSLPlaintext structure into an SSLCompressed structure. If the compression method is null, then the compression method is the identity operation, and hence the SSLPlaintext and SSLCompressed fragments are identical.

4.2.1.3 Cryptographic Protection

In the third step, the SSL Record Protocol protects a SSLCompressed structure according to the cipher spec specified in the SSL session state. According to Table 4.2, a *cipher spec* refers to a pair of algorithms that are used to cryptographically protect data. It consists of a message authentication and a data encryption algorithm. The cipher spec is complemented with a key exchange algorithm. A cipher spec together with a key exchange algorithm form a *cipher suite*, and the set of 31 cipher suites defined for SSL is summarized in Appendix A and Appendix C of the SSL 3.0 protocol specification. They are also illustrated in Table 4.4. In this table, the first column itemizes the names of the cipher suites. The suites written in italics used to be exportable from the United States (this criterion was important until the end of the 1990s). They were exportable only if the length of the Diffie-Hellman keys was not longer than 512 bits, and the key length of the block cipher was not longer than 40 bits. The other three columns decompose a cipher suite into its components in terms of key exchange algorithm, cipher (i.e., symmetric encryption system), and cryptographic hash function. For example, SSL_DH_RSA_WITH_3DES_EDE_CBC_SHA refers to the cipher suite that comprises RSA for key exchange, 3DES in CBC mode for encryption, and SHA-1 for message authentication. Each cipher suite is encoded in two bytes: the first byte is 0x00 and the second byte is the hexadecimal representation of the cipher suite number as they occur in Table 4.4 (starting with 0). All cipher suites whose first byte is 0xFF are considered private and can be used for experimentation. Interoperability of such types is a local matter. If the RFC editor's office agrees, then additional cipher suites may be publishing in informational or even standards track RFCs.

---

8 Of course, one hopes that compression shrinks rather than expands the fragment. However, for very short fragments, it is possible, because of formatting conventions, that the compression method actually provides output that is longer than the input.

Table 4.4
SSL Cipher Suites

CipherSuite	Key Exchange	Cipher	Hash
SSL_NULL_WITH_NULL_NULL	NULL	NULL	NULL
SSL_RSA_WITH_NULL_MD5	RSA	NULL	MD5
SSL_RSA_WITH_NULL_SHA	RSA	NULL	SHA
SSL_RSA_EXPORT_WITH_RC4_40_MD5	RSA_EXPORT	RC4_40	MD5
SSL_RSA_WITH_RC4_128_MD5	RSA	RC4_128	MD5
SSL_RSA_WITH_RC4_128_SHA	RSA	RC4_128	SHA
SSL_RSA_EXPORT_WITH_RC2_CBC_40_MD5	RSA_EXPORT	RC2_CBC_40	MD5
SSL_RSA_WITH_IDEA_CBC_SHA	RSA	IDEA_CBC	SHA
SSL_RSA_EXPORT_WITH_DES40_CBC_SHA	RSA_EXPORT	DES40_CBC	SHA
SSL_RSA_WITH_DES_CBC_SHA	RSA	DES_CBC	SHA
SSL_RSA_WITH_3DES_EDE_CBC_SHA	RSA	3DES_EDE_CBC	SHA
SSL_DH_DSS_EXPORT_WITH_DES40_CBC_SHA	DH_DSS_EXPORT	DES40_CBC	SHA
SSL_DH_DSS_WITH_DES_CBC_SHA	DH_DSS	DES_CBC	SHA
SSL_DH_DSS_WITH_3DES_EDE_CBC_SHA	DH_DSS	3DES_EDE_CBC	SHA
SSL_DH_RSA_EXPORT_WITH_DES40_CBC_SHA	DH_RSA_EXPORT	DES40_CBC	SHA
SSL_DH_RSA_WITH_DES_CBC_SHA	DH_RSA	DES_CBC	SHA
SSL_DH_RSA_WITH_3DES_EDE_CBC_SHA	DH_RSA	3DES_EDE_CBC	SHA
SSL_DHE_DSS_EXPORT_WITH_DES40_CBC_SHA	DHE_DSS_EXPORT	DES40_CBC	SHA
SSL_DHE_DSS_WITH_DES_CBC_SHA	DHE_DSS	DES_CBC	SHA
SSL_DHE_DSS_WITH_3DES_EDE_CBC_SHA	DHE_DSS	3DES_EDE_CBC	SHA
SSL_DHE_RSA_EXPORT_WITH_DES40_CBC_SHA	DHE_RSA_EXPORT	DES40_CBC	SHA
SSL_DHE_RSA_WITH_DES_CBC_SHA	DHE_RSA	DES_CBC	SHA
SSL_DHE_RSA_WITH_3DES_EDE_CBC_SHA	DHE_RSA	3DES_EDE_CBC	SHA
SSL_DH_anon_EXPORT_WITH_RC4_40_MD5	DH_anon_EXPORT	RC4_40	MD5
SSL_DH_anon_WITH_RC4_128_MD5	DH_anon	RC4_128	MD5
SSL_DH_anon_EXPORT_WITH_DES40_CBC_SHA	DH_anon	DES40_CBC	SHA
SSL_DH_anon_WITH_DES_CBC_SHA	DH_anon	DES_CBC	SHA
SSL_DH_anon_WITH_3DES_EDE_CBC_SHA	DH_anon	3DES_EDE_CBC	SHA
SSL_FORTEZZA_KEA_WITH_NULL_SHA	FORTEZZA_KEA	NULL	SHA
SSL_FORTEZZA_KEA_WITH_FORTEZZA_CBC_SHA	FORTEZZA_KEA	FORTEZZA_CBC	SHA
SSL_FORTEZZA_KEA_WITH_RC4_128_SHA	FORTEZZA_KEA	RC4_128	SHA

There is always an active cipher suite, but it is initially set to SSL_NULL_WITH _NULL_NULL, which does not provide any security service. In fact, this cipher suite refers to the identity operation for encryption and a MAC size of zero.

Cryptographic protection includes message authentication and encryption. So the first question that pops up is related to the order. In theory, there are three possibilities:

1. Authenticate the message, encrypt the message and the MAC, and send the resulting ciphertext (that now includes the MAC) to the recipient. This possibility is called *authenticate-then-encrypt* (abbreviated AtE), and it is used, for example, by the SSL/TLS protocols.

2. Encrypt the message, authenticate the ciphertext, and send the ciphertext along with the MAC to the recipient. This possibility is called *encrypt-then-authenticate* (abbreviated EtA), and it is used, for example, by the IPsec protocol.
3. Encrypt the message, authenticate the message, and send the ciphertext along with the MAC to the recipient. This possibility is called *encrypt-and-authenticate* (abbreviated E&A), and it is used, for example, by the SSH protocol.

It has been shown by Hugo Krawczyk and Ran Canetti [8, 9] that EtA is the generically secure method of combining secure message authentication and secure encryption, but that EtA is also secure if a block cipher in CBC mode or a stream cipher is used for encryption. This is the underlying reason why all ciphers in Table 4.4 are either block ciphers in CBC mode or stream ciphers. Let us now have a closer look at message authentication and encryption.

Message Authentication

First of all, we note that an SSL cipher suite specifies a cryptographic hash function (not a MAC algorithm), and hence some additional information is required to actually compute and verify a MAC. The algorithm used by SSL is a predecessor of the HMAC construction frequently used today (see Section 2.2.2.2). In fact, the SSL MAC algorithm is based on the original Internet-Draft for the HMAC construction, which used the concatenation instead of the XOR operation. Hence, the SSL MAC algorithm is conceptually similar and its security is assumed to be comparable to the one of the HMAC construction. Remember that the HMAC construction is defined as follows:

$$HMAC_k(m) = h(k \oplus opad \parallel h(k \oplus ipad \parallel m))$$

In this construction, h denotes a cryptographic hash function (i.e., MD5 or SHA-1), k the secret key (used for message authentication), m the message to be authenticated, $ipad$ (standing for "inner pad") the byte 0x36 (i.e., 00110110) repeated 64 times, $opad$ (standing for "outer pad") the byte 0x5C (i.e., 01011100) repeated 64 times, $\oplus$ the bit-wise addition modulo 2, and $\parallel$ the concatenation operation. Using a similar notation, the SSL MAC construction can be represented as

$$SSL\ MAC_k(SSLCompressed) = \\ h(k \parallel opad \parallel h(k \parallel ipad \parallel seq\_number \parallel \underbrace{type \parallel length \parallel fragment}_{SSLCompressed^*}))$$

where $SSLCompressed$ refers to the SSL structure that is authenticated (and that comprises $type$, $version$, $length$, and $fragment$ fields), $SSLCompressed^*$ represents the same structure without the $version$ field, h denotes a cryptographic hash function, and k refers to the (server or client) MAC write key. The two values $ipad$ and $opad$ are the same bytes repeated 48 times (for MD5) or 40 times (for SHA-1)—compare this to the 64 times that are required in the HMAC construction. Last but not least, the SSL MAC construction also takes into account a 64-bit sequence number seq_number for the message to be authenticated.[9]

Encryption

After having appended a MAC to the SSLCompressed structure, the SSL Record Protocol encrypts the SSLCompressed structure and the MAC to generate a SSLCiphertext structure. The situation is different in the case where a stream cipher is used and the case where a block cipher is used.

- If a stream cipher is used, then no padding and IV are needed. But a stream cipher is stateful, meaning that some cipher state must be maintained. In the case of the SSL protocol, the cipher state from the end of the encryption of one structure is used for the encryption of the next structure. According to Table 4.4, the SSL protocol envisions the use of the stream cipher RC4 with either a 40-bit or 128-bit key.

- If a block cipher is used, then things get more involved mainly for two reasons:

    - First, padding is needed to force the length of the plaintext to be a multiple of the cipher's block size. If, for example, DES is used for encryption, then the length of the plaintext must be a multiple of 64 bits or 8 bytes. The padding is in the form of a number of padding bytes followed by a 1-byte indication of the byte-length of the padding. The byte specifying the byte-length of the padding is then replicated for each byte in the padding. In the SSL protocol, the padding is assumed to be as short as possible (this is different in the TLS protocols).

    - Second, an IV is needed in some encryption modes. In the case of the CBC mode, for example, the SSL Handshake Protocol must provide an IV that also represents an SSL connection state element (see Table 4.3). This IV is used to encrypt the first structure. Afterwards, the last

---

[9] The sequence number is a count of the number of messages the parties have exchanged so far. Its value is set to zero with each CHANGECIPHERSPEC message, and it is incremented once for each subsequent SSL record layer message in the session.

ciphertext block of each structure is used as IV for the encryption of the next structure.

According to Table 4.4, the SSL protocol envisions the use of the block ciphers RC2 (with a 40-bit key), DES (with a 40 or 56-bit key), 3DES, IDEA, and Skipjack (named FORTEZZA). It goes without saying that, in principle, any other block cipher can also be used. Note, however, that the use of a block cipher is nontrivial, and that there are many difficulties and pitfalls to avoid if one uses a block cipher (some problems will be addressed in Sections 4.4 and 5.2).

Due to its simplicity, many SSL implementations prefer stream ciphers and employ RC4 by default. Consequently, if you use a standard browser and do not change your preferences or settings, then it is very likely that your browser employs RC4 for encryption.

At the bottom line, the algorithms specified in the cipher suite transform an SSLCompressed structure into an SSLCiphertext structure. Encryption should not increase the fragment length by more than another 1024 bytes, so the total length of the SSLCiphertext fragment (i.e., encrypted data and MAC) should not exceed $2^{14} + 2048$ bytes.

4.2.1.4 SSL Record Header

Last but not least, in the fourth step, the SSL Record Protocol appends an SSL record header to the SSLCiphertext structure. This turns a SSLCiphertext structure into an SSL record. In addition to the fragment (that is taken from the fragment of the SSLCiphertext structure), the SSL record header comprises three additional fields:

1. An 8-bit (content) *type* field that refers to the higher-layer SSL protocol. There are four predefined values:

    - 20 refers to the SSL Change Cipher Spec Protocol;
    - 21 refers to the SSL Alert Protocol;
    - 22 refers to the SSL Handshake Protocol;
    - 23 refers to the SSL Application Data Protocol.

2. A (protocol) *version* field that refers to the version of the SSL protocol in use. It is a two-byte value that consists of a major and a minor version number

separated with a comma. Hence, the value of the SSL protocol version the original specification refers to is 3,0.[10]

3. A 16-bit *length* field that refers to the byte-length of the following higher-layer protocol messages (that are transmitted in the fragment part of the SSL record). Remember that multiple higher-layer protocol messages that belong to the same type can be concatenated into a single SSL record, and that each of these higher-layer protocol messages must be self-delimiting, for example, by using an appropriate length field.

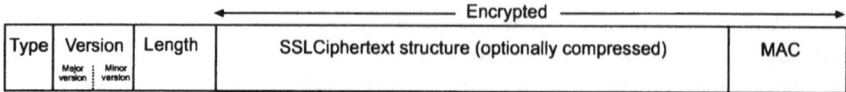

Figure 4.3 The outline of an SSL record.

The outline of an SSL record is illustrated in Figure 4.3. The fragment of the SSL records comprises an `SSLCiphertext` structure (optionally compressed) and a MAC in possibly encrypted form. The entire SSL record is sent to the recipient in a TCP segment. If multiple SSL records must be sent to the same recipient, then these records may be sent together in a single TCP segment.

4.2.2 SSL Handshake Protocol

The SSL Handshake Protocol is layered on top of the SSL Record Protocol. It allows a client and server to authenticate each other and to negotiate items like cipher suites and compression methods. The protocol and its message flows are illustrated in Figure 4.4. Messages that are written in square brackets are optional or situation-dependent, meaning that they are not always sent. Note that CHANGE-CIPHERSPEC is not actually an SSL Handshake Protocol message but represents an SSL protocol—and hence a content type—of its own. In Figure 4.4, the CHANGE-CIPHERSPEC message is therefore illustrated but written in italics. Also note that each SSL message is typed with a one-byte value (i.e., a decimal number between 0 and 255), and that these values are appended in brackets in the outline that follows (the different messages are more thoroughly discussed after the outline).

---

10 Remember from Section 3.2 that the PCT protocol's record format was compatible with that of the SSL protocol, and that in the case of PCT the most significant bit of the protocol version field was set to one.

SSL Protocol 95

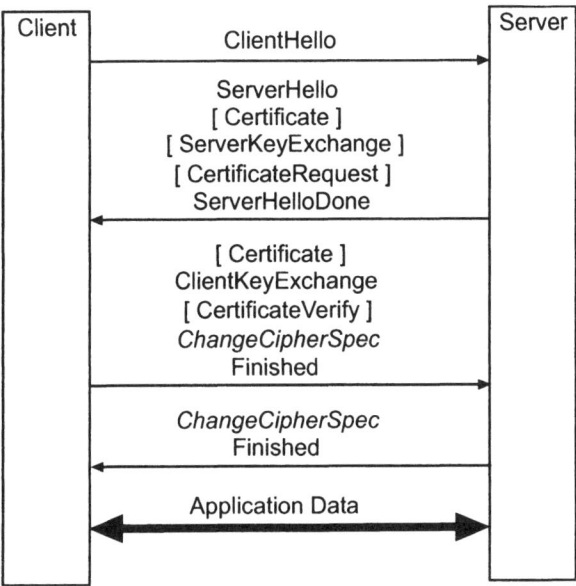

Figure 4.4 The SSL handshake protocol.

The SSL handshake protocol comprises four sets of messages—somtimes also termed *flights*[11]—that are exchanged between the client and server. Each set is typically transmitted in a separate TCP segment. There may be even a fifth set of messages that comprises a HELLOREQUEST message (type 0) that may be sent from the server to the client to actually invoke an SSL handshake. This message, however, is seldom used in practice and it is therefore ignored in the outline (but it is explained later on). In either case, the messages are presented in the order they are sent. Sending SSL handshake messages in unexpected order must result in a fatal error.

- The first set of messages is sent from the client to the server. It only comprises a CLIENTHELLO message (type 1).

- The second set of messages comprises 2–5 messages that are sent from the server to the client:

---

11 The term is not used in this book. It was introduced in the datagram TLS (DTLS) protocol specification addressed in Chapter 6.

1. A SERVERHELLO message (type 2) is sent in response to the CLIENT-HELLO message.
2. If the server is to authenticate itself (which is generally the case), it may send a CERTIFICATE message (type 11) to the client.
3. Under some circumstances (discussed below), the server may send a SERVERKEYEXCHANGE message (type 12) to the client.
4. If the server requires the client to authenticate itself with a certificate, it may send a CERTIFICATEREQUEST message (type 13) to the client.
5. Finally, the server sends a SERVERHELLODONE message (type 14) to the client.

After having exchanged CLIENTHELLO and SERVERHELLO messages, the client and server have negotiated a protocol version, a session identifier (ID), a cipher suite, and a compression method. Furthermore, two random values (i.e., `ClientHello.random` and `ServerHello.random`), have been generated and are now available for use.

- The third set of messages comprises 3–5 messages that are again sent from the client to the server:

    1. If the server has sent a CERTIFICATEREQUEST message, then the client sends a CERTIFICATE message (type 11) to the server.
    2. In the main step of the protocol, the client sends a CLIENTKEYEXCHANGE message (type 16) to the server. The content of this message depends on the key exchange algorithm in use.
    3. If the client has sent a certificate to the server, then it must also send a CERTIFICATEVERIFY message (type 15) to the server. This message is digitally signed with the private key that corresponds to the certificate's public key.
    4. The client sends a CHANGECIPHERSPEC message[12] to the server (using the SSL Change Cipher Spec Protocol) and copies its pending write state into the current write state.

---

12 The missing type indicates that the CHANGECIPHERSPEC message is not an SSL Handshake Protocol message. Instead, it is an SSL Change Cipher Spec Protocol message (identified with a content type value of 20).

5. The client sends a FINISHED message (type 20) to the server. As mentioned above, this is the first message that is cryptographically protected under the new cipher spec.

- Finally, the fourth set of messages comprises two messages that are sent from the server to the client:

   1. The server sends another CHANGECIPHERSPEC message to the client and copies its pending write state into the current write state.
   2. Finally, the server sends a FINISHED message (type 20) to the client. Again, this message is cryptographically protected under the new cipher spec.

At this point in time, the SSL handshake is complete and the client and server may begin exchanging application layer protocol data units (using the SSL Application Data Protocol).

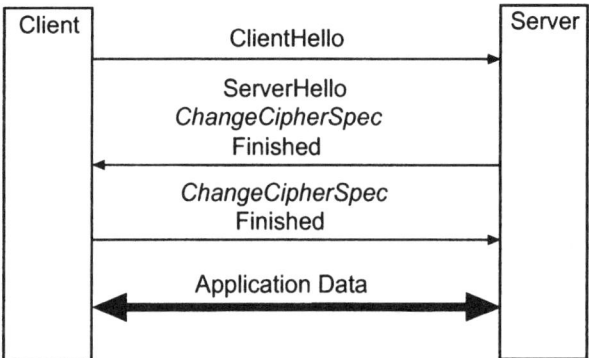

Figure 4.5 The simplied SSL handshake protocol (to resume a session).

When the client and server are willing to resume a previously established or duplicate an existing SSL session, then the SSL Handshake Protocol can be simplified considerably. The resulting (simplified) protocol is illustrated in Figure 4.5. The client sends a CLIENTHELLO message including the ID of the session to be resumed. The server then checks its session cache for a match. If a match is found and the server is willing to reestablish a connection under this session state, then it sends back a SERVERHELLO message with this particular session ID. The client and server can then directly move to the CHANGECIPHERSPEC and FINISHED messages. If a session ID match is not found, then the server must generate a new session ID and the client and server must go through a full SSL handshake negotiation.

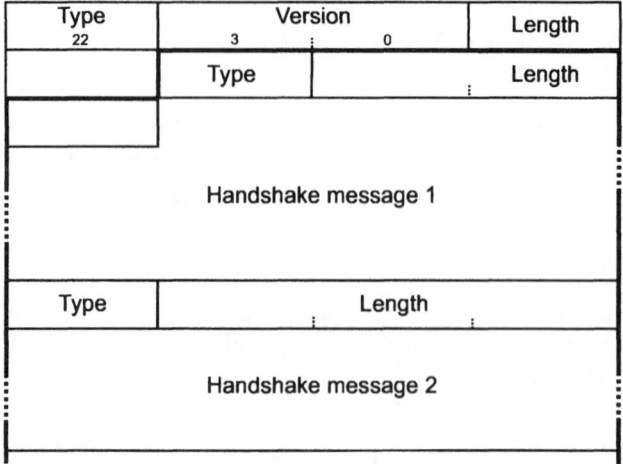

Figure 4.6 The structure of an SSL handshake protocol message.

Let us now have a closer look at the various messages that are exchanged in the course of an SSL handshake negotiation. Each message starts with a 1-byte *type* field that refers to the SSL handshake message and a 3-byte *length* field that refers to the byte length of the message. Remember that multiple SSL handshake messages can be sent in a single SSL record. The structure of such a message is illustrated in Figure 4.6. The strongly framed part of a message refers to the SSL handshake message(s), whereas the leading 5 bytes refer to the SSL record header. This header, in turn, always comprises a 1-byte type value 22 (referring to the SSL Handshake Protocol), a 2-byte version value 3,0 (standing for SSL 3.0), and a 2-byte length value referring to the byte length of the remaining part of the SSL record. If a value is fixed, then it is indicated below the respective field name.

4.2.2.1 HELLOREQUEST Message

As mentioned above, the HELLOREQUEST message allows a server to ask a client to restart an SSL handshake negotiation. The message is not often used, but it gives servers additional options. If, for example, an SSL connection has been in use for so long that its security is put in question, then the server may send a HELLOREQUEST message to actually force the client to negotiate new session keys.

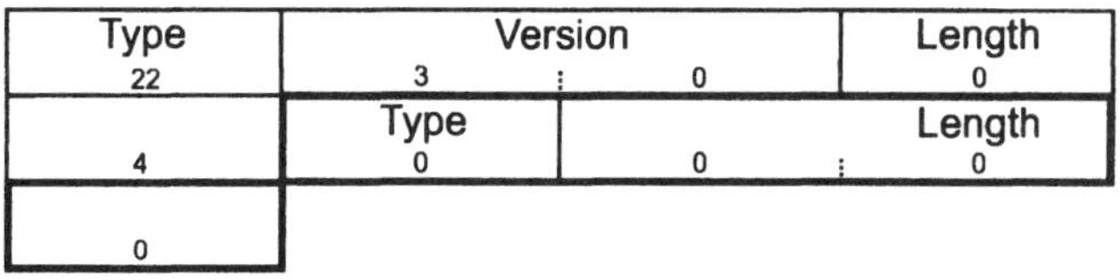

SSL Protocol 99

Type 22	Version 3 : 0	Length 0
4	Type 0 0	Length : 0
0		

Figure 4.7 An SSL HELLOREQUEST message.

As illustrated in Figure 4.7, an SSL HELLOREQUEST message starts with the usual 5-byte SSL record header. Afterwards, a type field value of zero refers to a HELLOREQUEST message. Since the message body is empty, the three bytes referring to the message length are also all set to zero. Because the HELLOREQUEST message is 4 bytes long, this value is also included in the length field of the SSL record header.

4.2.2.2 CLIENTHELLO Message

The CLIENTHELLO message is the first message that is sent from the client to the server in an SSL handshake negotiation. In fact, it is normally the message an SSL handshake negotiation begins with. As illustrated in Figure 4.8, an SSL CLIENT-HELLO message starts with the usual 5-byte SSL record header, a type field value of one (referring to a CLIENTHELLO message), and a 3-byte message length field value. In addition, a CLIENTHELLO message comprises the following fields:

- The 2 bytes immediately following the message length field refer to the highest SSL version supported by the client (typically 3,0). In the SSL protocol specification, this field is called `client_version`.
- The 32 bytes following the SSL version field comprise a client-generated random value. In the SSL protocol specification, this field is called `random`. It basically consists of two parts:

    - A 4-byte date and time (up to the second) string in standard UNIX format that is defined as the number of seconds elapsed since midnight

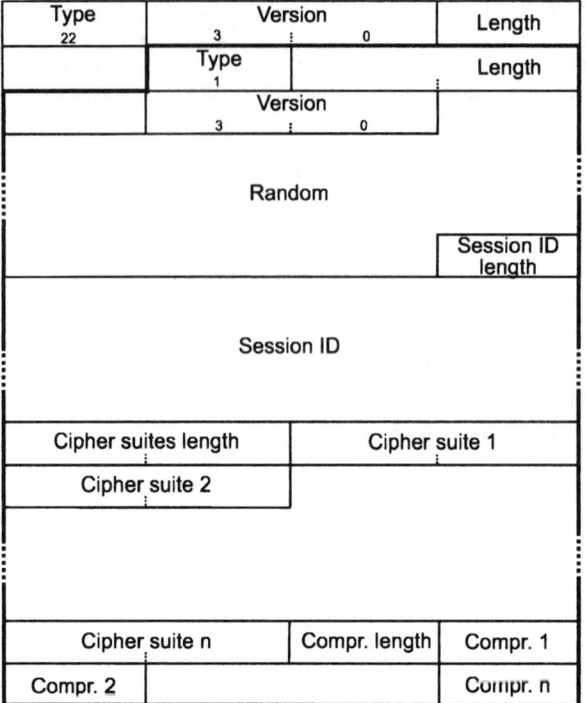

Figure 4.8 An SSL CLIENTHELLO message.

Coordinated Universal Time (UTC[13]) of January 1, 1970, not counting leap seconds[14] according to the sender's internal clock;[15]

– A 28-byte string that is randomly or pseudorandomly generated.

This value, together with a similar value created by the server, provides input for several cryptographic computations. Consequently, it is required that

---

13 Note that, for historical reasons, the term used at this point is sometimes Greenwich Mean Time (GMT), a predecessor of UTC.
14 A leap second is a one-second adjustment that keeps broadcast standards for time of day close to mean solar time.
15 The SSL protocol specification does not require a particular level of accuracy for this value, as it is not intended to provide an accurate time indication. Instead, the specification suggests using the date and time string as a way to ensure that the client does not reuse particular values.

it is unpredictable to some extent, and hence that a cryptographically strong random or pseudorandom bit generator is used to generate the second part.

- The byte immediately following the random value refers to the length of the session ID. If this value is set to zero, then there is no SSL session to resume or the client wants to generate new security parameters. In this case, the server is going to select an appropriate ID for the session. Otherwise, for example, if the session ID length is not equal to zero, then the client aims at resuming (and reusing) the identified session. Because a session ID may have a variable length, its value must be specified.

- If the session ID length is greater than zero, then the corresponding number of bytes following the session ID length represent the session ID. In the SSL protocol specification, this value—together with the session ID length—is called session_id. The SSL protocol limits session IDs (including length field) to 32 bytes or fewer, but it places no constraints on their content. Note though, that since session IDs are transmitted in CLIENTHELLO messages before any encryption is put in place, implementations should not place any information in the session ID that might, if revealed, compromise security.

- The 2 bytes immediately following the session ID refer to the number of cipher suites supported by the client. This number equals the length of the following list of cipher suites. The list is ordered according to the client's preferences (i.e., the client's first preference appears first).

- For every cipher suite supported by the client, there is a 2-byte code referring to it. In fact, the first byte of the code is always set to zero, whereas the second byte of the code refers to the index in Table 4.4. For example, SSL_NULL_WITH_NULL_NULL has a code 0,0, whereas SSL_RSA_WITH_3DES_EDE_CBC_SHA has a code 0,10. These codes are appended in a variable-length cipher suites field, called cipher_suites in the SSL protocol specification. If the session_id field is not empty (implying a session resumption request), then the value of the cipher_suites field must at least include the cipher suites from the session that is going to be resumed.

- After the cipher suites, a similar scheme applies to the compression methods supported by the client. In fact, the 2 bytes immediately following the cipher_suites field refer to the number of compression methods supported by the client. This number equals the length of the following list of compression methods. The list itself is ordered according to the client's preferences (i.e., the client's first preference appears first). For every compression method, a unique code is appended. The resulting value is written into the compression_methods field (as it is called in the SSL protocol specification). If the session_id field is not empty, then the compression_methods value must at least include the compression methods from that session. Due to the fact that SSL 3.0 only defines the null compression, all current implementations set the compression length to one and the following byte to zero, referring to null compression.

In the interest of forward compatibility, it is permitted for a CLIENTHELLO message to include extra data after the compression_methods field. This data must be included in the handshake hashes, but otherwise it must be ignored. This is the only handshake message for which this is legal (i.e., for all other messages, the amount of data in the message must match the description of the message precisely).

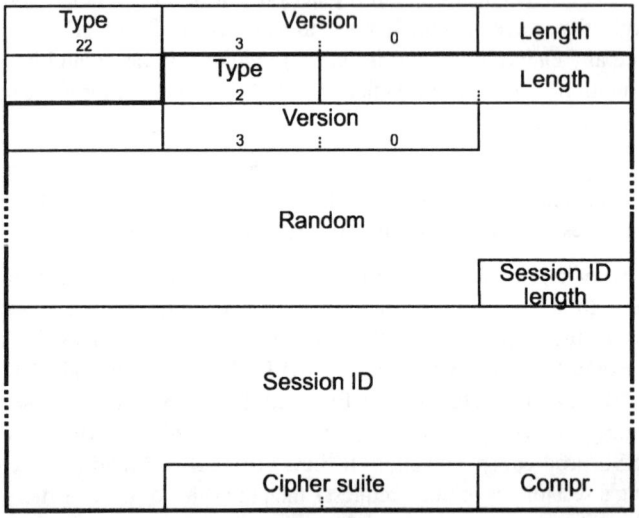

Figure 4.9 An SSL SERVERHELLO message.

4.2.2.3 SERVERHELLO Message

After having received a CLIENTHELLO message, it is up to the server to process and verify it, and to return a SERVERHELLO message in the positive case. As Figure 4.9 illustrates, the SERVERHELLO message closely resembles the CLIENTHELLO message. The only significant differences are the value of the SSL handshake message type (2 instead of 1) and the fact that the server specifies a single cipher suite and a single compression method (instead of lists of cipher suites and compression methods). Remember that the server must pick from among the choices proposed by the client, and hence the values specified by the server refer to the ones that are then used for the session.

More specifically, an SSL SERVERHELLO message starts with the usual 5-byte SSL record header, a type field value of two (referring to a SERVERHELLO message), and a 3-byte message length field. Afterwards, a SERVERHELLO message comprises the following fields:

- The 2 bytes immediately following the message length field refer to the SSL version that is going to be used. In the SSL protocol specification, this field is called server_version. It basically corresponds to the lower version of that suggested by the client in the CLIENTHELLO message and the highest version supported by the server. Typically, the server version is set to 3,0.

- The 32 bytes following the server version field comprise a 32-byte server-generated random value, again called random in the SSL protocol specification. The structure of the random value is identical to the one generated by the client; its actual value, however, must be independent and different from the client's value.

- The byte following the server random value field specifies the length of the session ID. Remember that the server may include, at its own discretion, a session ID in the SERVERHELLO message. If it does, then it allows the client to attempt to resume and reuse the session at some later point in time. Servers that don't wish to allow session resumption can omit a session ID by specifying a length of zero.

- If the session ID length is not equal to zero, then the corresponding number of bytes after the length field represent the session ID. If the session_id field of the CLIENTHELLO message was not empty, then the server is asked to look in its session cache for a match. If a match is found and the server is willing to establish a new connection using the old session state, then the server must respond with the same session_id value as supplied by the client. This indicates a resumed session and dictates that the parties must proceed to the CHANGECIPHERSPEC and FINISHED messages. Otherwise, if no match is found or the server is not willing to establish a new connection using the old session state, then the session_id field must contain a new value, and this new value is going to identify the new session.

- The 2 bytes immediately following the session ID field refer to the cipher suite selected by the server. This field is called `cipher_suite` in the SSL protocol specification (note the singular form in the field name). For resumed sessions, the value for the cipher suite field must be copied from the resumed session state.
- Finally, the last byte refers to the compression method selected by the server. This field is called `compression_method` in the SSL protocol specification (note the singular form). Again, for resumed sessions, the value for the compression method field must be copied from the resumed session state.

After the server has sent out an SSL SERVERHELLO message, it is assumed that the client and server have a common understanding about which SSL version and session to use, meaning that they know which session to resume or which algorithms to use to establish a new session.

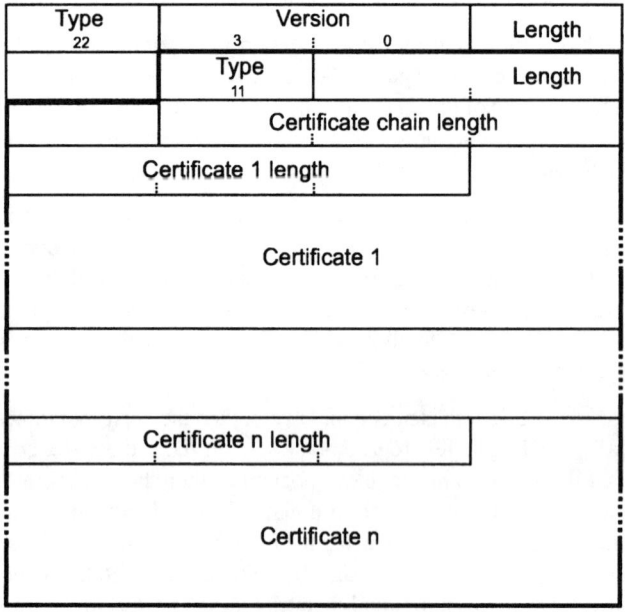

Figure 4.10 An SSL CERTIFICATE message.

4.2.2.4 CERTIFICATE Message

Most key exchange methods are nonanonymous, meaning that the server must authenticate itself to the client with a public key certificate (this applies to all key exchange methods except DH_anon). The server therefore sends a CERTIFICATE message to the client, immediately following a SERVERHELLO message. The same message type occurs later in the SSL handshake negotiation, when the server asks the client for a certificate with a CERTIFICATEREQUEST message and the client responds with another CERTIFICATE message. In either case, the aim of the CERTIFICATE message is to transfer a public key certificate, or—more generally—a set of public key certificates that form a certificate chain. In the SSL protocol specification, the field that may comprise a certificate chain is called certificate_list; it includes all certificates required to form the chain. Each chain is ordered with the sender's certificate first followed by a series of CA certificates proceeding sequentially upward until a root CA is reached. Note that support for certificate chains is a unique feature of SSL 3.0 that was not present in previous versions of the SSL protocol. Anyway, the certificate types must be appropriate for the key exchange algorithm in use. Typically, these are X.509 certificates (or some modified X.509 certificates as in the case of the FORTEZZA key exchange algorithm). All X.509 certificate profiles that are relevant in this context are specified by the IETF PKIX WG and further addressed in Chapter 8.

As illustrated in Figure 4.10, an SSL CERTIFICATE message starts with the usual 5-byte SSL record header, a type field value of value 11 (referring to an SSL CERTIFICATE message), and a 3-byte message length field. As mentioned above, the body of the message then contains a certificate chain that begins with 3 bytes that indicate the length of the entire chain (this value is always three less than the message length) and a certificate chain of exactly this length. Each certificate in the chain also begins with a 3-byte field referring to the length of this particular certificate. Depending on the length of the chain, the CERTIFICATE message may be considerably long.

In Section 2.1.6, we already mentioned that—due to the U.S. export controls that were in place until the end of the 1990s—Netscape Communications and Microsoft added features to their browsers that allowed them to use strong cryptography if triggered with specifically crafted certificates (otherwise support for strong cryptography was hidden from the server). These features were called *International Step-Up* (Netscape Communications) or *SGC* (Microsoft). In eiher case, the corresponding certificates were issued by officially approved CAs (e.g., VeriSign) and contained a special attribute in the extended key usage (extKeyUsage) field. In fact, an International Step-Up certificate included the OID 2.16.840.1.113730.4.1, whereas an SGC certificate included the OID 1.3.6.1.4.1.311.10.3.3. To keep things as simple as possible, a single certificate was typically issued that included both extended key usage objects (so the same certificate could be used to support International Step-Up and SGC).

In order to invoke International Step-Up or SGC, a normal initial SSL handshake took place. In the CLIENTHELLO message, the client claimed to support only export-strength cipher suites. So the server had no choice but to select a corresponding cipher suite. In fact, at this point in time, the server did not even know that the client supported strong cryptography in the first place. As soon as the server provided its CERTIFICATE message, however, the client knew that the server was capable of supporting strong cryptography. Depending on whether the client supported International Step-Up or SGC it proceeded the following way;

- In the case of International Step-Up, the client completed the initial handshake, but instead of beginning the exchange of application data, it started a new handshake with another CLIENTHELLO message. In this message, the client proposed full-strength cipher suites, and the server was to select one.
- In the case of SGC, the client aborted the initial handshake and sent a new CLIENTHELLO message to the server. This message proposed full-strength cipher suites, allowing the server to select one.

The bottom line of either International Step-Up or SGC is that a second SSL handshake takes place in which the server and client can negotiate the use of strong cryptography.

The use of International Step-Up and/or SGC was a compromise between the needs of the U.S. government to limit the use of full-strength cryptography abroad and the desire of browser manufacturers to offer the strongest possible product to the widest audience. Controlling the use of full-strength cryptography became a matter of controlling the issuance of International Step-Up or certificates SGC. Consequently, the U.S. government controlled which companies were allowed to purchase those certificates (mainly financial institutions that operated on a global scale).

Soon after International Step-Up and SGC were launched, a couple of local proxy servers for SSL, such as C2Net Software's *SafePassage Web Proxy*, popped up and were brought to market. As further addressed and put into perspective in Section 7.3, these proxies were able to transform export-grade cryptography into strong cryptography, independent from the browser. Even more interestingly, a tool named *Fortify*[16] was distributed internationally. The aim of the tool was to patch (or rather remove) the artificial barrier that precluded a browser from using strong cryptography (independent from the server certificate in use). This tool made

16 http://www.fortify.net.

International Step-Up and SGC obsolete, and the two initiatives silently sank into oblivion. They finally became obsolete when the U.S. government liberalized its export controls. Nevertheless, commercial CAs still sell SGC certificates, mainly because—as they argue—many elder export-version browsers that only employ strong cryptography if triggered with an appropriate certificate are still in use. These CAs can issue SGC certificates for all companies and organizations, not only financial ones.

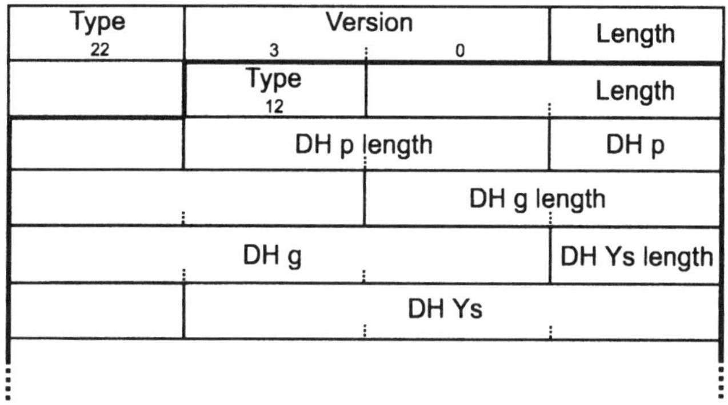

Type 22	Version 3 : 0	Length
	Type 12	Length
	DH p length	DH p
	DH g length	
	DH g	DH Ys length
	DH Ys	

Figure 4.11 The beginning of an SSL SERVERKEYEXCHANGE message using Diffie-Hellman.

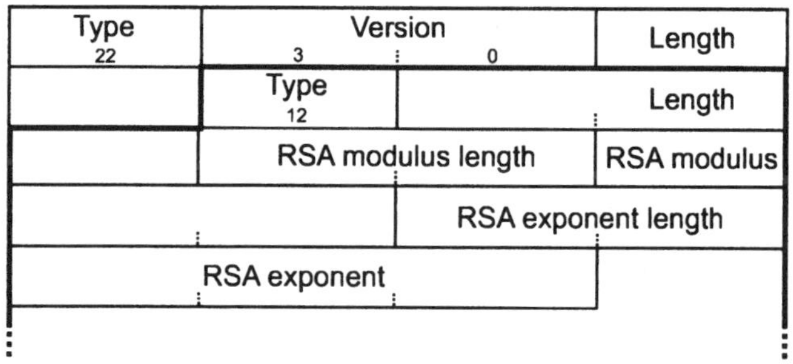

Type 22	Version 3 : 0	Length
	Type 12	Length
	RSA modulus length	RSA modulus
	RSA exponent length	
	RSA exponent	

Figure 4.12 The beginning of an SSL SERVERKEYEXCHANGE message using RSA.

4.2.2.5 SERVERKEYEXCHANGE Message

If RSA is used for key exchange, then the client can retrieve the public key from the server certificate and encrypt the premaster secret with this key. Similarly, if a fixed

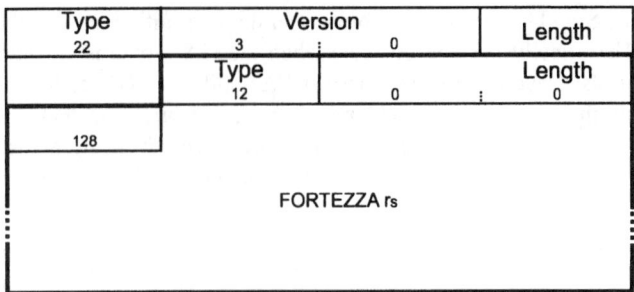

Figure 4.13 An SSL SERVERKEYEXCHANGE message using FORTEZZA.

Diffie-Hellman key exchange is used, then the client can retrieve the server's Diffie-Hellman parameters from the server certificate, employ these parameters to perform a Diffie-Hellman key exchange, and use the result as the premaster secret. In all of these cases, the server's CERTIFICATE message is sufficient and no additional information is required for the client to securely communicate a premaster secret to the server. In particular, no SERVERKEYEXCHANGE message is needed. In some other cases, however, the client needs some additional information, and this information must be delivered by the server in a SERVERKEYEXCHANGE message. This applies, for example, for an ephemeral or anonymous Diffie-Hellman key exchange and the FORTEZZA KEA.

A special case occurs if RSA_EXPORT is used for key exchange: in this case, a former U.S. export law may apply, according to which RSA keys larger than 512 bits could not directly be used for key exchange in software exported from the United States. Instead, these RSA keys could be used (as signature-only keys) to sign temporary shorter RSA keys for key exchange. Consequently, temporary 512-bit RSA keys were used and these keys were signed with the larger RSA keys (found in the certificate). Needless to say that this extra step is obsolete if the original RSA keys are 512 bits long or shorter. The bottom line is that one has to distinguish between two cases:

- If RSA_EXPORT is used for key exchange and the public key in the server certificate is longer than 512 bits, then the extra step must be taken and the SERVERKEYEXCHANGE message (that includes a signed shorter RSA key) must be sent.

- If, however, RSA_EXPORT is used for key exchange and the public key in the server certificate is 512 bits long or shorter, then the extra step need not be taken and the SERVERKEYEXCHANGE message need not be sent.

As illustrated in Figures 4.11 to 4.13, an SSL SERVERKEYEXCHANGE message always starts with the usual 5-byte SSL record header, a type field value of value 22 (referring to a SERVERKEYEXCHANGE message), and a 3-byte message length field. The rest of the SERVERKEYEXCHANGE message mainly depends on the key exchange algorithm in use (Diffie-Hellman, RSA, or FORTEZZA).

- If ephemeral or anonymous Diffie-Hellman is used, then the rest of the SERVERKEYEXCHANGE message comprises the server's Diffie-Hellman parameters, including a prime modulus p, generator g, and public exponent Y_s, as well as a digital signature for the parameters. The beginning of such a message is illustrated in Figure 4.11 (without signature part). Note that the fields for the Diffie-Hellman parameters have a variable length (consistently set to three in Figure 4.11).

- If RSA is used but the server has a signature-only RSA key, then the client cannot send a premaster secret encrypted with the server's public key. Instead, the server must create a temporary RSA public key pair and use the SERVERKEYEXCHANGE message to deliver the public key to the client. The SERVERKEYEXCHANGE message then includes the two parameters that together define a temporary RSA public key: the modulus and the exponent. Again, these parameters must come along with a digital signature. The beginning of such a message is illustrated in Figure 4.12 (without signature part). Note again that the fields for the RSA parameters have a variable length (consistently set to three in Figure 4.12).

- If FORTEZZA is used, then the SERVERKEYEXCHANGE message only carries the server's r_s value that is required by the FORTEZZA KEA. Since this value is always 128 bytes long, there is no need for a separate length parameter. Also, there is no need for a digital signature. A SERVERKEYEXCHANGE message is illustrated in Figure 4.13.

In the first two cases, the SERVERKEYEXCHANGE message may include a signature part. If server authentication is not part of a particular SSL session, then no signature part is required, and the SERVERKEYEXCHANGE message ends with the Diffie-Hellman, RSA, or FORTEZZA parameters. If the server is not acting anonymously and has sent a CERTIFICATE message, however, then the signed parameters format depends on the signature algorithm indicated in the server's certificate (RSA or DSA):

- If the server's certificate is for RSA signing, then the signed parameters consist of the concatenation of two hash values: an MD5 hash value and a SHA-1 hash value. Note that the two hash values are not individually signed, but one signature is generated for the combined hashes.

- If the server's certificate is for DSA signing, then the signed parameters consist solely of a SHA-1 hash value.

In either case, the input to the hash functions is a string that consists of ClientHello.random (i.e., the random value of the CLIENTHELLO message), ServerHello.random (i.e., the random value of the SERVERHELLO message), and the server key parameters mentioned above (all components are concatenated). The random values are included so old signatures and temporary keys cannot be replayed. The server key parameters refer to either the Diffie-Hellman parameters of Figure 4.11 or the RSA parameters of Figure 4.12. As mentioned above, no signed parameters are included for FORTEZZA.

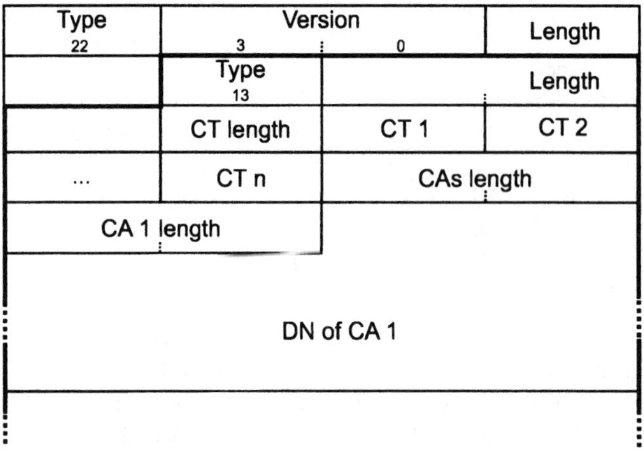

Type 22	Version 3 : 0		Length
	Type 13		Length
	CT length	CT 1	CT 2
...	CT n	CAs length	
	CA 1 length		
	DN of CA 1		

Figure 4.14   An SSL CERTIFICATEREQUEST message.

4.2.2.6 CERTIFICATEREQUEST Message

A nonanonymous server can optionally authenticate the client.[17] It therefore sends a CERTIFICATEREQUEST message to the client. This message not only asks the client to send a certificate (and to sign data using its corresponding private signing key later on), but it also informs the client which certificates are acceptable to the server.

---

17   Note that an anonymous server must not request a certificate from the client. Otherwise a fatal alert message (handshake failure) must be sent to the server.

Table 4.5
SSL Certificate Type Values

Value	Name	Description
1	rsa_sign	RSA signing and key exchange
2	dss_sign	DSA signing only
3	rsa_fixed_dh	RSA signing with fixed DH key exchange
4	dss_fixed_dh	DSA signing with fixed DH key exchange
5	rsa_ephemeral_dh	RSA signing with ephemeral DH key exchange
6	dss_ephemeral_dh	DSA signing with ephemeral DH key exchange
20	fortezza_kea	FORTEZZA signing and key exchange

As illustrated in Figure 4.14, an SSL CERTIFICATEREQUEST message starts with the usual 5-byte SSL record header, a type field value of value 13 (referring to a CERTIFICATEREQUEST message), and a 3-byte message length field. The remaining part of the CERTIFICATEREQUEST message begins with a list of acceptable certificate types (called `certificate_types` in the SSL protocol specification and acronymed CT in Figure 4.14). This type list has a length field of its own, and consists of one or more single-byte values that identify specific certificate types. The defined certificate type values and their meanings are summarized in Table 4.5. Note that the last three types are no longer needed in the TLS protocol.

After the certificate types, the CERTIFICATEREQUEST message also indicates which CAs the server considers appropriate. In the SSL protocol specification, this list is called `certificate_authorities`. It starts with a 2-byte length field and then contains one or more distinguished names (DNs). Each CA (or DN, respectively) has its own 2-byte length field that is put in front of the CA's DN. In Figure 4.14, only one CA is included. Keep in mind that this list may be very long.

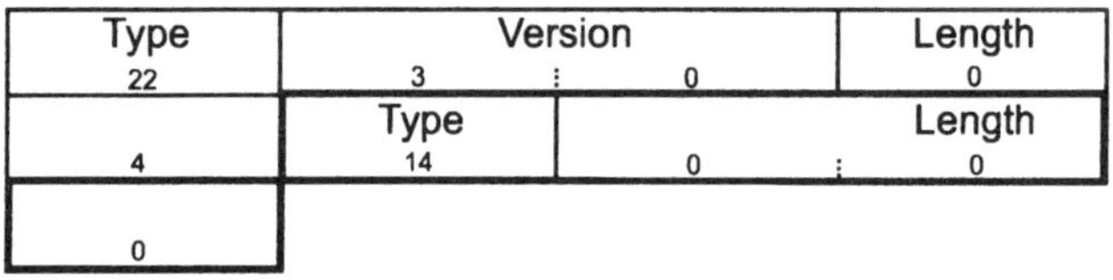

Type 22	Version 3 : 0	Length 0
4	Type 14 0 :	Length 0
0		

Figure 4.15 An SSL SERVERHELLODONE message.

4.2.2.7 SERVERHELLODONE Message

The SERVERHELLODONE message is sent by the server to indicate the end of the SERVERHELLO and associated messages. As illustrated in Figure 4.15, an SSL

SERVERHELLODONE message starts with the usual 5-byte SSL record header, a type field value of value 14 (referring to a SERVERHELLODONE message), and a 3-byte message length field. Since the body of the SERVERHELLODONE message is empty, the three bytes referring to the message length are all set to zero. The entire HELLOREQUEST message is 4 bytes long, and hence this value is included in the last byte of the length field of the SSL record header.

4.2.2.8 CERTIFICATE Message

After having received a SERVERHELLODONE message, it is up to the client to verify the server certificate (if required) and check that the values provided in the SERVERHELLO message are acceptable. If everything is fine, the client sends a couple of messages to the server. If the server requested a certificate, then the client would send a CERTIFICATE message to the server. This message would be structurally the same as the message sent from the server to the client (see Section 4.2.2.4). If the Diffie-Hellman key exchange algorithm is used, then the client-side Diffie-Hellman parameters must be compliant to the ones provided by the server, meaning that the Diffie-Hellman group and generator encoded in the client certificate must match the server's values.

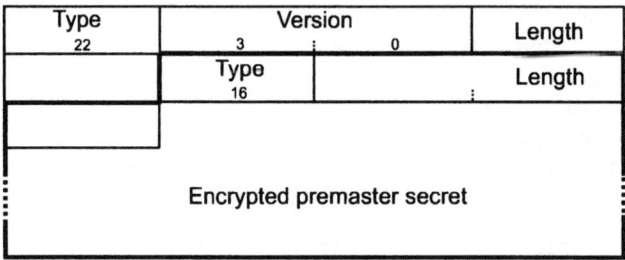

Figure 4.16   An SSL CLIENTKEYEXCHANGE message using RSA.

4.2.2.9 CLIENTKEYEXCHANGE Message

One of the most important messages in an SSL handshake is the CLIENTKEYEX-CHANGE message that is sent from the client to the server. It provides the server with the client-side keying material that is later used to secure communications. As illustrated in Figures 4.16 to 14.18, the format of the CLIENTKEYEXCHANGE message depends on the key exchange algorithm actually in use. In either case, it starts with the usual 5-byte SSL record header, a type field value of value 16

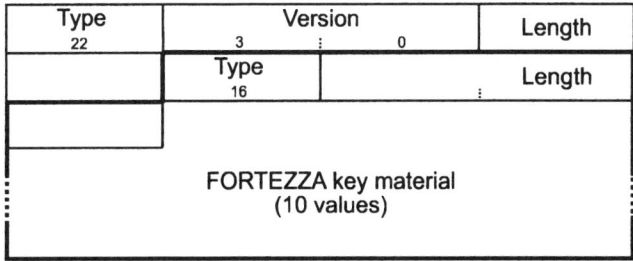

Figure 4.17 An SSL CLIENTKEYEXCHANGE message using FORTEZZA.

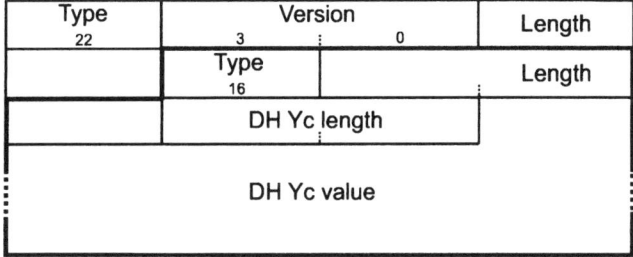

Figure 4.18 An SSL CLIENTKEYEXCHANGE message using Diffie-Hellman.

(referring to a CLIENTKEYEXCHANGE message), and a 3-byte message length field.[18] The body of the message then depends on the key exchange algorithm in use:

- If RSA or FORTEZZA is used, then the body of the CLIENTKEYEX-CHANGE message comprises an encrypted 48-byte premaster secret (i.e., pre_master_secret), that is sent from the client to the server. To detect version rollback attacks, the first 2 bytes from the 48 bytes refer to the latest (newest) version supported by the client and offered in the corresponding CLIENTHELLO message (note that this need not be the version that is actually

---

18 According to [10], some early SSL 3.0 implementations of Netscape Communications were buggy in the sense that the length field was omitted (because the length can be unambiguously determined anyway). This bug was mimicked by some early adopters and implementators of SSL 3.0. The bottom line was that some SSL 3.0 implementations omitted the length field in spite of the fact that it had been present in the protocol specification. Even today, it may happen that an SSL 3.0 implementation still omits the length field (for historical reasons).

in use[19]). Upon receiving the premaster secret, the server should check that this value matches the value transmitted by the client in the CLIENTHELLO message.

- In the case of RSA, the premaster secret is encrypted under the public RSA key from the server's certificate or temporary RSA key from the SERVERKEYEXCHANGE message. A coresponding SSL CLIENT-KEYEXCHANGE message using RSA is illustrated in Figure 4.16. The premaster secret is then used to generate a master secret, and the master secret is used to generate the various session keys.

- In the case of FORTEZZA, the KEA is used to derive a TEK, and the TEK is used to encrypt (and securely transmit) the premaster secret and a few other cryptographic parameters to the server. A corresponding SSL CLIENTKEYEXCHANGE message is illustrated in Figure 4.17. The FORTEZZA key material actually consists of 10 values, summarized in Table 4.6. Note that the client's Y_C value for the KEA calculation is between 64 and 128 bytes long, and that it is empty if Y_C is part of the client certificate.

Table 4.6
FORTEZZA Key Material

Parameter	Size
Length of Y_C	2 bytes
Client's Y_C value for the KEA calculation	0–128 bytes
Client's R_C value for the KEA calculation	128 bytes
DSA signature for the client's KEA public key	40 bytes
Client's write key, wrapped by the TEK	12 bytes
Client's read key, wrapped by the TEK	12 bytes
IV for the client write key	24 bytes
IV for the server write key	24 bytes
IV for the TEK used to encrypt the premaster secret	24 bytes
Premaster secret, encrypted by the TEK	48 bytes

- If ephemeral or anonymous Diffie-Hellman is used, then the CLIENTKEYEX-CHANGE message comprises the client's public Diffie-Hellman parameter Y_c. Such a message is illustrated in Figure 4.18. If, however, fixed Diffie-Hellman is used, then the client's public Diffie-Hellman parameters were already sent

---

19 There are implementations that employ the version in use instead of the latest version supported by the client. This is not a severe security problem, but there are some interoperability issues involved.

in a CERTIFICATE message, and hence a CLIENTKEYEXCHANGE message is not needed anymore.

If the server receives a CLIENTKEYEXCHANGE message, then it uses its private key to decrypt the premaster secret in the case of RSA or FORTEZZA, and it uses a Diffie-Hellman parameter of its own to compute a shared secret in the case of Diffie-Hellman.

4.2.2.10 CERTIFICATEVERIFY Message

If the client has provided a certificate with signing capabilities[20] in a SERVER-HELLODONE message, then it must still prove that it possesses the corresponding private key (the certificate alone cannot authenticate the client). Therefore, the client sends a CERTIFICATEVERIFY message to the server and this message basically comprises a digital signature generated with the client's private key.

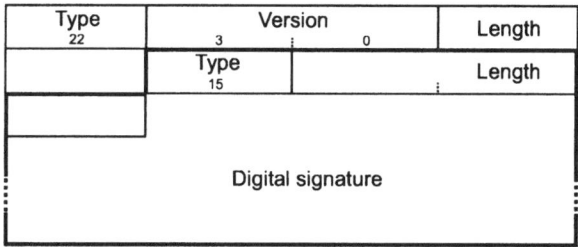

Figure 4.19 An SSL CERTIFICATEVERIFY message.

As illustrated in Figure 4.19, an SSL CERTIFICATEVERIFY message starts with the usual 5-byte SSL record header, a type field value of value 15 (referring to a CERTIFICATEVERIFY message), and a 3-byte message length field. The body of the CERTIFICATEVERIFY message comprises a digital signature, where the exact format of the signature depends on whether the client's certificate is for RSA or DSA.

- For RSA certificates, two separate hash values are combined and signed: an MD5 hash value and a SHA-1 hash values. The signature covers both values (there are not two separate signatures).

- For DSA certificates, only a SHA-1 hash value is signed.

20 This applies for all certificates except those containing fixed Diffie-Hellman parameters.

In either case, the information that serves as input to the hash functions (and hence is the information that is digitally signed) is the same. If *handshake_messages* refers to the concatenation of all SSL handshake messages that have been exchanged so far,[21] then the hash value is computed according to

$$h(k \parallel opad \parallel h(handshake\_messages \parallel k \parallel ipad))$$

where h is MD5 or SHA-1, k is the master secret, and $ipad$ and $opad$ are the values introduced earlier in this chapter. Again, the two values are repeated 48 times for MD5 and 40 times for SHA-1.

4.2.2.11 FINISHED Message

A FINISHED message is always sent immediately after a CHANGECIPHERSPEC message (as part of the SSL Change Cipher Spec Protocol) to verify that the key exchange and authentication processes have been successful. It is the first message protected with the newly negotiated algorithms and keys. No acknowledgment is required (i.e., parties may begin sending encrypted data immediately after sending the FINISHED message).

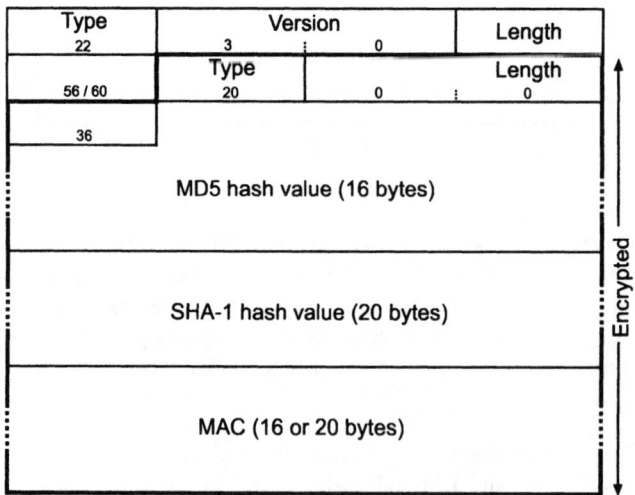

Figure 4.20 An SSL FINISHED message.

---

21 Note that CHANGECIPHERSPEC messages are not SSL handshake messages, and hence they are not included in the hash computations.

As illustrated in Figure 4.20, an SSL FINISHED message starts with the usual 5-byte SSL record header, and then continues with a body part that is cryptographically protected, meaning that it is encrypted most of the time (depending on the cipher suite in use). The encrypted body part comprises a header for the FINISHED message, with a type field value of value 20 (referring to a CERTIFICATEVERIFY message) and a 3-byte message length field, a 16-byte MD5 hash value, a 20-byte SHA-1 value, and a 16- or 20-byte MAC (the MAC length actually depends on the hash function in use). Both hash calculations use the same information and are computed according to

$$h(k \parallel opad \parallel h(handshake\_messages \parallel sender \parallel k \parallel ipad)),$$

where again h is MD5 or SHA-1, k is the master secret, $ipad$ and $opad$ are the values introduced earlier in this chapter, $handshake\_messages$ is the concatenation of all SSL handshake messages that have been exchanged so far (this value is different from the value used for the CERTIFICATEVERIFY message), and $sender$ refers to the entity that sends out the FINISHED message. If the client sends out the message, then this value is 0x434C4E54. Otherwise, if the server sends out the message, then this value is 0x53525652. Note the similarity between this calculation and the hash calculation for the CERTIFICATEVERIFY message; the only differences refer to the inclusion of the sender and the different base for the construction of $handshake\_messages$. The length of the FINISHED message body is 36 bytes, whereas the length of the FINISHED message is 40 bytes. Depending on whether MD5 or SHA-1 is used for message authentication, the length of the SSL record fragment is 56 or 60 bytes. This value is included in the SSL record header's length field.

4.2.3 SSL Change Cipher Spec Protocol

As mentioned above, the SSL Change Cipher Spec Protocol is a protocol of its own that allows the communicating peers to signal transitions in ciphering strategies. The protocol itself is very simple. It consists of a single message (i.e., a CHANGE-CIPHERSPEC message), that is compressed and encrypted according to the current (not pending) cipher spec. The placement of the CHANGECIPHERSPEC messages in a normal SSL handshake is illustrated in Figure 4.4. When resuming a previously established SSL session, the CHANGECIPHERSPEC message is just sent after the hello messages (see Figure 4.5).

As illustrated in Figure 4.21, an SSL CHANGECIPHERSPEC message starts with a 5-byte SSL record header, this time referring to type 20 (standing for the SSL Change Cipher Spec Protocol). The rest of the SSL record header remains unchanged and includes a version and a length field. The length field value is actually

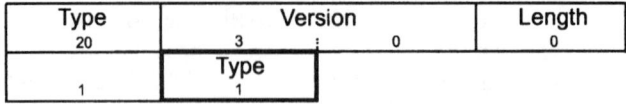

Figure 4.21 An SSL CHANGECIPHERSPEC message.

set to one, because the CHANGECIPHERSPEC message only includes a single type byte. This byte, in turn, is a placeholder that can currently only have a single value of one.

The CHANGECIPHERSPEC message is unique in that it is not properly part of the SSL handshake but rather has its own content type and hence represents an SSL (sub-)protocol of its own. Because the CHANGECIPHERSPEC message must not be encrypted and the FINISHED message must be encrypted, they cannot be transmitted in the same SSL record. Using separate content types is one way of achieving this. But it is useful only if an implementation attempts to send multiple handshake messages in a single SSL record. In fact, it is sometimes a performance improvement to send multiple handshake messages in the same TCP segment, and sending them in the same SSL record is one way of doing so. However, many implementations instead opt to transmit multiple records in the same TCP segment, which has very much the same effect (an example will be given in the following section). For such implementations, the use of separate content types is an inconvenience that unnecessarily complicates the state machine of the SSL Handshake Protocol. The bottom line is that the use of a separate content type for the CHANGECIPHERSPEC message can be (and sometimes is) discussed controversially.

4.2.4 SSL Alert Protocol

As mentioned above, the SSL Alert Protocol allows the communicating peers to exchange alert messages. Each alert message carries an alert level and an alert description:

- The *alert level* comprises 1 byte, where the value 1 stands for "warning" and the value 2 stands for "fatal." For all errors messages for which a particular alert level is not explicitly specified, the sender may determine at its discretion whether it is fatal or not. Similarly, if an alert with an alert level of warning is received, the receiver may decide at its discretion whether to treat this as a fatal error. Anyway, all messages that are transmitted with an alert level of fatal

Table 4.7
SSL Alert Messages

Alert	Code	Brief description
close_notify	0	The sender notifies the recipient that it will not send any more messages on the connection. This alert is always a warning.
unexpected_message	10	The sender notifies the recipient that an inappropriate message was received. This alert is always fatal and should never be observed in communication between proper implementations.
bad_record_mac	20	The sender notifies the recipient that a record with an incorrect MAC was received. This alert is always fatal and should never be observed in communication between proper implementations.
decompression_failure	30	The sender notifies the recipient that the decompression function received improper input, meaning that it could not decompress the received data. This alert is always fatal and should never be observed in communication between proper implementations.
handshake_failure	40	The sender notifies the recipient that it was not able to negotiate an acceptable set of security parameters given the options available. This alert is always fatal.
no_certificate	41	The sender (which is always a client) notifies the recipient (which is always a server) that it has no certificate that can satisfy the server's certificate request. Note that this alert is only used in SSL (it is no longer used in any version of TLS).
bad_certificate	42	The sender notifies the recipient that the certificate provided is corrupt (e.g., its signature cannot be verified).
unsupported_certificate	43	The sender notifies the recipient that the certificate provided is not supported.
certificate_revoked	44	The sender notifies the recipient that the certificate provided has been revoked by the issuing CA.
certificate_expired	45	The sender notifies the recipient that the certificate provided has expired and is no longer valid.
certificate_unknown	46	The sender notifies the recipient that some unspecified issue arose in processing the certificate provided, rendering it unacceptable.
illegal_parameter	47	The sender notifies the recipient that a field in the SSL handshake message was out of range or inconsistent with some other field. This alert is always fatal.

must be treated accordingly, meaning that they must result in the immediate termination of the connection.

- The *alert description* also comprises 1 byte, where a numeric code refers to a specific situation. The SSL alert messages are summarized in Table 4.7 (or Appendix A.3 of the SSL 3.0 specification). For example, code 0 stands for the closure alert close_notify that notifies the recipient that the sender will not send any more messages. Note that the sender and the server must share knowledge that a connection is ending in order to avoid a truncation attack, and that either party may initiate a closure by sending a close_notify alert accordingly. Any data received after such an alert must be ignored. In addition to the closure alert, there are a number of error alerts. In fact, all other SSL alert messages refer to error alerts. When an error is detected, the detecting party sends a message to the other party. Upon transmission or receipt of an fatal alert message, both parties immediately close the connection and drop any information related to it.

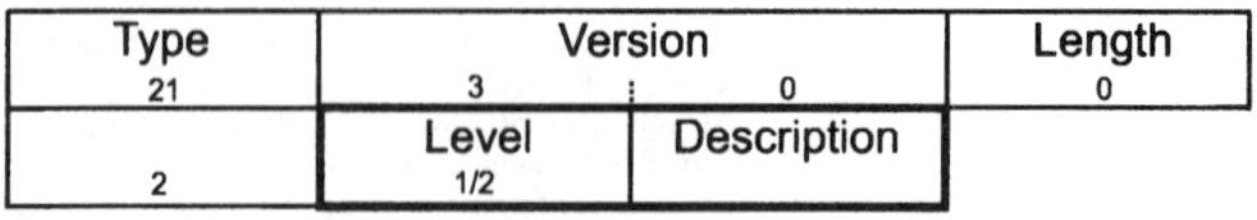

Type 21	Version 3 ; 0	Length 0
2	Level 1/2	Description

Figure 4.22 An SSL ALERT message.

As illustrated in Figure 4.22, an SSL ALERT message starts with a 5-byte SSL record header, this time referring to type 21 (standing for the SSL Alert Protocol). The rest of the SSL record header remains the same and includes a version and a length field. The length is actually set to two, because the ALERT message includes only two bytes (one byte referring to the alert level and the other byte referring to the alert description code).

4.2.5 SSL Application Data Protocol

As mentioned earlier in this chapter, the SSL Application Data Protocol allows the communicating peers to exchange data according to some application layer protocol. More specifically, it takes application data and feeds it into the SSL Record Protocol for fragmentation, compression, and cryptographic protection. The resulting SSL records are then sent to the recipient, where they are decrypted, verified, decompressed, and reassembled.

Figure 4.23 illustrates some application data encapsulated in an SSL record. As usual, the SSL record starts with a 5-byte header, including a type field (this time referring to 23 standing for the SSL Application Data Protocol), a version field, and a length field. Everything after the SSL record header is encrypted and can only be decrypted using the appropriate key. This applies to the actual application data, but it also applies to the MAC (that is either 16 or 20 bytes long). As mentioned above, things are slightly more involved if a block cipher is used. In this case, some message padding must be appended to the SSL record, and the last byte in the record must then refer to the padding length. The corresponding format of an SSL record for a block cipher is illustrated in Figure 4.24.

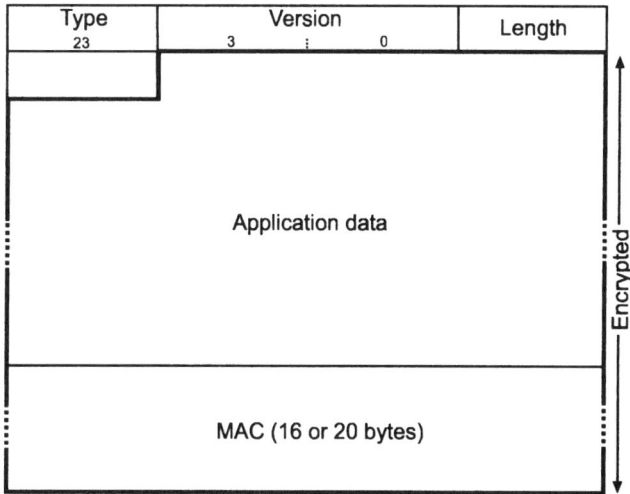

Figure 4.23 Application data encapsulated in an SSL record (stream cipher).

4.3 TRAFFIC ANALYSIS OF AN SSL SESSION

To illustrate the functioning of the SSL protocol, we provide a traffic analysis of an SSL session. We therefore consider a setting in which a client (i.e., a Web browser) tries to access an SSL-enabled Web server, and we use a network protocol analyzer (Wireshark) to capture the SSL records that are sent back and forth. The dissection of these records is well suited to show what is going on behind the scenes (i.e., at the protocol level). Before the SSL protocol can be invoked, the client must establish a TCP connection to the server. We jump over this step and assume such a TCP connection between the client and server already exists.

In our example, the client takes the initiative and sends a CLIENTHELLO message to the server. This message is encapsulated in an SSL record that looks as follows (in hexadecimal notation):

```
16 03 00 00 41 01 00 00    3d 03 00 48 b4 54 9e 00
6b 0f 04 dd 1f b8 a0 52    a8 ff 62 23 27 c0 16 a1
59 c0 a9 21 4a 4e 3e 61    58 ed 25 00 00 16 00 04
00 05 00 0a 00 09 00 64    00 62 00 03 00 06 00 13
00 12 00 63 01 00
```

The SSL record starts with a type field that comprises the value 0x16 (representing 22 in decimal notation, and hence standing for the SSL Handshake Protocol), a

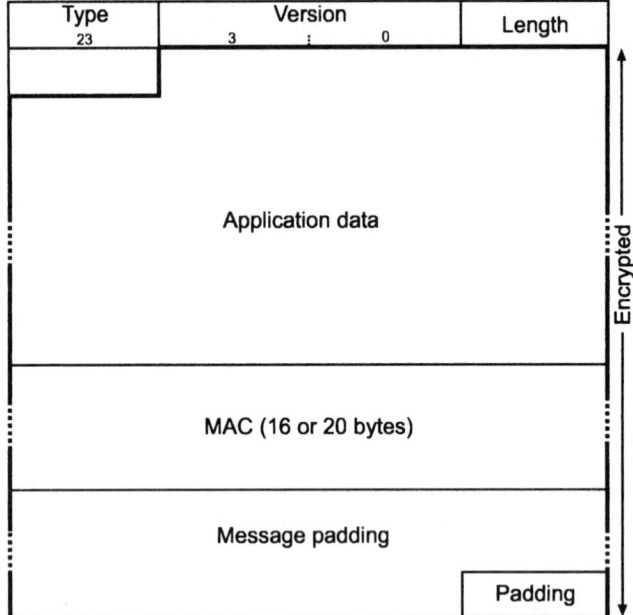

Figure 4.24 Application data encapsulated in an SSL record (block cipher).

version field that comprises the value 0x0300 (referring to SSL 3.0), and a length field that comprises the value 0x0041 (representing 65 in decimal notation). This basically means that the fragment of the SSL record is 65 bytes long, and that the following 65 bytes thus represent the CLIENTHELLO message. This message, in turn, starts with 0x01 standing for the SSL handshake message type 1 (referring to a CLIENTHELLO message), 0x00003d standing for a message length of 61 bytes, and 0x0300 again representing SSL 3.0. The subsequent 32 bytes—from 0x48b4 to 0xed25—represent the random value chosen by the client (remember that the first 4 bytes represent the date and time). Because there is no SSL session to resume, the session ID length is set to zero (0x00) and no session ID is appended. Instead, the next value 0x0016 (representing 22 in decimal notation) indicates that the subsequent 22 bytes refer to the 11 cipher suites that are supported by the client. Each pair of bytes represents a cipher suite. The second-to-last byte 01 indicates that there is a single compression method supported by the client, and the last byte 0x00 refers to this compression method (which actually refers to no compression).

SSL Protocol

After having received the CLIENTHELLO message, the server is to respond with a series of SSL handshake messages. If possible, then all messages are merged into a single SSL record and transmitted in a single TCP segment to the client. In our example, such an SSL record comprsies a SERVERHELLO, a CERTIFICATE, and a SERVERHELLODONE message. The corresponding SSL record starts with the following byte sequence:

```
16 03 00 0a 5f
```

Again, 0x16 refers to the SSL Handshake Protocol, 0x0300 refers to SSL version 3.0, and 0x0a5f refers to the length of the SSL record (which is actually 2655 bytes). The three above-mentioned messages are then encapsulated in the rest of the SSL record.

- The SERVERHELLO message looks as follows:

```
02 00 00 46 03 00 48 b4    54 9e da 94 41 94 59 a9
64 bc d6 15 30 6c b0 08    30 8a b2 e0 6d ea 8f 7b
6b df d5 a7 3c d4 20 48    b4 54 9e 26 8b a1 9d 26
59 1b 5e 31 4c fe d3 2b    a7 96 26 99 55 55 41 7c
d8 e8 44 8a 3e f9 d5 00    05 00
```

The message starts with 0x02 standing for the SSL Handshake Protocol message type 2 (referring to a SERVERHELLO message), 0x000046 standing for a message length of 70 bytes, and 0x0300 again standing for SSL 3.0. The subsequent 32 bytes

```
48 b4 54 9e da 94 41 94    59 a9 64 bc d6 15 30 6c
b0 08 30 8a b2 e0 6d ea    8f 7b 6b df d5 a7 3c d4
```

represent the random value chosen by the server (note again that the first 4 bytes represent the date and time). Afterwards, 0x20 refers to a session ID length of 32 bytes, and hence the subsequent 32 bytes

```
48 b4 54 9e 26 8b a1 9d    26 59 1b 5e 31 4c fe d3
2b a7 96 26 99 55 55 41    7c d8 e8 44 8a 3e f9 d5
```

represent the session ID. Remember that this ID is going to be used if the client wants to resume the SSL session at some later point in time (before the session expires). Following the session ID, 0x0005 refers to the selected cipher suite (which is TLS_RSA_WITH_RC4_128_SHA in this example) and 0x00 refers to the selected compression method (which is the null compression).

- Next, the CERTIFICATE message comprises the server's public key certificate. It is quite comprehensive and begins with the followiung byte sequence:

```
0b 00 0a 0d 00 0a 0a
```

In this byte sequence, `0x0b` stands for the SSL Handshake Protocol message type 11 (referring to a CERTIFICATE message), `0x000a0d` stands for a message length of 2573 bytes, and `0x000a0a` stands for the length of the certificate chain. Note that the length of the certificate chain must equal the message length minus 3 (the length of the length field). The remaining 2570 bytes of the message then comprise the certificate chain required to validate the server's public key certificate (these bytes are not illustrated above).

- Last but not least, the SSL record also comprises a SERVERHELLODONE message. This message is very simple and only consists of 4 bytes:

```
0e 00 00 00
```

`0x0e` stands for the SSL Handshake Protocol message type 14 (referring to a SERVERHELLODONE message) and `0x000000` stands for a message length of zero bytes.

After having received the SERVERHELLODONE message, it is up to the client to submit a series of messages to the server. In our example, this series comprises a CLIENTKEYEXCHANGE, a CHANGECIPHERSPEC, and a FINISHED message. Each of these messages is transmitted in an SSL record of its own, but all three records can be transmitted in a single TCP segment to the server.

- The CLIENTKEYEXCHANGE message is transmitted in the first SSL record. In our example, this record looks as follows:

```
16 03 00 00 84 10 00 00    80 18 4a 74 7e 92 66 72
fa ee ac 4b f8 fb 7c c5    6f b2 55 61 47 4e 1e 4a
ad 5f 4b f5 70 fe d1 b4    0b ef 36 52 4f 7b 33 34
ad 23 67 f0 60 ec 67 67    35 5a cf 50 f8 d0 3d 28
4e fb 01 88 56 06 86 3c    c7 c3 85 8c 81 2c 0d d8
20 a6 1b 09 ee 86 c5 6c    37 e5 e8 56 96 cc 46 44
58 ee c1 9b 73 53 ff 88    ab 90 19 53 3d f2 23 5b
8f 57 d2 b0 74 2a bd 05    f9 9e dd 6a 50 69 50 4a
55 8a f1 5b 9b 6d ba 6f    b0
```

In the SSL record header, `0x16` stands for the SSL Handshake Protocol, `0x0300` refers to SSL version 3.0, and `0x0084` represents the length of the SSL record (132 bytes). After this header, the byte `0x10` stands for the SSL Handshake Protocol message type 16 (referring to a CLIENTKEYEXCHANGE message), and the following three bytes `0x000080` refer to the message length (128 bytes or 1024 bits). Consequently, the remaining 128 bytes of the message represent the premaster secret (as chosen by the client) encrypted under the server's public RSA key. The RSA encryption is line with PKCS #1.

- The CHANGECIPHERSPEC message is transmitted in the second SSL record. This record is very simple and consists of only 6 bytes:

  ```
  14 03 00 00 01 01
  ```

  In the SSL record header, 0x14 (20 in decimal notation) stands for the SSL Change Cipher Spec Protocol, 0x0300 refers to SSL version 3.0, and 0x0001 represents the message length of one single byte. This byte (i.e., 0x01), in turn, is the last byte in the record.

- The FINISHED message is the first message that is cryptographically protected according to the newly negotiated cipher spec. Again, it is transmitted in an SSL record of its own. This record looks as follows:

  ```
  16 03 00 00 3c 38 9c 10    98 a9 d3 89 30 92 c2 41
  52 59 e3 7f c7 b3 88 e6    5f 6f 33 08 59 84 20 65
  55 c2 82 cb e2 a6 1c 6f    dc c1 13 4b 1a 45 30 8c
  e5 f4 01 1a 71 08 06 eb    5c 54 be 35 66 52 21 35
  f1
  ```

  In the SSL record header, 0x16 stands for the SSL Handshake Protocol, 0x0300 refers to SSL version 3.0, and 0x003c represents the length of the SSL record (60 bytes). These 60 bytes are encrypted and look like gibberish to somebody not holding the appropriate decryption key.

After having received the CHANGECIPHERSPEC and FINISHED messages, the server must respond with the same pair of messages (not illustrated in our example). Afterwards, application data can be exchanged in SSL records. Such a record may start as follows:

```
17 03 00 02 73
```

In the SSL record header, 0x17 (23 in decimal notation) stands for the SSL Application Data Protocol, 0x0300 stands for SSL version 3.0, and 0x0273 (627) stands for the length of the encrypted data fragment. It goes without saying that an arbitrary number of SSL records can be exchanged between the client and the server.

4.4 SECURITY ANALYSIS

Many researchers have investigated the security of the SSL protocol. For example, soon after Netscape Communications released its first browsers supporting the SSL protocol in 1996, David Wagner and Ian Goldberg showed that the method used to seed the PRBG (to generate the premaster secrets) was cryptographically weak.[22] In fact, the seeds were derived from a few predictable (or at least easily guessable) quantitities, such as the time of day, the process ID, and the parent process ID. These values do not provide enough entropy, and hence the premaster secrets generated by the browsers were partially predictable. This result became a press headline and casted a damning light on the security of the evolving SSL protocol. This was unfortunate, because the real problem was not the SSL protocol, but the way it was implemented by Netscape Communications. It goes without saying that the problem could easily be remedied by strengthening the PRBGs in use. This was quickly done by Netscape Communications, but the story still illustrated the well-known fact that even a secure protocol can be implemented in an insecure way.

Later in 1996, David Wagner and Bruce Schneier were the first who did an informal security analysis of the SSL protocol. They found a number of minor flaws and new active attacks, but their overall assessment was still positive. They concluded that "on the whole SSL 3.0 is a valuable contribution towards practical communications security" [11]. In the aftermath of the Wagner-Schneier analysis, a few other researchers tried to do more formal analyses by applying formal methods for the security analysis of SSL 3.0 [12, 13]. Again, the results and key findings were positive in the sense that no major vulnerability was found. This reaffirmed the community that SSL 3.0 was indeed a reasonably secure protocol.

In addition to the general security analyses of SSL 3.0, some researchers have cryptanalyzed specific implementations or parts thereof. For example, in 1998, Daniel Bleichenbacher found an adaptive chosen ciphertext attack[23] against certain cryptographic protocols that—like SSL 3.0—are based on PKCS #1 version 1.5 [14]. The attack is based on two well-known facts about RSA when used as asymmetric encryption system:

- RSA encryption (in its native form) is susceptible to a chosen ciphertext attack [15]: An adversary who wants to find the decryption of $m \equiv c^d \pmod{n}$ of a given ciphertext c can choose a random integer r and ask for the decryption of the innocent-looking ciphertext $c' \equiv r^e c \pmod{n}$. From the answer $m' \equiv (c')^d \pmod{n}$, the adversary can easily recover the plaintext original message, because $m \equiv m' s^{-1} \pmod{n}$.

- The least significant bit (LSB) of an RSA encryption is as secure as the whole message [16]. This fact—also known as bit security-property of RSA—can be extended in the sense that all individual RSA bits are secure [17]. This

---

22 http://www.ddj.com/windows/184409807.
23 In the cryptographic literature, a chosen ciphertext attack is acronymed CCA and an adaptive chosen ciphertext attack is acronymed CCA2.

basically means that there exists an algorithm that can decrypt a ciphertext if there exists another algorithm that can predict the LSB or any other bit of a message given only the corresponding ciphertext and the public key. Hence, it is not necessary for an adversary to learn the complete decrypted message in a chosen ciphertext attack; single bits per chosen ciphertext may be sufficient.

Bleichenbacher turned these theoretical results into a practical attack that allows one private-key RSA operation to be performed if the adversary has access to an oracle that, for any chosen ciphertext, returns one bit telling whether the ciphertext corresponds to some unknown block of data encrypted using PKCS #1.

| 00 | 02 | Padding | 00 | Data block |

Figure 4.25 PKCS #1 block format for encryption (block type 2).

To make the point more clear, we say that a ciphertext is *PKCS #1 conforming*, if its decryption is formed according to PKCS #1 (block type 2). The PKCS #1 block format is illustrated in Figure 4.25. Such a data block starts with a zero byte, a byte referring to block type 2, a variable length padding string, a zero byte, and the actual data block that is encrypted. The Bleichenbacher attack exploits the fact that a PKCS #1 conforming block must always start with two characteristic bytes (i.e., 0x00 and 0x02) and can be recognized accordingly. The adversary can use the above-mentioned oracle to decrypt a given ciphertext c (i.e., compute c^d (mod n)). This ciphertext can, for example, be a previously transmitted SSL CLIENTKEYEXCHANGE message. In this case, the adversary can retrieve the corresponding premaster secret and derive the master secret and the SSL encryption keys accordingly.

Theoretically, an adversary can use the algorithm given in the reduction proof of [17] to find c. In [14], however, Bleichenbacher proposed a different algorithm that tries to minimize the number of chosen ciphertexts. More specifically, if the adversary wants to find $m \equiv c^d \pmod{n}$ for a given ciphertext c, he or she can choose an integer $r < n$, compute $c' \equiv r^e c \pmod{n}$, and send c' to the oracle. If the oracle says that c' is PKCS #1 conforming, then—according to the rationale given above—the adversary automatically knows that the first two bytes of $mr \pmod{n}$ refer to 0x00 and 0x02. This, in turn, implies that

$$2B \leq mr \pmod{n} < 3B$$

for $B = 2^{8(k-2)}$ and k referring to the byte length of n. The adversary now has an interval for $mr \pmod{n}$ (and hence for m), and he or she can iterate the procedure to narrow down the interval. After sufficiently many steps, he or she is able to determine the original plaintext message m. Typically (and according to the analysis given in [14]), 2^{20}—which is slightly more than one million—chosen ciphertexts will be sufficient, but this number may vary widely depending on numerous implementation details.

Due to the fact that the Bleichenbacher attack requires a huge quantity of oracle queries, it can usually be detected quite easily in an online setting. Also, a feasible way to avoid vulnerability to this attack is to treat incorrectly formatted blocks in a manner indistinguishable from correctly formatted blocks. Thus, when the server receives an incorrectly formatted RSA block, it should generate a random 48-byte value and proceed using it as the premaster secret. The server then acts identically whether the received RSA block is correctly encoded or not. This easily defeats the Bleichenbacher attack. But in spite of its easy detection and circumvention, the attack still demonstrated the feasibility and potential severity of adaptive chosen ciphertext attacks, and as such, it has had (and continues to have) a deep impact on cryptographic research. Before the attack, people had only theoretically argued about the possibility of chosen ciphertext attacks, but it was not generally perceived as a real threat. After its publication, there was strong concensus that chosen ciphertext attacks indeed pose a threat, and that it makes a lot of sense to use (asymmetric) encryption systems that protect against it. Consequently, PKCS #1 was rapidly updated in version 2.0 [6], adapting a technique known as *optimal asymmetric encryption padding* (OAEP) [18]. Unlike ad-hoc schemes such as the padding used in PKCS #1 version 1.5, OAEP had been proven secure against chosen ciphertext attacks in the random oracle model. In addition to OAEP, the research community has come up with other asymmetric encryption systems provably secure against chosen ciphertext attacks—the most important system being proposed by Ronald Cramer and Victor Shoup [19]. The Cramer-Shoup system was the first asymmetric encryption system that was provably secure against chosen ciphertext attacks in the standard model (i.e., without requiring random oracles).

In the aftermath of the Bleichenbacher attack, many researchers tried to extend or optimize it, or to find similar attacks. For example (and in spite of the fact that RSA-OAEP is theoretically secure against chosen ciphertext attacks in the random oracle model), James Manger found possibilities to mount highly efficient chosen ciphertext attacks against several implementations of PKCS #1 version 2.0 in 2001 [20]. Again, PKCS #1 had to be updated to reduce the likelihood of success for the Manger attack. The resulting PKCS #1 version 2.1 [7] refers to the state-of-the-art and is the version in use today. Similarly, three Czech cryptologists—Vlastimil Klíma, Ondrej Pokorný, and Tomás Rosa—came up with another extension of the Bleichenbacher attack in 2003 [21].

Both extensions of the Bleichenbacher attack reaffirmed the well-known fact that even a theoretically (or provably) secure cryptosystem can be vulnerable and successfully attacked as soon as it gets implemented in practice. This fact is also supported by the huge quantity of side-channel attacks that have been developed and proposed in the last decade. There are even some side-channel attacks that can be mounted remotely (i.e., against network servers), such as, for example, the timing attacks demonstrated by Dan Boneh and David Brumley [22]. Due to this insight, implementations that use RSA for key exchange should use RSA blinding or some other technique that protects against timing attacks.

In addition to the Bleichenbacher attack and its extensions, some researchers have found other (mostly subtle) security problems in the CBC padding scheme used by the SSL protocol. In 2002, for example, Serge Vaudenay published a paper in which he explained how CBC padding as used in SSL induces a side channel that may be exploited in a chosen ciphertext attack [23]. In the following year, Vaudenay and a few other researchers published a follow-up paper in which they showed that the CBC padding problem can actually be turned into a feasible attack [24]. In 2004, Gregory Bard found another vulnerability in CBC padding that can be exploited in a blockwise adaptive chosen plaintext attack [25]. The bottom line was that TLS 1.0 had to be revised and that TLS 1.1 had to take precautions to protect against these attacks (see Section 5.3). Both problems can easily be circumnavigated by not using a block cipher in CBC mode in the first place. Fortunately, most Web browsers routinely invoke the stream cipher RC4 by default.

4.5 FINAL REMARKS

In this chapter, we introduced, overviewed, and went through the details of the SSL protocol and its use in practice. We saw that the protocol is simple and straightforward—especially if RSA or Diffie-Hellman are used for key exchange (the use of a Diffie-Hellman key exchange is advantageous, because it makes sure that both parties participate in the generation of the cryptographic keys). There are only a few details that can be discussed controversially, such as the use of a separate content type for CHANGECIPHERSPEC messages, and these details may even change in the future. But from a security perspective, simplicity and straightforwardness are always advantageous properties, and hence the starting position of the SSL protocol with regard to security is very good. All attempts to break the security of the SSL protocol have failed so far, and—as outlined in the previous section—the few attacks that are known are not particularly worrisome or can be remedied easily. Against this background, the SSL protocol has established itself as the leading security protocol for Internet and Web-based applications.

In fact, the SSL protocol is slowly eliminating alternative and partly competing cryptographic security protocols, such as IPsec/IKE. If we consider virtual private networking, for example, we observe a trend from IPsec/IKE-based virtual private networks (VPNs) to SSL/TLS-based VPNs. A similar trend can be observed in many other areas, and all of these trends emphasize the key role the SSL protocol is playing in the security scene.

Like any other security technology, the SSL protocol also has a few disadvantages and pitfalls. For example, the use of the SSL protocol makes content screening impossible. If a data stream is encrypted using, for example, the SSL protocol with a cryptographically strong cipher, then it is no longer possible to subject the data stream to content screening. This is because the content screener only "sees" encrypted data in which it cannot efficiently find malicious content. In order to screen content, it is necessary to temporarily decrypt the data stream and to reencrypt it just after the screening process. This calls for an SSL proxy (see Section 7.3). Another problem that pops up when the SSL protocol is used in the field is the need for public key certificates. As mentioned before, an SSL-enabled Web server always needs a certificate and must be configured in a way that it can make use of it. Additionally, a Web server can also be configured in a way that it requires clients to authenticate themselves with a public key certificate. In this case, the clients must also be equipped with public key certificates. As there are many potential clients for a Web server, the process of equipping clients with certificates is involved and tricky. It is also the reason why the original designers of the SSL protocol opted to make client authentication optional in the first case. There is much more to say about public key certificates and PKIs, and we therefore allocate a separate chapter for this important topic.

References

[1] Khare, R., and S. Lawrence, "Upgrading to TLS Within HTTP/1.1," Standards Track Request for Comments 2817, May 2000.

[2] Rescorla, E., "HTTP Over TLS," Informational Request for Comments 2818, May 2000.

[3] Hoffman, P., "SMTP Service Extension for Secure SMTP over TLS," Standards Track Request for Comments 2487, January 1999.

[4] Klensin, J., Freed, N., Rose, M., Stefferud, E., and D. Crocker, "SMTP Service Extensions," Standards Track Request for Comments 1869 (STD 10), November 1995.

[5] Kaliski, B., "PKCS #1: RSA Encryption Version 1.5," Informational Request for Comments 2313, March 1998.

[6] Kaliski, B., and J. Staddon, "PKCS #1: RSA Cryptography Specifications Version 2.0," Informational Request for Comments 2437, October 1998.

[7] Jonsson, J., and B. Kaliski, "Public-Key Cryptography Standards (PKCS) #1: RSA Cryptography Specifications Version 2.1," Informational Request for Comments 3447, February 2003.

[8] Canetti, R., and H. Krawczyk, "Analysis of Key-Exchange Protocols and Their Use for Building Secure Channels," *Proceedings of EUROCRYPT '01*, Springer-Verlag, LNCS 2045, 2001, pp. 453–474.

[9] Krawczyk, H., "The Order of Encryption and Authentication for Protecting Communications (Or: How Secure is SSL?)," *Proceedings of CRYPTO '01*, Springer-Verlag, LNCS 2139, 2001, pp. 310–331.

[10] Rescorla, E., *SSL and TLS: Designing and Building Secure Systems*. Addison-Wesley, Reading, MA, 2000.

[11] Wagner, D., and B. Schneier, "Analysis of the SSL 3.0 Protocol," *Proceedings of the Second USENIX Workshop on Electronic Commerce*, USENIX Press, November 1996, pp. 29–40.

[12] Mitchell, J., Shmatikov, V., and U. Stern, "Finite-State Analysis of SSL 3.0," *Proceedings of the Seventh USENIX Security Symposium*, USENIX, 1998, pp. 201–216.

[13] Paulson, L.C., "Inductive Analysis of the Internet Protocol TLS," *ACM Transactions on Computer and System Security*, Vol. 2, No. 3, 1999, pp. 332–351.

[14] Bleichenbacher, D., "Chosen Ciphertext Attacks Against Protocols Based on the RSA Encryption Standard PKCS #1," *Proceedings of CRYPTO '98*, Springer-Verlag, LNCS 1462, August 1998, pp. 1–12.

[15] Davida, G.I., "Chosen Signature Cryptanalysis of the RSA (MIT) Public Key Cryptosystem," TR-CS-82-2, Deptartment of Electrical Engineering and Computer Science, University of Wisconsin, Milwaukee, 1982.

[16] Alexi, W., Chor, B., Goldreich, O., and C.P. Schnorr, "RSA and Rabin Functions: Certain Parts are as Hard as the Whole," *SIAM Journal on Computing*, Vol. 17, No. 2, 1988, pp. 194–209.

[17] Hastad, J., and M. Naslund, "The Security of all RSA and Discrete Log Bits," *Journal of the ACM*, Vol. 51, No. 2, March 2004, pp. 187–230.

[18] Bellare, M., and P. Rogaway, "Optimal Asymmetric Encryption," *Proceedings of EUROCRYPT '94*, Springer-Verlag, LNCS 950, 1994, pp. 92–111.

[19] Cramer, R., and V. Shoup, "A Practical Public Key Cryptosystem Provably Secure Against Adaptive Chosen Ciphertext Attack," *Proceedings of CRYPTO '98*, Springer-Verlag, LNCS 1462, August 1998, pp. 13–25.

[20] Manger, J., "A Chosen Ciphertext Attack on RSA Optimal Asymmetric Encryption Padding (OAEP) as Standardized in PKCS#1 v2.0," *Proceedings of CRYPTO '01*, Springer-Verlag, August 2001, pp. 230–238.

[21] Klíma, V., Pokorný, O., and T. Rosa, "Attacking RSA-Based Sessions in SSL/TLS," *Proceedings of Cryptographic Hardware and Embedded Systems (CHES)*, Springer-Verlag, September 2003, pp. 426–440.

[22] Boneh, D., and D. Brumley, "Remote Timing Attacks are Practical," *Proceedings of the 12th USENIX Security Symposium*, 2003, pp. 1–14.

[23] Vaudenay, S., "Security Flaws Induced by CBC Padding—Applications to SSL, IPSEC, WTLS ... ," *Proceedings of EUROCRYPT '02*, Amsterdam, Netherland, Springer-Verlag, LNCS 2332, 2002, pp. 534–545.

[24] Canvel, B., Hiltgen, A., Vaudenay, S., and M. Vuagnoux, "Password Interception in a SSL/TLS Channel," *Proceedings of CRYPTO '03*, Springer-Verlag, LNCS 2729, 2003, pp. 583–599.

[25] Bard, G.V., "Vulnerability of SSL to Chosen-Plaintext Attack," Cryptology ePrint Archive, Report 2004/111, 2004.

Chapter 5

TLS Protocol

In this chapter, we elaborate on the TLS protocol—the designated successor of the SSL protocol. We assume the reader to be familiar with the SSL protocol, and hence we confine ourselves to elaborating on the differences between the SSL and the various versions of the TLS protocol. See Section 3.2 for an outline of the TLS protocol evolution, comprising version 1.0 [1], version 1.1 [2], and—most importantly—version 1.2 [3]. In the sequel, we provide an introduction in Section 5.1, and we then focus on TLS 1.0 in Section 5.2, TLS 1.1 in Section 5.3, and TLS 1.2 in Section 5.4. After these specification-related parts, we provide a traffic analysis of a TLS session in Section 5.5, briefly analyze its security in Section 5.6, and conclude with some final remarks in Section 5.7.

5.1 INTRODUCTION

The TLS protocol is structurally identical to the SSL protocol: it is a client/server protocol that is stacked on top of a reliable transport layer protocol, such as TCP in the case of the TCP/IP, and that consists of the same two layers and protocols as SSL (the only exception is that the prefix "SSL" in the protocols' names is replaced with the prefix "TLS").

- On the lower layer, the *TLS Record Protocol* is to fragment, optionally compress, and cryptographically protect higher-layer protocol data. The corresponding data structures are called `TLSPlaintext`, `TLSCompressed`, and `TLSCiphertext`. As with SSL, each of these data structures comprises four fields:
  - A *type* field that refers to the higher-layer protocol;

- A *version* field that refers to the protocol version (e.g., 3,1 for TLS 1.0);
- A *length* field that refers to the byte length of the fragment;
- An arbitrarily (up to 2^{14} bytes) long *fragment* field that comprises the higher-layer protocol data (typically a `TLSCiphertext` data structure).

Remember that data of different content types may be interleaved in a single TLS record, and that application data is generally of lower precedence for transmission than other content types.

- On the higher layer, the TLS protocol comprises the following four protocols we already know from the SSL protocol:
  - The *TLS Change Cipher Spec Protocol* (20);
  - The *TLS Alert Protocol* (21);
  - The *TLS Handshake Protocol* (22);
  - The *TLS Application Data Protocol* (23).

Each protocol is identified with a unique content type (for which the corresponding value is appended in brackets). To allow future extensions, additional record types may be defined and supported by the TLS Record Protocol.

Again, we use the term *TLS protocol* to refer to all four protocols itemized above, and we use a more specific term to refer to a particular protocol.

Table 5.1
Security Parameters for a TLS Connection

connection end	Information whether the entity is considered the "client" or the "server" in the connection
bulk encryption algorithm	Algorithm used for bulk data encryption (including its key size, how much of that key is secret, whether it is a block or stream cipher, the block size of the cipher if it is a block cipher, and whether the cipher is exportable)
MAC algorithm	Algorithm used for message authentication
compression algorithm	Algorithm used for data compression
master secret	48-byte secret shared between the client and the server
client random	32-byte value provided by the client
server random	32-byte value provided by the server

Similar to the SSL protocol, the TLS protocol also makes a distinction between a TLS session and a connection:

Table 5.2
TLS Connection State Elements

compression state	The current state of the compression algorithm
cipher state	The current state of the encryption algorithm
MAC secret	MAC secret for this connection
sequence number	64-bit sequence number for the records transmitted under a particular connection state (initially set to zero)

- A *TLS connection* represents the operating environment of the TLS protocol;
- Several TLS connection may correspond to a single *TLS session*.

As with SSL, there are always four connection states outstanding: the *current* read and write states, as well as the *pending* read and write states. All TLS records are processed under the current (read and write) states, whereas the security parameters and elements for the pending states are negotiated and set during the execution of the TLS Handshake Protocol.

The state elements of a TLS session are basically the same as the state element of an SSL session (see Table 4.2), so we don't have to repeat them here. At the connection level, however, the specifications of the SSL and TLS protocols are slightly different: while the TLS protocol distinguishes between the security parameters summarized in Table 5.1 and the state elements summarized in Table 5.2, the SSL protocol does not make this distinction and only considers state elements (see Table 4.3). But taking the security parameters and state elements together, the differences between SSL and TLS connections are rather minor and not very profound. In addition to the security parameters summarized in Table 5.1, the PRF algorithm in use is another security parameter that must be considered separately since TLS version 1.2.

The most obvious difference between the SSL and TLS protocols is related to the way the protocols generate the keying material. In Section 4.1, we saw that SSL uses a unique construction for the generation of the master secret and key block (that is then used to generate the keying material). TLS 1.0 also uses a unique construction, but this construction is centered around a TLS-specific PRF. Let us therefore first introduce the TLS PRF, before we delve into the details of how the TLS protocol actually generates the keying material needed. The subtle differences between TLS 1.0 and TLS 1.1, on the one hand, and TLS 1.2, on the other hand, are only briefly raised.

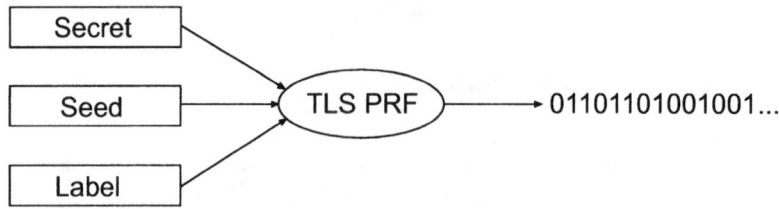

Figure 5.1 Overview of the TLS PRF.

5.1.1 TLS PRF

As overviewed in Figure 5.1, the TLS protocol employs a PRF that takes as input a secret, a seed, and a label (sometimes termed "identifying label"), and that generates as output an arbitrarily long bit sequence. To make the TLS PRF as secure as possible, it combines two cryptographic hash functions—MD5 and SHA-1—in a way that is supposed to be secure at least as long as one of the two hash functions remains secure. This is true for TLS 1.0 and 1.1; as discussed later, it is no longer true for TLS 1.2. The TLS PRF (used for TLS 1.0 and 1.1) is based on an auxiliary data expansion function, termed P_hash(secret,seed) in the TLS protocol specification. This function uses a single cryptographic hash function hash (which can be MD5 or SHA-1) to expand a secret and a seed seed into an arbitrarily long output value. In particular, the data expansion function is defined as follows:

```
P_hash(secret,seed) = HMAC_hash(secret,A(1)+seed) +
                      HMAC_hash(secret,A(2)+seed) +
                      HMAC_hash(secret,A(1)+seed) +
                      ...
```

As usual, + denotes the string concatenation operator. The A-function, in turn, is recursively defined as follows:

```
A(0) = seed
A(i) = HMAC_hash(secret,A(i-1)) for i>0
```

Using this recursive definition, the A-values that are necessary to evaluate the expansion function can be computed as follows:

```
A(1) = HMAC_hash(secret,A(0))
     = HMAC_hash(secret,seed)
A(2) = HMAC_hash(secret,A(1))
     = HMAC_hash(secret,HMAC_hash(secret,seed))
```

```
A(3) = HMAC_hash(secret,A(2))
     = HMAC_hash(secret,HMAC_hash(secret,
                        HMAC_hash(secret,seed)))
...
```

The A-function of the TLS PRF is illustrated in Figure 5.2. The output of the function consists of `A(1)`, `A(2)`, `A(3)`, ... For each iteration of the expansion function `P_hash(secret,seed)`, one additional output value of the A-function is needed. This can theoretically be continued an infinite number of times.

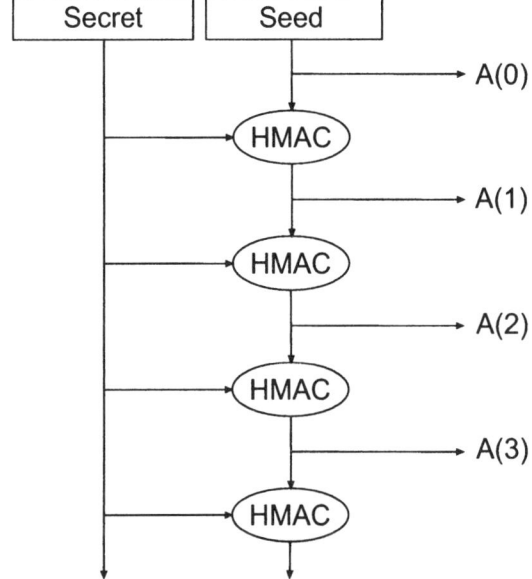

Figure 5.2 The A-function of the TLS PRF.

More specifically, the expansion function `P_hash(secret,seed)` is iteratively applied as many times as necessary to generate the required output data. Let us assume that we need 64 bytes of output data. If MD5 is used, then four iterations of the hash function are sufficient, since $4 \cdot 16 = 64$ bytes. If, however, SHA-1 is used, then four iterations yield $4 \cdot 20 = 80$ bytes. In this case, the first 64 output bytes are effectively used, whereas the last 16 bytes are silently discarded and remain unused.

The expansion function `P_hash(secret,seed)` is the major ingredient of the TLS PRF. As mentioned above and illustrated in Figure 5.1, the TLS PRF

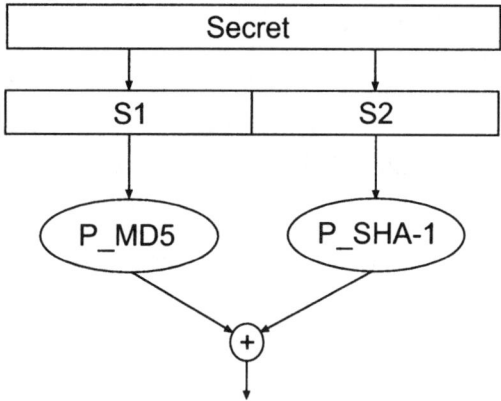

Figure 5.3 The internal structure of the TLS PRF (as used for TLS 1.0 and TLS 1.1).

takes as input a secret, a seed, and a label, and it generates as output a block of data of appropriate length. The secret and the seed are the parameters that are input to P_hash(secret, seed), whereas the label represents an arbitrary ASCII string. The string should be included in the exact form, without a length byte or trailing null character. For example, the label "eSECURITY" would be processed by hashing the following sequence of bytes (in hexadecimal notation): 65 53 45 43 55 52 49 54 59.

The internal structure of the TLS PRF (as used for TLS 1.0 and TLS 1.1) is illustrated in Figure 5.3. First, the secret is split into two halves (i.e., S1 and S2). S1 is taken from the first half of the secret, whereas S2 is taken from the second half of the secret. Their length is created by rounding up the length of the secret divided by two. If the secret happens to be an odd number of bytes long, then the last byte of S1 will be repeated and be the same as the first byte of S2. S1 and the concatenation of the label and the seed are then input to P_MD5, whereas S2 and the concatenation of the label and the seed are input to P_SHA-1. At the end, both output values are subject to a bitwise addition modulo 2 (XOR). Hence, the TLS PRF can be formally expressed as follows:

```
PRF(secret,label,seed) =
   P_MD5(S1,label+seed) XOR P_SHA-1(S2,label+seed)
```

Note that MD5 produces an output value of 16 bytes, whereas SHA-1 produces an output value of 20 bytes. Therefore, the boundaries of the iterations of P_MD5 and P_SHA-1 are not aligned, and the expansion functions must be iterated differently many times. To generate an output of 80 bytes, for example, P_MD5 must be iterated 5 times, whereas P_SHA-1 must be iterated only 4 times.

As already mentioned above, the TLS PRF overviewed so far is used in TLS 1.0 and TLS 1.1. Since TLS 1.2, however, the combined use of MD5 and SHA-1 has been abandoned, and a single—but hopefully more secure—cryptographic hash function is used. In this case, the PRF construction is conceptually simpler and more straightforward. It can be expressed as follows:

```
PRF(secret,label,seed) = P_hash(secret,label+seed)
```

The cryptographic hash function hash is part of the cipher suite. For the typical case of using SHA-256, P_hash actually refers to P_SHA256. Independent from the TLS PRF in use (be it the PRF for TLS 1.0 and 1.1 or the PRF for TLS 1.2), the keying material is generated in a specific way that is addressed next.

5.1.2 Generation of Keying Material

The primary use of the TLS PRF is to generate the keying material needed for a TLS connection. First, the variable-length premaster secret that is the output of the key exchange algorithm and part of the TLS session state is used to generate a 48-byte long master secret:

```
master_secret =
   PRF(pre_master_secret,"master secret",
      client_random+server_random)
```

In this step, the string "master secret" refers to the label, and the concatenation of the two random values client_random and client_random represents the seed. Note that client_random is the same value as client random in Table 5.1. The use of the underscore character is used inconsistently in the SSL and TLS protocol specifications, and we use both terms synonymously and interchangeably. The bottom line is that the master secret and the server and client random values are security parameters for the TLS connection (see Table 5.1).

Next, the 48-byte master secret is used as a source of entropy to determine the various keys that are needed for the TLS connection. The keys are taken from a key block of appropriate size that is generated as follows:

```
key_block =
   PRF(master_secret,"key expansion",
      server_random+client_random)
```

This time, the master secret is the secret, the string "key expansion" refers to the label, and the concatenation of the two random values client_random and client_random represents the seed. The key block can then be partitioned into the following values that are appropriately sized:

```
client_write_MAC_secret
server_write_MAC_secret
client_write_key
server_write_key
client_write_IV
server_write_IV
```

Any additional material in the key block is discarded. For example, a cipher suite that uses 3DES in CBC mode and SHA-1 requires $2 \cdot 24 = 48$ bytes for the 3DES keys, $2 \cdot 8 = 16$ bytes for the IVs, and $2 \cdot 20 = 40$ bytes for the MAC keys. Hence, a total of 104 bytes of keying material is needed. If the key block is longer, then the spare bytes can be discarded.

If the cipher in use is exportable (basically meaning that the Boolean predicate `is_exportable` of the cipher in use is true), then the write keys are used to generate the final write keys:

```
final_client_write_key =
   PRF(client_write_key,"client write key",
       server_random+client_random)
final_server_write_key =
   PRF(server_write_key,"server write key",
       client_random+server_random)
```

Also, if the cipher happens to be an exportable block cipher, then the IVs are derived solely from the random values of the TLS Handshake Protocol's hello messages (i.e., without any secret). In this case, instead of using the `client_write_IV` and `server_write_IV` values mentioned above, an IV block is generated from which the IVs are actually taken. The IV block is generated as follows:

```
iv_block =
   PRF("","IV block",client_random+server_random)
```

In this construction, the secret is empty and the label refers to the string "IV block." The resulting IV block is then partitioned into two appropriately sized IVs:

```
client_write_IV
server_write_IV
```

An example to generate the keying material for an exportable block cipher (i.e., RC2 with 40-bit keys) can be found in the TLS 1.0 protocol specification [1]. It is not repeated here (mainly because exportable block ciphers are not widely used anymore).

A number of protocols wish to leverage TLS to perform key establishment but then use some of the keying material for their own purposes. There is work going on within the IETF TLS WG to describe a general mechanism for allowing that.[1] In this setting, the keying material is called *Exported Keying Material* (EKM). It is generated using the TLS PRF in the following way:

```
EKM = PRF(master_secret,label,
          server_random+client_random+
          context_value_length+context_value)
```

In this formula, the label refers to a disambiguating string and context value refers to an application-specific value. Assuming the PRF having good pseudorandomness properties, it is prohibitively difficult to distinguish the EKM from random data (independent from the length of the EKM).

In addition to the TLS PRF and the generation of the keying material, there are other differences between the SSL protocol and the various versions of the TLS protocol. These differences are outlined and discussed next. For each difference, we give some background information and the rationale that has led to the respective design.

5.2 TLS 1.0

It has been mentioned several times so far that TLS 1.0 is very close to and backward-compatible with SSL 3.0, and that it can therefore be viewed as essentially SSL 3.1. This viewpoint is reflected in the version field that is included in each TLS record. In fact, this field comprises the two bytes 3 and 1, where 3 stands for the major version and 1 stands for the minor version. This suggests that TLS 1.0 is actually the same as SSL 3.1. In addition to the version, there are a few other differences between 3.0 and TLS 1.0. For example, we have seen that both protocols employ different PRFs to determine the keying material. Also the TLS protocol distinguishes between security parameters and state elements for TLS connections, whereas the SSL protocol only considers state elements. In addition to these obvious differences, there are also some differences that are more subtle and require further explanation; they are addressed next.

5.2.1 Cipher Suites

As with SSL, a TLS cipher spec refers to a pair of algorithms that are used to authenticate messages and encrypt data, whereas a cipher suite additionally comprises a key exchange algorithm. TLS 1.0 supports the same cipher suites as

---

1 http://www.ietf.org/internet-drafts/draft-ietf-tls-extractor-*.txt

SSL 3.0 (see Table 4.4). Only the three cipher suites that employ FORTEZZA, that is,

- SSL_FORTEZZA_KEA_WITH_NULL_SHA;
- SSL_FORTEZZA_KEA_WITH_FORTEZZA_CBC_SHA;
- SSL_FORTEZZA_KEA_WITH_RC4_128_SHA;

are no longer supported and have no counterpart in TLS 1.0. This means that there is a total of 28 cipher suites supported by TLS 1.0. Also, for obvious reasons, the names of the cipher suites have changed from SSL_* to TLS_*, so the cipher suite SSL_DHE_RSA_WITH_3DES_EDE_CBC_SHA has effectively become TLS_DHE_RSA_WITH_3DES_EDE_CBC_SHA without any substantial change with regard to content. But there are still a few subtle changes that need to be mentioned at this point. The changes refer to message authentication and data encryption. The key exchange algorithms have not changed and remain exactly the same.

5.2.1.1 Message Authentication

The MAC construction employed by the SSL protocol (see Section 4.2.1.3) is conceptually similar to the HMAC construction, but it is not exactly the same. For TLS 1.0, it was therefore decided to consistently use the HMAC construction for message authentication. The input parameters to the HMAC construction are the MAC key K, as well as the concatenation of the sequence number seq_number and the four components of the TLSCompressed structure (i.e., $type$, $version$, $length$, and $fragment$). Hence, the HMAC value is generated as follows:

$$HMAC_K(TLSCompressed) = \\ h(K \parallel opad \parallel h(K \parallel ipad \parallel seq\_number \parallel \\ \underbrace{type \parallel version \parallel length \parallel fragment}_{TLSCompressed}))$$

In this notation, h refers to the cryptographic hash function in use (as specified by the MAC algorithm parameter of the TLS connection). If one associates the concatenation of seq_number and the four components of the TLSCompressed structure with the message to be authenticated, then it is clear that the method specified above really refers to the HMAC construcion. Using this method, TLS 1.0 is now in line with international standardization.

5.2.1.2 Data Encryption

SSL 3.0 was specified prior to the enactment of the new U.S. export controls (see Section 2.1.6). Consequently, the preferred ciphers were DES (in the case of a block cipher) and RC4 (in the case of a stream cipher). When TLS 1.0 was specified in 1999, the situation regarding the U.S. export controls was about to change, and hence stronger ciphers could be prescribed. The AES was not yet standardized, and hence 3DES represented the greatest common denominator. In the absence of an application profile standard specifying otherwise, a TLS 1.0-compliant application must implement the cipher suite TLS_DHE_DSS_WITH_3DES_EDE_CBC_SHA. In fact, TLS_DHE_DSS_WITH_3DES_EDE_CBC_SHA is the only cipher suite that is mandatory to implement according to the TLS 1.0 specification.

If a cipher suite comprises a block cipher operated in CBC mode (such as TLS_DHE_DSS_WITH_3DES_EDE_CBC_SHA), then there is a subtle change to be mentioned here: while SSL 3.0 assumes the padding (that forces the length of the plaintext that comprises the fragment of a TLSCompressed structure to be a multiple of the cipher's block size) to be as short as possible, TLS 1.0 does not make this assumption. In fact, TLS 1.0 provides the possibility to add more padding (up to 255 bytes) prior to encryption. This allows the sender of a message to better hide the actual length of the message, and hence to better protect against traffic analysis attacks.

Table 5.3
The Camellia-Based Cipher Suites for TLS [4]

Cipher suite	Value
TLS_RSA_WITH_CAMELLIA_128_CBC_SHA	{ 0x00, 0x41 }
TLS_RSA_WITH_CAMELLIA_128_CBC_SHA	{ 0x00, 0x41 }
TLS_DH_DSS_WITH_CAMELLIA_128_CBC_SHA	{ 0x00, 0x42 }
TLS_DH_RSA_WITH_CAMELLIA_128_CBC_SHA	{ 0x00, 0x43 }
TLS_DHE_DSS_WITH_CAMELLIA_128_CBC_SHA	{ 0x00, 0x44 }
TLS_DHE_RSA_WITH_CAMELLIA_128_CBC_SHA	{ 0x00, 0x45 }
TLS_DH_anon_WITH_CAMELLIA_128_CBC_SHA	{ 0x00, 0x46 }
TLS_RSA_WITH_CAMELLIA_256_CBC_SHA	{ 0x00, 0x84 }
TLS_DH_DSS_WITH_CAMELLIA_256_CBC_SHA	{ 0x00, 0x85 }
TLS_DH_RSA_WITH_CAMELLIA_256_CBC_SHA	{ 0x00, 0x86 }
TLS_DHE_DSS_WITH_CAMELLIA_256_CBC_SHA	{ 0x00, 0x87 }
TLS_DHE_RSA_WITH_CAMELLIA_256_CBC_SHA	{ 0x00, 0x88 }
TLS_DH_anon_WITH_CAMELLIA_256_CBC_SHA	{ 0x00, 0x89 }

In addition to the move from DES to 3DES, a complementary RFC was released in 2005 [4] that proposed a couple of cipher suites that employ the Camellia block cipher. The RFC has been submitted to the IETF Standards Track and is still valid (even for TLS 1.1 and TLS 1.2). The Camellia-based cipher suites and their respective values are itemized in Table 5.3. Note that all cipher suites employ the cryptographic hash function SHA-1. The Camellia-based cipher suites are mainly used in Japan and partly in Europe.

Last but not least, we note that all TLS cipher suites are itemized in Appendix A (in numerical order). This applies for the TLS 1.0 cipher suites, but it also applies for the TLS 1.1 and TLS 1.2 cipher suites.

Table 5.4
TLS 1.0 Certificate Type Values

Value	Name	Description
1	rsa_sign	RSA signing
2	dss_sign	DSA signing
3	rsa_fixed_dh	RSA signing with fixed DH key exchange
4	dss_fixed_dh	DSA signing with fixed DH key exchange

5.2.2 Certificate Management

With regard to certificate management, there are two far-reaching differences between SSL 3.0 and TLS 1.0:

- First, SSL 3.0 requires complete certificate chains, meaning that certificates must go back to a root CA, whereas TLS 1.0 accepts certificate chains that go back "only" to an intermediate CA. This simplifies the verification and validation of certificates considerably.
- Second, TLS 1.0 supports a reduced and slightly different set of certificate types used for CERTIFICATEREQUEST messages. In fact, TLS 1.0 only supports the four certificate types itemized in Table 5.4:

  – RSA signing (1);
  – DSA signing (2);
  – RSA signing with fixed Diffie-Hellman key exchange (3);
  – DSA signing with fixed Diffie-Hellman key exchange (4).

  The numbers in brackets refer to their respective type values. These types correspond to the first four certificate types supported by SSL (see Table

4.5). So TLS 1.0 does no longer support RSA signing with ephemeral Diffie-Hellman key exchange (5), DSA signing with ephemeral Diffie-Hellman key exchange (6), and FORTEZZA signing and key exchange (20). The first two certificate types (5 and 6) are not really needed, because a certificate that can be used to generate RSA (DSA) signatures can also be used to sign ephemeral Diffie-Hellman keys. Also, the last certificate type (20) is no longer needed, because the FORTEZZA-type cipher suites have been removed from TLS 1.0 anyway.

Later in this chapter, we will see that the certificate types missing in TLS 1.0 have been reintroduced in TLS 1.1 as reserved values (see Section 5.3).

Table 5.5
TLS Alert Messages (Part 1)

Alert	Code	Brief description (if new)
close_notify	0	
unexpected_message	10	
bad_record_mac	20	
decryption_failed	21	The sender notifies the recipient that a ciphertext (received in the fragment of a TLSCiphertext record) decrypted in an invalid way. This alert is always fatal.
record_overflow	22	The sender notifies the recipient that a record was too long (i.e., either a TLSCiphertext record was longer than $2^{14} + 2048$ bytes or a TLSCompressed record was longer than $2^{14} + 1024$ bytes. This alert is always fatal and should never be observed in communication between proper implementations.
decompression_failure	30	
handshake_failure	40	
bad_certificate	42	
unsupported_certificate	43	
certificate_revoked	44	
certificate_expired	45	
certificate_unknown	46	
illegal_parameter	47	
unknown_ca	48	The sender notifies the recipient that a valid certificate chain was received, but at least one certificate was not accepted because the CA cerificate could not be located or could not be matched with a trusted CA. This alert is always fatal.
access_denied	49	The sender notifies the recipient that a valid certificate was received, but when access control was applied, the sender decided not to proceed with negotiation. This alert is always fatal.

5.2.3 Alert Messages

TLS 1.0 uses a set of alert messages that is slightly different from SSL 3.0. In fact, the 23 Alert Protocol message types of TLS 1.0 are summarized in Tables 5.5 (Part

Table 5.6
TLS Alert Messages (Part 2)

Alert	Code	Brief description (if new)
decode_error	50	The sender notifies the recipient that a message could not be decoded because some field was out of the specified range or the length of the message was incorrect. This alert is always fatal.
decrypt_error	51	The sender notifies the recipient that a handshake cryptographic operation failed, including being unable to verify a signature, decrypt a key exchange, or validate a finished message.
export_restriction	60	The sender notifies the recipient that a negotiation not in compliance with export restrictions was detected. This alert is always fatal.
protocol_version	70	The sender notifies the recipient that the protocol version the client has attempted to negotiate is recognized but not supported (for example, an older protocol version might be avoided for security reasons). This alert is always fatal.
insufficient_security	71	Returned instead of handshake_failure when a negotiation has failed specifically because the server requires ciphers more secure than those supported by the client. This alert is always fatal.
internal_error	80	The sender notifies the recipient that an internal error unrelated to the peer or the correctness of the protocol makes it impossible to continue. This alert is always fatal.
user_canceled	90	The sender notifies the recipient that this handshake is being canceled for some reason unrelated to a protocol failure. If the user cancels an operation after the handshake is complete, just closing the connection by sending a close_notify is more appropriate. This alert should be followed by a close_notify. This alert is generally a warning.
no_renegotiation	100	The sender notifies the recipient that a renegotiation is not appropriate. This alert is always a warning.

1) and 5.6 (Part 2). In these tables, only the message types that are new (related to SSL 3.0) come along with a description. In addition to the new message types, there is also one message type that has become obsolete and is now marked as reserved (i.e., no_certificate or no_certificate_RESERVED with an alert code of 41).

5.2.4 Other Differences

TLS 1.0 uses simplified and streamlined formats and ways of computing the hash values for the CERTIFICATEVERIFY and the FINISHED messages.

- With regard to the CERTIFICATEVERIFY message, the handshake messages are simply hashed (using MD5 or SHA-1) and digitally signed using the appropriate signing key. Compare this to the relatively complex construction of the SSL CERTIFICATEVERIFY message (see Section 4.2.2.10).

- With regard the the FINISHED message, the TLS PRF is used to generate

```
PRF(master_secret,finished_label,
    MD5(handshake_messages)+
    SHA-1(handshake_messages)),
```

where `finished_label` refers to the string "client finished" (if the client sends the FINISHED message) or "server finished" (if the sever sends the FINISHED message), and `handshake_messages` comprises all handshake messages (except any HELLOREQUEST message) up to but not including the current message. This includes only data visible at the handshake layer and does not include any record layer header. From the output of this PRF, only the first 12 bytes are used to form the actual FINISHED message.

5.3 TLS 1.1

The official TLS 1.0 protocol specification was released approximately one decade ago. It is therefore not particularly surprising that more recent developments have led to changes in the TLS protocol specification. In April 2006, some of these changes were approved and the specification of the TLS 1.1 protocol was officially released [2]. This version of the TLS protocol is referenced as 3,2. Let us start with some preliminary remarks, before we delve more deeply into the differences between TLS 1.0 and TLS 1.1.

5.3.1 Preliminary Remarks

At the end of Section 4.4, we mentioned that some researchers have found (mostly subtle) security problems in the CBC padding scheme employed by the SSL protocol. In 2002, for example, Vaudenay published a paper in which he explained how CBC padding used by SSL induces a side channel that may be exploited in a chosen ciphertext attack [5]. Note that the existence of this attack is in seeming contrast to the theoretical result that EtA is secure if a block cipher in CBC mode or a stream cipher is used for encryption. This, in turn, attests to the fact that a theoretically secure scheme need not remain secure when implemented in practice. Anyway, Vaudenay's side channel attack starts from the fact that most cryptographic security protocols employ some form of padding before messages are subject to block cipher encryption. When a recipient receives a ciphertext, he or she usually decrypts it and verifies the format of the padding, before further processing the message (verifying, for example, the MAC that comes along with the message). Consequently, validity of the format often leaks from a security protocol in a chosen ciphertext attack, since the recipient typically sends an acknowledgment or an error message (e.g., `decryption_failed` in the case of the SSL protocol). If the adversary is able to tell the two situations apart, then he or she has a side channel that may be exploited. Note that a MAC does not protect against such an attack, because message padding is performed after the computation of the MAC (so the MAC cannot be verified before the padding in the decryption).

Vaudenay's side channel attacks are theoretically interesting but not practically feasible in a typical SSL/TLS setting. This is because the error messages (i.e., `decryption_failed` messages) are usually encrypted and the adversary has no access to the logfile. So, in general, the adversary cannot tell an acknowledgment and an error message apart. To make things worse, an SSL/TLS connection is usually aborted prematurely once an error has occured. Both problems limit the feasibility of the attacks. But there may still be situations in which such an attack is feasible. For example, in a 2003 follow-up paper, Vaudenay and some of his colleagues showed how a multisession attack can be used to intercept a password transmitted over an SSL/TLS connection (the target situation is an IMAP client that uses the SSL/TLS protocols to securely connect to an IMAP server) [6]. This paper became a headline in the trade press, and hence the designers of the TLS protocol were strongly encouraged (if not forced) to take precautions to protect the TLS protocol against the attack. More specifically, they had to update TLS 1.0 and come up with TLS 1.1.

In a 2002 posting, Bodo Möller[2] argued that the distinction between alert messages for `bad_record_mac` (code 20) and `decryption_failed` (code 21) is disadvantageous from a security viewpoint as it improves the odds of an adversary. He therefore recommended to neglect the distinction and return a `bad_record_mac` alert in either case. Consequently, a `bad_record_mac` alert message must also be returned if a TLSCiphertext decrypts in an invalid way; either because its length is not an even multiple of the block length, or its padding values, when checked, are not correct. This recommendation was adopted in TLS 1.1,[3] in spite of the fact that it was challenged in [6]. The doubts are caused by the fact that timing differences may still exist to tell the two situations apart. Instead of suppressing `decryption_failed` alert messages, one can try to make alert messages time-invariant by simulating a MAC verification even if a padding error has already occured. One can even go one step further and add random noise to the time delay. The first of these recommendations found its way into the TLS 1.1 protocol specification (at least as an implementation note). In addition, TLS 1.1 also replaces the implicit IV used in TLS 1.0 with an explicit random IV. This is in response to another vulnerability in CBC padding that was found by Gregory Bard, and that can be exploited in a blockwise adaptive chosen plaintext attack

2 http://www.openssl.org/~bodo/tls-cbc.txt.
3 The TLS 1.1 protocol specification says that the decryption_failed error alert "MAY be returned if a TLSCiphertext decrypted in an invalid way."

[7]. This means that for each `TLSCompressed` fragment that is encryted there is a seperate IV that is randomly chosen and sent along with the corresponding `TLSCiphertext` fragment. Since the IVs are now explicit and sent along with the `TLSCiphertext` fragments, there is no need to initially generate IVs. So the key generation process overviewed in Section 5.1.2 can be simplified to only generate the `client_write_MAC_secret` and the `server_write_MAC_secret`, as well as the `client_write_key` and the `server_write_key`.

Table 5.7
TLS 1.1 Standard Cipher Suites

Cipher suite	Value
TLS_NULL_WITH_NULL_NULL	{ 0x00,0x00 }
TLS_RSA_WITH_NULL_MD5	{ 0x00,0x01 }
TLS_RSA_WITH_NULL_SHA	{ 0x00,0x02 }
TLS_RSA_WITH_RC4_128_MD5	{ 0x00,0x04 }
TLS_RSA_WITH_RC4_128_SHA	{ 0x00,0x05 }
TLS_RSA_WITH_IDEA_CBC_SHA	{ 0x00,0x07 }
TLS_RSA_WITH_DES_CBC_SHA	{ 0x00,0x09 }
TLS_RSA_WITH_3DES_EDE_CBC_SHA	{ 0x00,0x0A }
TLS_DH_DSS_WITH_DES_CBC_SHA	{ 0x00,0x0C }
TLS_DH_DSS_WITH_3DES_EDE_CBC_SHA	{ 0x00,0x0D }
TLS_DH_RSA_WITH_DES_CBC_SHA	{ 0x00,0x0F }
TLS_DH_RSA_WITH_3DES_EDE_CBC_SHA	{ 0x00,0x10 }
TLS_DHE_DSS_WITH_DES_CBC_SHA	{ 0x00,0x12 }
TLS_DHE_DSS_WITH_3DES_EDE_CBC_SHA	{ 0x00,0x13 }
TLS_DHE_RSA_WITH_DES_CBC_SHA	{ 0x00,0x15 }
TLS_DHE_RSA_WITH_3DES_EDE_CBC_SHA	{ 0x00,0x16 }
TLS_DH_anon_WITH_RC4_128_MD5	{ 0x00,0x18 }
TLS_DH_anon_WITH_DES_CBC_SHA	{ 0x00,0x1A }
TLS_DH_anon_WITH_3DES_EDE_CBC_SHA	{ 0x00,0x1B }

5.3.2 Cipher Suites

The cipher suites supported by TLS 1.1 have been changed considerably. This is not true for the HMAC construction, but it is true for a number of other things. First and foremost, all cipher suites that comprise an export-grade key exchange algorithm or cipher may still be offered for backward compatibility, but they must not be negotiated in TLS 1.1. This applies to all cipher suites written in italics in Table 4.4 (except SSL_NULL_WITH_NULL_NULL) and the export-grade Kerberos-based cipher suites from RFC 2712 [8]. The other Kerberos- and AES-based cipher suites specified in RFC 2712 and RFC 3268 [9] have been included in TLS 1.1. The

Table 5.8
TLS 1.1 Kerberos-Based Cipher Suites

Cipher suite	Value
TLS_KRB5_WITH_DES_CBC_SHA	{ 0x00, 0x1E }
TLS_KRB5_WITH_3DES_EDE_CBC_SHA	{ 0x00, 0x1F }
TLS_KRB5_WITH_RC4_128_SHA	{ 0x00, 0x20 }
TLS_KRB5_WITH_IDEA_CBC_SHA	{ 0x00, 0x21 }
TLS_KRB5_WITH_DES_CBC_MD5	{ 0x00, 0x22 }
TLS_KRB5_WITH_3DES_EDE_CBC_MD5	{ 0x00, 0x23 }
TLS_KRB5_WITH_RC4_128_MD5	{ 0x00, 0x24 }
TLS_KRB5_WITH_IDEA_CBC_MD5	{ 0x00, 0x25 }

Table 5.9
TLS 1.1 AES-Based Cipher Suites

Cipher suite	Value
TLS_RSA_WITH_AES_128_CBC_SHA	{ 0x00, 0x2F }
TLS_DH_DSS_WITH_AES_128_CBC_SHA	{ 0x00, 0x30 }
TLS_DH_RSA_WITH_AES_128_CBC_SHA	{ 0x00, 0x31 }
TLS_DHE_DSS_WITH_AES_128_CBC_SHA	{ 0x00, 0x32 }
TLS_DHE_RSA_WITH_AES_128_CBC_SHA	{ 0x00, 0x33 }
TLS_DH_anon_WITH_AES_128_CBC_SHA	{ 0x00, 0x34 }
TLS_RSA_WITH_AES_256_CBC_SHA	{ 0x00, 0x35 }
TLS_DH_DSS_WITH_AES_256_CBC_SHA	{ 0x00, 0x36 }
TLS_DH_RSA_WITH_AES_256_CBC_SHA	{ 0x00, 0x37 }
TLS_DHE_DSS_WITH_AES_256_CBC_SHA	{ 0x00, 0x38 }
TLS_DHE_RSA_WITH_AES_256_CBC_SHA	{ 0x00, 0x39 }
TLS_DH_anon_WITH_AES_256_CBC_SHA	{ 0x00, 0x3A }

resulting cipher suites supported by TLS 1.1 are summarized in Tables 5.7 to 5.9 (together with their respective code values). The Camellia-based cipher suites itemized in Table 5.3 still apply and can be used for TLS 1.1. Again, refer to the appendix for a complete listing of all TLS cipher suites and their respective code values.

5.3.3 Certificate Management

As mentioned above and summarized in Table 5.10, the certificate type values 5, 6, and 20 were reintroduced in TLS 1.1 as reserved values (meaning that they should no longer be used).

Table 5.10
TLS 1.1 Certificate Type Values

Value	Name	Description
1	rsa_sign	RSA signing and key exchange
2	dss_sign	DSA signing only
3	rsa_fixed_dh	RSA signing with fixed DH key exchange
4	dss_fixed_dh	DSA signing with fixed DH key exchange
5	rsa_ephemeral_dh_RESERVED	RSA signing with ephemeral DH key exchange
6	dss_ephemeral_dh_RESERVED	DSA signing with ephemeral DH key exchange
20	fortezza_dms_RESERVED	FORTEZZA signing and key exchange

5.3.4 Alert Messages

In addition to alert message 41 (i.e., no_certificate or no_certificate_RESERVED) that has become obsolete in TLS 1.0, alert message 60 (i.e., export_restriction or export_restriction_RESERVED) has also become obsolete in TLS 1.1. This is because export-grade encryption is no longer supported by TLS 1.1 (as mentioned above), and hence there is no need for corresponding alert messages anymore.

5.3.5 Other Differences

There are at least two other differences between TLS 1.0 and TLS 1.1 that deserve to be mentioned:

- First, a premature closure (i.e., a closure without a mutual exchange of close_notify messages) no longer causes a TLS session to be nonresumable. Put in other words: even if a connection is closed without having the communicating peers properly exchange close_notify, it may still be resumable under certain conditions. But keep in mind that any connection terminated with a fatal alert must not be resumed.

- Second, a number of new registries have been created by the Internet Assigned Numbers Authority (IANA[4]) for parameter values, such as certificate types, cipher suites, content types, alert values, and handshake types. The goal is to add flexibility to the TLS protocol. If a parameter must be added or changed, then it is no longer necessary to modify the protocol specification. Instead, adding or changing the parameter in the registry is sufficient.

---

4 The IANA is responsible for the global coordination of the DNS Root, IP addressing, and other Internet protocol resources.

In theory, there are many possibilities for assigning the parameter values mentioned above. In practice, however, the assignments are usually in line with RFC 2434 (BCP 26) [10] and conform with one of the following three policies given in this document:

- Values that are assigned via *Standards Action* are reserved for Standards Track RFCs approved by the Internet Engineering Steering Group (IESG).

- Values that are assigned via *Specification Required* must at least be documented in an RFC or other permanent and readily available reference, in sufficient detail so that interoperability between independent implementations is possible.

- Values that are assigned via *Private Use* need not fulfill any requirement. In fact, there is no need for IANA to review such assignments and they are not generally useful for interoperability.

For example, the certificate types supported by TLS 1.1 are divided into three groups: values in the range 0–63 inclusive are assigned via Standards Action, values in the range 64–223 inclusive are assigned via Specification Required, and values in the range 224–255 inclusive are assigned via Private Use. Similarly, the cipher suites supported by TLS 1.1 are also divided into three groups: values with the first byte in the range 0–191 are assigned via Standards Action (e.g., all cipher suites mentioned so far), values with the first byte in the range 192–254 are assigned via Specification Required (e.g., cipher suites that employ ECC as mentioned below), and values with the first byte 255 are assigned via Private Use. Last but not least, all content type, alert value, and handshake type values are allocated via Standards Action.

5.4 TLS 1.2

After the offical release of TLS 1.1 in 2006, the respective standardization activities continued and many people working in the field continued to make proposals on how TLS could be extended and evolved. In 2008, the next version of the TLS protocol—TLS 1.2—became ready and was officially released in RFC 5246 [3]. It is referenced as version 3,3.

As mentioned at the end of Section 5.1, TLS 1.2 uses a new PRF that is simpler and more straightforward than its predecessor (mainly because it uses only one cryptographic hash function instead of combining two functions). Similarly, for digital signatures, the combined use of MD5 and SHA-1 has been replaced with the use of a single cryptographic hash value. Again, we start with some preliminary remarks regarding TLS extensions, before we delve more deeply into the specific differences between TLS 1.1 and TLS 1.2.

5.4.1 TLS Extensions

Remember from Section 3.2 that the specification of TLS 1.2 [3] not only made RFC 4346 [2] obsolete, but also RFC 3268 [9] and RFC 4366 [11]:

- RFC 3268 introduces AES-based cipher suites for TLS (that can be used by all versions of the TLS protocol).
- As TLS is used in an increasing variety of new operational environments (e.g., wireless networks[5]), RFC 4366 introduces a couple of extensions that may be used to add functionality (and hence flexibility) to the TLS protocol.

More specifically, RFC 4366 provides both generic extension mechanisms for the TLS handshake client and server hello messages, as well as specific extensions using these mechanisms. The extensions may be used by TLS clients and servers; they are backward-compatible, meaning that communication is possible between TLS clients that support the extensions and TLS servers that do not support the extensions, and vice versa.

A client may request the use of extensions via an extended CLIENTHELLO message. An extended CLIENTHELLO message, in turn, is just a "normal" CLIENT-HELLO message with an additional block of data that comprises a list of extensions. Remember that additional information can be appended to a CLIENTHELLO message, and hence an extended CLIENTHELLO message that conforms to the specification does not "break" existing TLS servers. A TLS server is to accept such a message, even if it does not properly understand the extensions. The presence of extensions can be detected by determining whether there are bytes following the compression methods at the end of the CLIENTHELLO message. This method of detecting optional data is not in line with the usual method of having a variable length field, but it is used for compatibility with TLS before extensions were defined. Anyway, if the server understands the extensions, it sends back an extended SERVERHELLO message in place of a "normal" SERVERHELLO message. Again, the extended SERVERHELLO message may comprise a list of extensions. Note that the extended SERVERHELLO message is only sent in response to an extended CLIENTHELLO message. This prevents the possibility that the extended SERVER-HELLO message "breaks" existing TLS clients. Also note that there is no upper

---

5 Endpoint devices that connect to wireless networks often suffer from a number of constraints not commonly present in wired networks, such as limitations in terms of bandwidth, computational power, or battery lifetime.

bound for the length of the list of extensions. So it may happen that a client floods a server by sending a very long list of extensions. If this poses a problem, then it is possible and very likely that future server implementations will limit the maximum length of an extended CLIENTHELLO message.

Table 5.11
TLS Extension Types and Values

Extension type	Values	Description	References
server_name	0	Server name	[11]
max_fragment_length	1	Maximal fragment length	[11]
client_certificate_url	2	Client certificate URL	[11]
trusted_ca_keys	3	Trusted CA keys	[11]
truncated_hmac	4	Truncated HMAC	[11]
status_request	5	Status request	[11]
user_mapping	6	User mapping	[12, 13]
—	7,8	Reserved	
cert_type	9	Certificate types	[14]
elliptic_curves	10	Elliptic curves	[15]
ec_point_formats	11	Elliptic curve point formats	[15]
srp	12	SRP protocol	[16]
supported_signature_algorithms	13	Signature algorithms	[3]
—	14–34	Unassigned	
SessionTicket	35	Session tickets	[17]

Each extension consists of a type and a data field that is specific for the type (it may also be empty). As mentioned at the end of the previous section, the IANA maintains a registry of available content type values.[6] The values are assigned via IETF Concensus, meaning that new assignments are made via RFCs approved by the IESG. The registry is a moving target and subject to change. The currently valid TLS extension types and values are summarized in Table 5.11.

The first six extension types 0–5 are defined in RFC 4366 [11] and a follow-up document that is currently in the status of an Internet-Draft.[7] The extension type 6 is defined in RFC 4680 [12] and RFC 4681 [13], the extension type 9 is defined in RFC 5081 [14], the extensions types 10 and 11 are defined in RFC 4492 [15], the extension type 12 is defined in RFC 5054 [16], and the extension type 13 is defined in the original TLS 1.2 protocol specification [3]. Last but not least, the extension type 35 is defined in RFC 5077 [17]. In the sequel, we briefly overview these extension types and finish up this section with a summary. Before we do so, we note that RFC

6 http://www.iana.org/assignments/tls-extensiontype-values/.
7 draft-ietf-tls-rfc4366-bis-*.txt

Table 5.12
New TLS Alert Messages Introduced in RFC 4366 [11]

Alert	Code	Brief description (if new)
`unsupported_extension`	110	The sender (client) notifies the recipient (server) that it does not support an extension contained in an extended SERVERHELLO message. This alert message is always fatal.
`certificate_unobtainable`	111	The sender (server) notifies the recipient (client) that it is unable to retrieve a certificate (chain) from the URL supplied in a CERTIFICATEURL message. This alert message may be fatal.
`unrecognized_name`	112	The sender (server) notifies the recipient (client) that it does not recognize the server specified in a server name extension. This alert message may be fatal.
`bad_certificate_status_response`	113	The sender (client) notifies the recipient (server) that it has received an invalid certificate status response. This alert message is always fatal.
`bad_certificate_hash_value`	114	The sender (server) notifies the recipient (client) that a certificate hash does not match a client-provided value. This alert message is always fatal.

4366 also introduces a number of new TLS alert messages (overviewed in Table 5.12). Meanwhile, the `unsupported_extension` alert message has become part of the TLS 1.2 protocol specification (the other messages are not yet part of the TLS protocol specification).

5.4.1.1 Server Name

Virtual hosting is a commonly used method to host multiple servers (e.g., Web servers) with different domain names on the same computer, sometimes on the same IP address. To make use of virtual hosting, a client typically establishes a TCP session to the hosting computer, establishes an HTTP/1.1 connection on top of this TCP session, and specifies the Web server's domain name in the `Host` header of a subsequent HTTP request message. This works perfectly fine for HTTP. If, however, HTTPS is used instead of HTTP, then a SSL/TLS connection must be established prior to the invocation of HTTP. This basically means that the client must employ other means to support virtual hosting. SSL 3.0, TLS 1.0, and TLS 1.1 have no other means, so these protocols do not support virtual hosting, meaning that each SSL/TLS-enabled Web server must have a unique IP address. This is a severe disadvantage when it comes to the large-scale deployment of the SSL/TLS protocol, and it is probably one of the main reasons why SSL/TLS-enabled Web servers are not as widely deployed as they could be. In fact, the disadvantage is so severe that TLS 1.2 has been extended to support virtual hosting. More specifically, an extension type `server_name` (value 0) has been defined that can be used by a client to tell the Web server the domain name of the server it is trying to connect to. The bottom line is that a particular computer with a unique IP address server can now host multiple virtual SSL/TLS-enabled Web servers. This is important for the large-scale deployment of the TLS protocol.

5.4.1.2 Maximal Fragment Length

We have already seen in Section 4.2 that the maximum fragment length of an SSL record is 2^{14} bytes. This also applies to TLS. In many situations, it is reasonable to work with fragments of exactly this length. There are, however, also situations in which the clients are constrained and need to operate on fragments of smaller length. This is where the extension type max_fragment_length (value 1) comes into play. It can be used by a client to tell the server that it needs to negotiate a smaller maximal fragment length. The actual maximum fragment length is sent in the data field of the extension. Supported values are 1 (standing for 2^9 bytes), 2 (standing for 2^{10} bytes), 3 (standing for 2^{11} bytes), and 4 (standing for 2^{12} bytes).

5.4.1.3 Client Certificate URL

Normally, when client authentication is required in the execution of the SSL/TLS protocols, the client sends a CERTIFICATE message to the server and this message includes a certificate. In many situations this works perfectly fine. But there are also situations in which the transmission of a full-fledged certificate or certificate chain is too expensive, and in which it is advantageous to transmit only a certificate URL in place of a certificate. The aim is that the server can retrieve the client certificate from the corresponding URL. This is computationally and communicationally less expensive for the client. More specifically, the extension type client_certificate_url (value 2) can be used by a client to provide a certificate URL. The data field of the extension is empty. If and only if the server has agreed on this extension, the client provides a CERTIFICATEURL message (type 21) instead of a "normal" CERTIFICATE message (type 11) to the server. CERTIFICATEURL is one of the two new message types introduced in RFC 4366 [11].

5.4.1.4 Trusted CA Keys

In the "normal" execution of the SSL/TLS protocol, the server has no clue about what root CAs the client trusts. So when the server provides its certificate (chain) in the CERTIFICATE message, it may be the case that the certificate is not accepted by the client. This means that the SSL/TLS handshake needs to be repeated. In the most extreme case, it may happen that SSL/TLS handshakes need to be repeated multiple times. This is not efficient, especially if clients are configured to trust only a few (or only very specific) root CAs. Repeated SSL/TLS handshakes are particularly undesirable in low bandwidth scenarios, and this is where the extension type `trusted_ca_keys` (value 3) comes into play: it can be used by a client to tell the server which root CAs it actually trusts (to avoid repeated handshake failures). The information about the root CAs is actually sent in the data field of the extension. This also imposes a bandwidth penalty, but compared to repeated SSL/TLS handshakes this penalty is negligible.

5.4.1.5 Truncated HMAC

In Section 2.2.2.2, we mentioned that the output of the HMAC construction may be truncated to a value that is shorter than the output of the hash value in use, and that there are situations in which the truncated HMAC construction is advantageous. Against this background, the extension type `truncated_hmac` (value 4) has been defined. It can be used by a client to tell the server that it supports truncated HMACs, meaning that it that it can handle HMACs that are truncated, for example, to 80 bits. The data field of this extension is empty.

5.4.1.6 Status Request

Normally, when a participating entity of an SSL/TLS protocol execution receives a certificate, it is up to him or her to verify the validity of the certificate. Most importantly, the certificate revocation list (CRL) of the certificate issuing-CA must be retrieved and checked. Normally, this poses no problem, especially if the certificate-receiving entity is a server. But if the certificate-receiving entity is a constrained client, it may still happen that retrieving and checking the CRL is computationally too expensive, and that an alternative that burdens the server would be preferred. This is where the extension type `status_request` (value 5) comes into play: it can be used by a client to tell the server that it wishes to receive certificate status information, such as an Online Certificate Status Protocol (OCSP) response. Additional information related to OCSP is sent in the data field of the extension. The certificate status information, in turn, is provided by the server in a CERTIFICATE-STATUS message (type 22). This is the other new message type introduced in RFC 4366 [11].

5.4.1.7 User Mapping

The user mapping extension is based on a general mechanism defined in RFC 4680 [12]. This mechanism can be used by a client to exchange supplemental application data in an extended CLIENTHELLO message. If the server is willing to accept the supplemental application data, then it must respond with an extended SERVERHELLO message and a corresponding SUPPLEMENTALDATA message (type 23). The TLS implementation cannot do anything else with a SUPPLEMENTALDATA message than to forward it to the application layer. The client may also provide a SUPPLEMENTALDATA message, but otherwise the TLS protocol message flow remains the same.

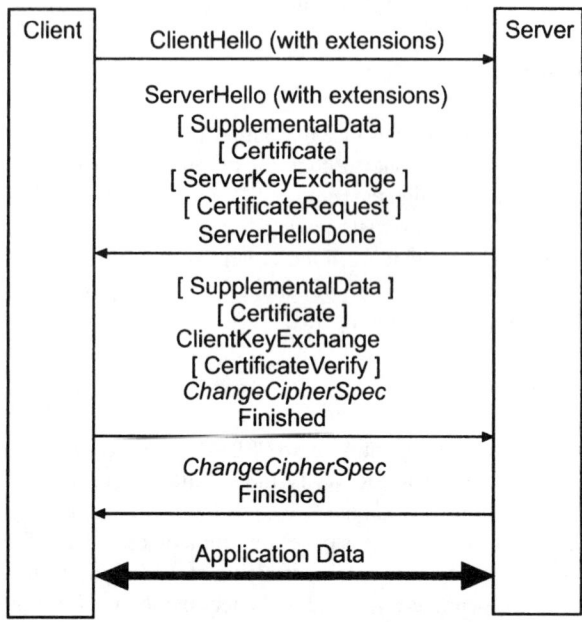

Figure 5.4 The TLS handshake protocol supporting the exchange of supplemental application data.

The resulting TLS handshake protocol supporting the exchange of supplemental application data is illustrated in Figure 5.4. If the server is not willing to accept the supplemental application data unless the client is properly authenticated, then a double handshake technique must be used. Using this technique, a first TLS handshake is performed to establish a first TLS session, and this session is then used to protect a second TLS handshake. The supplemental application data is actually transmitted as part of the second TLS handshake.

Based on RFC 4680, RFC 4681 [13] defines a TLS extension and a payload for the SUPPLEMENTALDATA message in a TLS handshake that can be used to accommodate mapping of users to their accounts when using TLS client authentication.

The extension type user_mapping (value 6) is therefore sent in the CLIENT-HELLO message, and—in the positive case—it is also included in the SERVER-HELLO message (to inform the client that the server understands the extension). The user mapping data is then included in the SUPPLEMENTALDATA message that is sent from the client to the server. It is up to the server to parse this message, extract the client's domain, and store it in the context for use when mapping the certificate to the user's directory account.

5.4.1.8 Certificate Types

In Section 8.1, we will see that there are two sets of standards for public key certificates supported by the IETF: X.509 and PGP (or OpenPGP, respectively). The SSL/TLS protocols natively support X.509 certificates, but there are situations in which X.509 certificates are not readily available and the participants are equipped with non-X.509 (e.g., OpenPGP) certificates instead. To support situations like these, the IETF TLS WG has specified both an extension type cert_type (value 9) and an Experimental RFC 5081 [14] that elaborates on the use of such non-X.509 certificates in a TLS setting. As usual, the extension is backward-compatible with TLS, so that existing implementations that make "normal" use of X.509 certificates are not negatively affected. This also means that no cipher suite is required to use non-X.509 certificates, but that all cipher suites may be used in combination with such certificates (if the key exchange method is compatible with them). The cert_type extension comes along with a data field that carries the encodings of the corresponding certificate types as registered by the IANA.

The values 0 (X.509) and 1 (OpenPGP) are defined in RFC 5081. The values between 2 and 223 (in decimal notation) are unassigned and can be assigned via IETF Concensus, whereas the values between 224 and 255 (again, in decimal notation) are reserved for Private Use. Consequently, there is room for future extensions and complementary certificate types.

If a client wants to indicate the support of multiple certificate types, it must include a cert_type extension in the CLIENTHELLO message. The data field of the extension must carry a list of supported certificate types, sorted by client preference. If the server receives a CLIENTHELLO message with the cert_type extension and chooses a cipher suite that requires a certificate, then it must either select a certificate type from the list of client-supported certificate types or terminate the connection with a fatal alert of type unsupported_certificate (alert code 43). In the first case, the server must encode the selected certificate type in an extended SERVERHELLO message (with another cert_type extension). X.509

certificates are assumed by default, meaning that servers that only support X.509 certificates may also omit including the `cert_type` extension in the SERVERHELLO message.

In addition to the CLIENTHELLO and SERVERHELLO messages, the contents of the CERTIFICATE messages sent from the server to the client and vice versa are also determined by the negotiated certificate type and the selected key exchange algorithm (that is part of the cipher suite). In particular, if the OpenPGP certificate type is negotiated, then it is required to include an OpenPGP certificate in the CERTIFICATE message with a public key that matches the selected key exchange algorithm. If RSA is used for key exchange, then the OpenPGP certificate must contain an RSA public key that can be used for encryption. Similarly, if DHE_DSS (DHE_RSA) is used for key exchange, then the OpenPGP certificate must contain a DSS (RSA) public key that can be used for authentication. Anyway, any OpenPGP certificate appearing in a CERTIFICATE message must be sent in the standardized binary OpenPGP format. Optionally, it is also possible to send only a fingerprint of the OpenPGP certificate, instead of the entire certificate.

All other TLS handshake messages remain unaffected by the `cert_type` extension. There is, however, a subtle remark to be made with regard to the CERTIFICATEREQUEST message that may be sent from the server to the client (see Section 4.2.2.6). If such a message is sent, then it may specify certificate types and CAs that are accepted by the server. In the case of OpenPGP certificates, the list of CAs that are accepted by the server must be empty (because OpenPGP certificates are typically issued by peers instead of CAs).

5.4.1.9 Elliptic Curves and Elliptic Curve Point Formats

We already mentioned in Chapter 2 that ECC is an emerging public key cryptographic technology, because it offers equivalent security with smaller key sizes and smaller key sizes result in savings for power, memory, bandwidth, and computational costs. This makes ECC particularly interesting for constrained resource environments. Against this background, the IETF TLS WG has worked on incorporating ECC into TLS. The result of this work is documented in Informational RFC 4492 [15] officially released in May 2006. It is applicable to both TLS 1.0 and TLS 1.1, and it may even be applicable to TLS 1.2 (note that TLS 1.2 was specified after the official release of RFC 4492).

More specifically, RFC 4492 introduces five new ECC-based key exchange algorithms for the TLS handshake protocol. All of them use the ECDH key exchange to compute the TLS premaster secret, and they differ only in the lifetime of ECDH keys (long-term or ephemeral) and the mechanism used to authenticate them. The derivation of the TLS master secret from the premaster secret and the subsequent generation of the keying material and initialization vectors is independent from the key exchange algorithm and not impacted by the use of ECC. The five ECC-based key exchange algorithms can be characterized as follows:

- ECDH_ECDSA uses long-term ECDH keys and ECDSA-signed certificates. More specifically, the server's certificate must contain a long-term ECDH public key signed with ECDSA, and hence a SERVERKEYEXCHANGE message need not be sent. The client generates an ECDH key pair on the same elliptic curve as the server's long-term public key and may send its own public key in the CLIENTKEYEXCHANGE message. Both client and server then perform an ECDH key exchange and use the result as the premaster secret.

- ECDHE_ECDSA uses ephemeral ECDH keys and ECDSA-signed certificates. More specifically, the server's certificate must contain an ECDSA public key signed with ECDSA. The server sends it ephemeral ECDH public key and a specification of the corresponding elliptic curve in a SERVERKEYEXCHANGE message. The parameters are digitally signed with ECDSA using the private key corresponding to the public key in the server's certificate. The client generates another ECDH key pair on the same curve and sends its public key to the server in a CLIENTKEYEXCHANGE message. Again, both the client and the server perform an ECDH key exchange and use the result as the premaster secret.

- ECDH_RSA uses long-term ECDH keys and RSA-signed certificates. This key exchange algorithm is essentially the same as ECDH_ECDSA, except that the server's certificate is signed with RSA instead of ECDSA.

- ECDHE_RSA uses ephemeral ECDH keys and RSA-signed certificates. This key exchange algorithm is essentially the same as ECDHE_ECDSA, except that the server's certificate must contain an RSA public key authorized for signing, and the signature in the SERVERKEYEXCHANGE message must be generated with the corresponding private RSA key. Also, the server certificate must be signed with RSA instead of ECDSA.

- ECDH_anon uses an anonymous ECDH key exchange without any authentication. This basically means that no signature must be provided, and hence no certificate must be in place. The ECDH public keys are exchanged in SERVERKEYEXCHANGE and CLIENTKEYEXCHANGE messages.

The ECDHE_ECDSA and ECDHE_RSA key exchange algorithms provide PFS. With ECDHE_RSA, a server can reuse its existing RSA certificate and still comply with a constrained client's ECC preferences. But the computational cost for the server is higher than for traditional RSA key exchange.

Table 5.13
TLS 1.2 Cipher Suites That Employ ECC (According to [15])

Cipher Suite	Value
TLS_ECDH_ECDSA_WITH_NULL_SHA	{ 0xC0, 0x01 }
TLS_ECDH_ECDSA_WITH_RC4_128_SHA	{ 0xC0, 0x02 }
TLS_ECDH_ECDSA_WITH_3DES_EDE_CBC_SHA *	{ 0xC0, 0x03 }
TLS_ECDH_ECDSA_WITH_AES_128_CBC_SHA *	{ 0xC0, 0x04 }
TLS_ECDH_ECDSA_WITH_AES_256_CBC_SHA	{ 0xC0, 0x05 }
TLS_ECDHE_ECDSA_WITH_NULL_SHA	{ 0xC0, 0x06 }
TLS_ECDHE_ECDSA_WITH_RC4_128_SHA	{ 0xC0, 0x07 }
TLS_ECDHE_ECDSA_WITH_3DES_EDE_CBC_SHA	{ 0xC0, 0x08 }
TLS_ECDHE_ECDSA_WITH_AES_128_CBC_SHA	{ 0xC0, 0x09 }
TLS_ECDHE_ECDSA_WITH_AES_256_CBC_SHA	{ 0xC0, 0x0A }
TLS_ECDH_RSA_WITH_NULL_SHA	{ 0xC0, 0x0B }
TLS_ECDH_RSA_WITH_RC4_128_SHA	{ 0xC0, 0x0C }
TLS_ECDH_RSA_WITH_3DES_EDE_CBC_SHA	{ 0xC0, 0x0D }
TLS_ECDH_RSA_WITH_AES_128_CBC_SHA	{ 0xC0, 0x0E }
TLS_ECDH_RSA_WITH_AES_256_CBC_SHA	{ 0xC0, 0x0F }
TLS_ECDHE_RSA_WITH_NULL_SHA	{ 0xC0, 0x10 }
TLS_ECDHE_RSA_WITH_RC4_128_SHA	{ 0xC0, 0x11 }
TLS_ECDHE_RSA_WITH_3DES_EDE_CBC_SHA *	{ 0xC0, 0x12 }
TLS_ECDHE_RSA_WITH_AES_128_CBC_SHA *	{ 0xC0, 0x13 }
TLS_ECDHE_RSA_WITH_AES_256_CBC_SHA	{ 0xC0, 0x14 }
TLS_ECDH_anon_WITH_NULL_SHA	{ 0xC0, 0x15 }
TLS_ECDH_anon_WITH_RC4_128_SHA	{ 0xC0, 0x16 }
TLS_ECDH_anon_WITH_3DES_EDE_CBC_SHA	{ 0xC0, 0x17 }
TLS_ECDH_anon_WITH_AES_128_CBC_SHA	{ 0xC0, 0x18 }
TLS_ECDH_anon_WITH_AES_256_CBC_SHA	{ 0xC0, 0x19 }

Each of the five key exchange algorithms can be combined with no encryption, RC4, 3DES, and AES (with either 128-bit or 256-bit keys), as well as the cryptographic hash function SHA-1. The resulting TLS 1.2 cipher suites that employ ECC are summarized in Table 5.13. In RFC 4492, it is recommended that server implementations should support all cipher suites, whereas client implementations should support at least one of the cipher suites marked with a star in Table 5.13.

In addition to the ECC-based key exchange algorithms and cipher suites mentioned so far, RFC 4492 also defines three new client authentication mechanisms, each named after the type of client certificate involved: ECDSA_sign, ECDSA_fixed_ECDH, and RSA_fixed_ECDH. The ECDSA_sign mechanism can be used with any of the nonanonymous ECC-based key exchange algorithms itemized above, as well as other nonanonymous key exchange algorithms defined in the TLS protocol specification. Contrary to that, the ECDSA_fixed_ECDH and RSA_fixed_ECDH mechanisms can be used only with ECDH_ECDSA and ECDH_RSA. In either case, the server can request ECC-based client authentication by including one or more of these certificate types in its CERTIFICATEREQUEST message. If the client has an appropriate certificate and is willing to use it for authentication, then it must send that certificate in a CERTIFICATE message and prove possession of the corresponding private key. For ECDSA_sign, this proof is explicit and comprises a digitally signed CERTIFICATEVERIFY message. For ECDSA_fixed_ECDH and RSA_fixed_ECDH, the proof is implicit and no CERTIFICATEVERIFY message needs to be sent.

To actually invoke ECC, RFC 4492 defines two new extension types that allow negotiating the use of ECC during a TLS handshake: the supported elliptic curves extension and the supported point formats extension:

- The supported elliptic curves extension `elliptic_curves` (vales 10) that may be sent in an extended CLIENTHELLO message allows the client to indicate the set of elliptic curves it supports. The curves defined in RFC 4492 are the ones that are specified by the Standards for Efficient Cryptography Group (SECG[8]) in [18]. Many of these curves are also recommended by other standardization bodies, such as ANSI and NIST.

- Similarly, the supported point formats extension `ec_point_formats` (value 11) is also sent in an extended CLIENTHELLO message and allows the client to indicate the set of point formats it can parse.

For both extensions, it is up to the server to select an elliptic curve and a corresponding point format in an extended SERVERHELLO message.

5.4.1.10 SRP Protocol

In Section 2.2.3.3, we mentioned that the Diffie-Hellman key exchange is susceptible to man-in-the-middle attacks, and hence the participating peers need to authenticate themselves in one way or another (this applies to any key agreement protocol). Consequently, there are multiple ways to design and come up with an authenticated Diffie-Hellman key exchange, and the use of a password is certainly the most simple and straightforward choice. But many proposals for a password-authenticated Diffie-Hellman key exchange have turned out to be susceptible to dictionary attacks, meaning that an adversary can simply try out all possible password candidates (until he or she finds the correct one). Against this background, Steven M. Bellovin and Michael Merritt introduced the notion of an *Encrypted Key Exchange* (EKE) in the early 1990s to defeat dictionary attacks [19, 20]. In the most general form of EKE,

---

[8] http://www.secg.org.

at least one party encrypts an ephemeral (one-time) public key using a password, and sends it to a second party, who decrypts it and uses it to negotiate a shared key with the first party. The password is not susceptible to dictionary attacks, because it is used to encrypt a randomly looking value, and hence an adversary is not able to decide whether a password candidate is actually correct. The notion of an EKE was later refined by many researchers, and one of these refinements has become known as the *Secure Remote Password* (SRP) [21, 22].[9]

The use of the SRP protocol for client authentication in a TLS handshake is addressed in an Informational RFC 5054 [16]. It complements the use of public key certificates, preshared keys, and/or Kerberos for client authentication. The SRP extension allows the use of user names and passwords over unencrypted channels without revealing the password to an eavesdropper. Since SRP is based on a Diffie-Hellman key exchange, it also supplies a shared secret at the end of the authentication process. This shared secret can then be used to generate the keying material that is required.

Table 5.14
SRP-Based Cipher Suites for the TLS Protocol (According to [16])

Cipher Suite	Value
TLS_SRP_SHA_WITH_3DES_EDE_CBC_SHA	{ 0xC0, 0x1A }
TLS_SRP_SHA_RSA_WITH_3DES_EDE_CBC_SHA	{ 0xC0, 0x1B }
TLS_SRP_SHA_DSS_WITH_3DES_EDE_CBC_SHA	{ 0xC0, 0x1C }
TLS_SRP_SHA_WITH_AES_128_CBC_SHA	{ 0xC0, 0x1D }
TLS_SRP_SHA_RSA_WITH_AES_128_CBC_SHA	{ 0xC0, 0x1E }
TLS_SRP_SHA_DSS_WITH_AES_128_CBC_SHA	{ 0xC0, 0x1F }
TLS_SRP_SHA_WITH_AES_256_CBC_SHA	{ 0xC0, 0x20 }
TLS_SRP_SHA_RSA_WITH_AES_256_CBC_SHA	{ 0xC0, 0x21 }
TLS_SRP_SHA_DSS_WITH_AES_256_CBC_SHA	{ 0xC0, 0x22 }

When the client sends the CLIENTHELLO message to the server, it basically adds an srp extension (type value 12) to the message. This is to initiate an execution of the SRP protocol. The client and server then exchange SRP-specific SERVERKEYEXCHANGE and SERVERKEYEXCHANGE messages. In the end, the client and server are able to compute a shared secret (and the SRP password ensures that an eavesdropper cannot mount a dictionary attack against the password in use). The SRP-based cipher suites for the TLS protocol are itemized in Table 5.14. Implementations conforming to RFC 5054 must implement the cipher suite TLS_SRP_SHA_WITH_3DES_EDE_CBC_SHA. They should

[9] http://srp.stanford.edu.

also implement TLS_SRP_SHA_WITH_AES_128_CBC_SHA and TLS_SRP_SHA_WITH_AES_256_CBC_SHA, and they may implement the remaining cipher suites.

5.4.1.11 Signature Algorithms

There are multiple hash and signature algorithms that may or may not be supported by different clients. The extension type `supported_signature_algorithms` (type 13) is defined in the original TLS 1.2 protocol specification [3]. It can be used by a client to tell the server which hash and signature algorithms it actually supports. The IANA maintains registries for these algorithms that are in line with RFC 2434 [10]. Supported hash algorithms are none (0),[10] MD5 (1), SHA-1 (2), SHA-224 (3), SHA-256 (4), SHA-384 (5), and SHA-512 (6), whereas supported signature algorithms are anonymous (0), RSA (1),[11] DSA (2), and ECDSA (3). The corresponding code values are appended in brackets. Because not all hash and signature algorithms may be accepted by an implementation, algorithms are always listed in pairs (for example, DSA with SHA-1 may be accepted, but DSA with SHA-256 typically is not). Each pair of algorithms specifies a way to generate and verify signatures. Due to this flexibility, the TLS 1.2 CERTIFICATEREQUEST message must also list the hash and signature algorithm pairs the server accepts, and hence the message must include an additional `supported_signature_algorithms` parameter that yields this information. This parameter is in addition to `certificate_types` and `certificate_authorities`. The interaction of the `certificate_types` and `supported_signature_algorithms` parameters is tricky and much of the functionality of the first parameter is superseded by the second.

5.4.1.12 Session Tickets

The extension type `SessionTicket` (value 35) introduced in [17] can be used by a server to resume sessions without having to keep per-client session state. It is based on ideas originally proposed in [23, 24]. A client can indicate support for session tickets by including a `SessionTicket` extension in the CLIENTHELLO message. If the client does not already possess a ticket, then the data field of the extension must be empty. The server, in turn, returns another empty `SessionTicket` extension to the client. As such, it indicates that it will send a new session ticket to the client in a NEWSESSIONTICKET handshake message (type 4). The ticket basically comprises the session state, including, for example, the cipher suite and master secret in use. It is encrypted and integrity-protected with a key that needs to be

---

10 The "none" value is provided for future extensibility, in case of a signature algorithm that does not require hashing before signing.
11 The "RSA" value actually refers to RSA using PKCS version 1.5.

known only to the server. This simplifies key management considerably. Normally, the NEWSESSIONTICKET message is sent by the server during the handshake before the CHANGECIPHERSPEC message, after it has successfully verified the client's FINISHED message. The corresponding protocol message flow is illustrated in Figure 5.5.

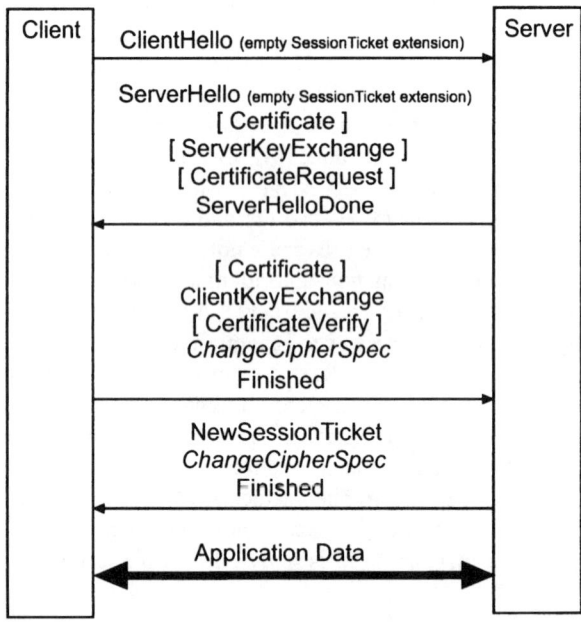

Figure 5.5 The message flow of the TLS handshake protocol issuing a new session ticket.

After having received the NEWSESSIONTICKET message, the client caches the session ticket along with the master secret and some other parameters associated with the current session. When it wishes to resume the session at some later point in time, it includes the ticket in the SessionTicket extension within the CLIENT-HELLO message. The server decrypts the received ticket (using its respective key), verifies the ticket's validity, retrieves the session state, and uses this state to resume the session. If the server successfully verifies the session ticket provided by the client, then it may also renew the ticket by including a NEWSESSIONTICKET message after its SERVERHELLO message. The corresponding message flow is illustrated in Figure 5.6.

If, in the setting sketched above, the server cannot or does not want to accept the session ticket provided by the client, then it can initiate a full TLS handshake

TLS Protocol

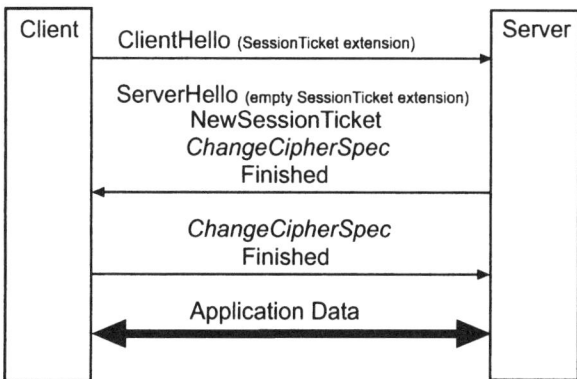

Figure 5.6 The message flow for an abbreviated TLS handshake protocol using a new session ticket.

with the client. If the server does not wish to issue a new ticket, then it can complete the TLS handshake without including a SessionTicket extension or NEWSESSIONTICKET message. The corresponding message flow is the same as the one illustrated in Figure 4.4 (for the SSL handshake protocol). The only difference is that the initial CLIENTHELLO message comprises a SessionTicket extension.

Last but not least, it is also possible that a client submits a session ticket in a simplified TLS handshake protocol in order to resume a session (similar to Figure 4.5 for the SSL handshake protocol). In this case, the client also uses a SessionTicket extension. If the server accepts the ticket, then everything is fine. If, however, the server does not accept the ticket, then there are basically two situations to distinguish:

- If the server does not accept the ticket and does not wish to issue a new ticket, then it simply does not send back a SERVERHELLO message with a SessionTicket extension.

- If the server does not accept the ticket but still wishes to issue a new ticket, then it may perform a full handshake. The resulting message flow is the same as the one illustrated in Figure 5.5, except that the SessionTicket extension in the CLIENTHELLO is not empty.

As mentioned above, a session ticket is signaled by the SessionTicket extension and sent in the corresponding data field. It comprises an opaque data structure and a lifetime (in seconds) to specify the temporal validity. Anyway, the session ticket is part of the CLIENTHELLO and/or SERVERHELLO messages, and as such it is also included in the hash value used to create and verify the FINISHED messages of the TLS handshake.

It is sometimes argued that session tickets are vulnerable to a similar set of exploits as the kind that are directed at cookie implementations. This argument is flawed, mainly because a session ticket is cryptographically protected with a key that is held only by the server and the use of the ticket requires some client-side state. Consequently, an adversary who is able to capture a session ticket is neither able to decrypt it nor use it for another purpose (because it does not have the appropriate state). There are proposals to encrypt cookies in a similar way [25], but as of this writing such secure cookies are not yet widely deployed.

5.4.1.13 Summary

In this section, we have seen that TLS 1.2 introduces and comes along with many possible extensions. For most extensions, it is sufficient to extend the CLIENT-HELLO and/or SERVERHELLO messages. For some extensions, however, it is also necessary to use new TLS handshake messages. This is particularly true for the NEWSESSIONTICKET message (type 4), CERTIFICATEURL message (type 21), CERTIFICATESTATUS message (type 22), and SUPPLEMENTALDATA message (type 23). These messages have no counterparts in the SSL protocol or previous versions of the TLS protocol.

5.4.2 Cipher Suites

TLS 1.0 and TLS 1.1 include cipher suites based on single-DES and IDEA. Both block ciphers are no longer recommended for general use in TLS, and have been entirely removed from TLS 1.2. There is an Internet-Draft[12] (targeted as an Informational RFC) that specifies these cipher suites for completeness, and discusses reasons why their use is no longer recommended. According to Table 5.7, this applies to

- TLS_RSA_WITH_DES_CBC_SHA,
- TLS_DH_DSS_WITH_DES_CBC_SHA,
- TLS_DH_RSA_WITH_DES_CBC_SHA,
- TLS_DHE_DSS_WITH_DES_CBC_SHA,
- TLS_DHE_RSA_WITH_DES_CBC_SHA, and
- TLS_DH_anon_WITH_DES_CBC_SHA

12 http://www.ietf.org/internet-drafts/draft-ietf-tls-des-idea-*.txt.

for single-DES, and

- TLS_RSA_WITH_IDEA_CBC_SHA

for IDEA.

Table 5.15
TLS 1.2 Cipher Suites That Require a Server-Side RSA Certificate for Key Exchange

Cipher Suite	Value
TLS_RSA_WITH_NULL_MD5	{ 0x00,0x01 }
TLS_RSA_WITH_NULL_SHA	{ 0x00,0x02 }
TLS_RSA_WITH_NULL_SHA256	{ 0x00,0x3B }
TLS_RSA_WITH_RC4_128_MD5	{ 0x00,0x04 }
TLS_RSA_WITH_RC4_128_SHA	{ 0x00,0x05 }
TLS_RSA_WITH_3DES_EDE_CBC_SHA	{ 0x00,0x0A }
TLS_RSA_WITH_AES_128_CBC_SHA	{ 0x00,0x2F }
TLS_RSA_WITH_AES_256_CBC_SHA	{ 0x00,0x35 }
TLS_RSA_WITH_AES_128_CBC_SHA256	{ 0x00,0x3C }
TLS_RSA_WITH_AES_256_CBC_SHA256	{ 0x00,0x3D }

The cipher suites supported by TLS 1.2 are listed in Tables 5.15 to 5.17. Note that the cipher suites that employ an anonymous Diffie-Hellman key exchange (see Table 5.17) must not be used by TLS 1.2 implementations unless the application layer has specifically requested to allow anonymous key exchange. In addition to the cipher suites listed in Tables 5.15 to 5.17, TLS 1.2 also supports the default cipher suite TLS_NULL_WITH_NULL_NULL with its value {0x00,0x00}. This is similar to all previous versions of the SSL and TLS protocols. In the absence of an application profile standard specifying otherwise, a TLS-compliant application must implement and actively support the cipher suite TLS_RSA_WITH_AES_128_CBC_SHA.

Also, note that some TLS 1.2 cipher suites have been extended to support SHA-256 in addition to SHA-1, and that TLS 1.2 also supports modes of operation for authenticated encryption [26]. The term used in the specifications is AEAD, an acronym standing for authenticated encryption with additional data. Examples are the counter with CBC-MAC mode (CCM) [27] and the Galois/counter mode (GCM) [28] as specified by NIST. The use of the AES in GCM in specified in a pair of RFCs [29, 30]. Generally speaking, AEAD ciphers take as input the following components:

- A single key;
- A nonce;
- A plaintext;
- Some additional data to be included in the authentication check.

Table 5.16
TLS 1.2 Cipher Suites That Employ a Nonanonymous Diffie-Hellman Key Exchange

Cipher Suite	Value
TLS_DH_DSS_WITH_3DES_EDE_CBC_SHA	{ 0x00,0x0D }
TLS_DH_RSA_WITH_3DES_EDE_CBC_SHA	{ 0x00,0x10 }
TLS_DHE_DSS_WITH_3DES_EDE_CBC_SHA	{ 0x00,0x13 }
TLS_DHE_RSA_WITH_3DES_EDE_CBC_SHA	{ 0x00,0x16 }
TLS_DH_DSS_WITH_AES_128_CBC_SHA	{ 0x00,0x30 }
TLS_DH_RSA_WITH_AES_128_CBC_SHA	{ 0x00,0x31 }
TLS_DHE_DSS_WITH_AES_128_CBC_SHA	{ 0x00,0x32 }
TLS_DHE_RSA_WITH_AES_128_CBC_SHA	{ 0x00,0x33 }
TLS_DH_DSS_WITH_AES_256_CBC_SHA	{ 0x00,0x36 }
TLS_DH_RSA_WITH_AES_256_CBC_SHA	{ 0x00,0x37 }
TLS_DHE_DSS_WITH_AES_256_CBC_SHA	{ 0x00,0x38 }
TLS_DHE_RSA_WITH_AES_256_CBC_SHA	{ 0x00,0x39 }
TLS_DH_DSS_WITH_AES_128_CBC_SHA256	{ 0x00,0x3E }
TLS_DH_RSA_WITH_AES_128_CBC_SHA256	{ 0x00,0x3F }
TLS_DHE_DSS_WITH_AES_128_CBC_SHA256	{ 0x00,0x40 }
TLS_DHE_RSA_WITH_AES_128_CBC_SHA256	{ 0x00,0x67 }
TLS_DH_DSS_WITH_AES_256_CBC_SHA256	{ 0x00,0x68 }
TLS_DH_RSA_WITH_AES_256_CBC_SHA256	{ 0x00,0x69 }
TLS_DHE_DSS_WITH_AES_256_CBC_SHA256	{ 0x00,0x6A }
TLS_DHE_RSA_WITH_AES_256_CBC_SHA256	{ 0x00,0x6B }

The key is either `client_write_key` or `server_write_key`; no MAC key is used. Each AEAD cipher suite must specify how the nonce is constructed and how long it should be. The plaintext is the fragment of the `TLSCompressed` structure. Last but not least, the additional data is the concatenation of the sequence number and the type, version, and length fields of the `TLSCompressed` structure. Anyway, the output of an AEAD cipher is a ciphertext that can be uniquely decrypted using the same values.

There are situations in which public key operations are too expensive or have other management disadvantages. In these situations it may be advantageous to use symmetric keys, shared in advance among communicating parties, to establish a TLS connection. For example, Standards Track RFC 4279 [31] specifies three sets of cipher suites for the TLS protocol that support authentication based on *preshared keys* (PSKs). As its name suggests, a PSK is a symmetric key that is shared in advance among communicating parties. The three sets of cipher suites that employ a PSK are summarized in Table 5.18. They can be described as follows:

Table 5.17
TLS 1.2 Cipher Suites That Employ an Anonymous Diffie-Hellman Key Exchange

Cipher Suite	Value
TLS_DH_anon_WITH_RC4_128_MD5	{ 0x00, 0x18 }
TLS_DH_anon_WITH_3DES_EDE_CBC_SHA	{ 0x00, 0x1B }
TLS_DH_anon_WITH_AES_128_CBC_SHA	{ 0x00, 0x34 }
TLS_DH_anon_WITH_AES_256_CBC_SHA	{ 0x00, 0x3A }
TLS_DH_anon_WITH_AES_128_CBC_SHA256	{ 0x00, 0x6C }
TLS_DH_anon_WITH_AES_256_CBC_SHA256	{ 0x00, 0x6D }

Table 5.18
TLS Cipher Suites That Employ a PSK (According to [31])

Cipher Suite	Value
TLS_PSK_WITH_RC4_128_SHA	{ 0x00, 0x8A }
TLS_PSK_WITH_3DES_EDE_CBC_SHA	{ 0x00, 0x8B }
TLS_PSK_WITH_AES_128_CBC_SHA	{ 0x00, 0x8C }
TLS_PSK_WITH_AES_256_CBC_SHA	{ 0x00, 0x8D }
TLS_DHE_PSK_WITH_RC4_128_SHA	{ 0x00, 0x8E }
TLS_DHE_PSK_WITH_3DES_EDE_CBC_SHA	{ 0x00, 0x8F }
TLS_DHE_PSK_WITH_AES_128_CBC_SHA	{ 0x00, 0x90 }
TLS_DHE_PSK_WITH_AES_256_CBC_SHA	{ 0x00, 0x91 }
TLS_RSA_PSK_WITH_RC4_128_SHA	{ 0x00, 0x92 }
TLS_RSA_PSK_WITH_3DES_EDE_CBC_SHA	{ 0x00, 0x93 }
TLS_RSA_PSK_WITH_AES_128_CBC_SHA	{ 0x00, 0x94 }
TLS_RSA_PSK_WITH_AES_256_CBC_SHA	{ 0x00, 0x95 }

- The first set of cipher suites (with the PSK key exchange algorithm) use only secret key algorithms and are thus especially suitable for performance-constrained environments.

- The second set of cipher suites (with DHE_PSK key exchange algorithm) use a PSK to authenticate an ephemeral Diffie-Hellman key exchange.

- The third set of cipher suites (with RSA_PSK key exchange algorithm) combine RSA-based authentication of the server with client-based authentication using a PSK.

Note that the SRP-based cipher suites addressed in Section 5.4.1.10 can also be thought of as cipher suites belonging to the first set. The SRP protocol is computationally more expensive than a PSK-based key exchange method, but it is also cryptographically more sound (mainly because it protects against dictionary attacks).

Table 5.19
TLS Cipher Suites With No Encryption That Employ a PSK (According to [32])

Cipher Suite	Value
TLS_PSK_WITH_NULL_SHA	{ 0x00, 0x2C }
TLS_DHE_PSK_WITH_NULL_SHA	{ 0x00, 0x2D }
TLS_RSA_PSK_WITH_NULL_SHA	{ 0x00, 0x2E }

In addition to RFC 4279, RFC 4785 [32] specifies three TLS cipher suites with no encryption that employ a PSK. The cipher suites are itemized in Table 5.19. They are useful when authentication and integrity protection is desired, but confidentiality is not needed or not permitted. Anyway, clients and servers may have PSKs with several different parties. The client therefore indicates which key to use by including a *PSK identity* in the CLIENTKEYEXCHANGE message. To help the client in selecting which identity to use, the server can provide a *PSK identity hint* in the SERVERKEYEXCHANGE message. If no hint is provided, then the SERVERKEYEXCHANGE message can be omitted (at least for the PSK and RSA_PSK key exchange algorithms). If the client provides a PSK identity but the server is not able to make any use of it, then the server may return an unknown_psk_identity alert message (with alert code 115).

Table 5.20
TLS Cipher Suites That Combine a PSK and ECC (Work in Progress)

Cipher Suite
TLS_ECDHE_PSK_WITH_RC4_128_SHA
TLS_ECDHE_PSK_WITH_3DES_EDE_CBC_SHA
TLS_ECDHE_PSK_WITH_AES_128_CBC_SHA
TLS_ECDHE_PSK_WITH_AES_256_CBC_SHA
TLS_ECDHE_PSK_WITH_AES_128_CBC_SHA256
TLS_ECDHE_PSK_WITH_AES_256_CBC_SHA384
TLS_ECDHE_PSK_WITH_NULL_SHA
TLS_ECDHE_PSK_WITH_NULL_SHA256
TLS_ECDHE_PSK_WITH_NULL_SHA384

Furthermore, in addition to RFCs 4279 and 4785, there is work going on within the IETF TLS WG to combine a PSK and ECC, and to specify a set of cipher suites that use a PSK to authenticate an ephemeral ECDH key exchange.[13]

---

[13] http://www.ietf.org/internet-drafts/draft-ietf-tls-ecdhe-psk-*.txt.

The corresponding cipher suites are itemized in Table 5.20. Their values still have to be assigned from the TLS cipher suite registry. Also, there is related work that seeks to define sets of cipher suites in which SHA-1 is replaced with some stronger cryptographic hash functions (i.e., SHA-256 or SHA-384) and/or cipher suites that use the AES in GCM.[14] The corresponding cipher suites are itemized in Table 5.21. Again, their values still have to be assigned from the TLS cipher suite registry.

Table 5.21
TLS Cipher Suites That Combine a PSK With AES-GCM and Stronger Cryptographic Hash Functions (Work in Progress)

Cipher Suite
TLS_PSK_WITH_AES_128_GCM_SHA256
TLS_PSK_WITH_AES_256_GCM_SHA384
TLS_PSK_WITH_NULL_SHA256
TLS_PSK_WITH_NULL_SHA384
TLS_DHE_PSK_WITH_AES_128_GCM_SHA256
TLS_DHE_PSK_WITH_AES_256_GCM_SHA384
TLS_DHE_PSK_WITH_NULL_SHA256
TLS_DHE_PSK_WITH_NULL_SHA384
TLS_RSA_PSK_WITH_AES_128_GCM_SHA256
TLS_RSA_PSK_WITH_AES_256_GCM_SHA384
TLS_RSA_PSK_WITH_NULL_SHA256
TLS_RSA_PSK_WITH_NULL_SHA384

5.4.3 Certificate Management

The certificate types of TLS 1.1 are listed in Table 5.10. Due to the fact that TLS 1.2 supports ECC, there is need for additional certificate types. For example, while dss_sign refers to a certificate for a DSA public key, ecdsa_sign refers to a certificate for an ECDSA public key. Similarly, rsa_fixed_ecdh and ecdsa_fixed_ecdh refer to certificates for an ECDH key exchange. In all cases, the certificate must use the same elliptic curve as the server's key and a point format actually supported by the server. Also, it must be signed with an appropriate hash and signature generation algorithm pair.

5.4.4 Alert Messages

In addition to alert message 41 (no_certificate_RESERVED) that has become obsolete in TLS 1.0 and alert message 60 (export_restriction_RESERVED)

---

14 http://www.ietf.org/internet-drafts/draft-ietf-tls-psk-new-mac-aes-gcm-*.txt.

that has also become obsolete in TLS 1.1, alert message 21 has become obsolete and is now referred to as decryption_failed_RESERVED in TLS 1.2. Also—as mentioned above—the unsupported_extension alert message (see Table 5.12) is included in the TLS 1.2 protocol specification.

5.4.5 Other Differences

Compression algorithms for TLS 1.2 are specified in RFC 3749 [33]. In addition to value 0 (referring to null compression), this RFC also introduces value 1 (referring to the DEFLATE compression method and encoding format specified in Informational RFC 1951 [34]).

Remember from Section 5.2 that a TLS FINISHED message always uses 12 bytes from the output of the PRF. Since TLS 1.2, the length of the PRF output taken into account depends on the cipher suite in use. The default value is still 12 and all existing cipher suites adopt this value. But future cipher suites may specify other lengths (that are greater than 12).

5.5 TRAFFIC ANALYSIS OF A TLS SESSION

To illustrate the functioning of the TLS protocol, we provide a traffic analysis of a TLS session. We therefore consider the same setting as described in Section 4.3. The client takes the initiative and launches the TLS protocol by sending a CLIENTHELLO message to the server. The message looks as follows (in hexadecimal notation):

```
16 03 01 00 41 01 00 00    3d 03 01 49 47 77 14 b9
02 5d e6 35 ff 49 d0 65    cb 89 93 7d 68 9b 55 e7
b6 49 e6 93 e9 e9 48 c0    b7 d2 13 00 00 16 00 04
00 05 00 0a 00 09 00 64    00 62 00 03 00 06 00 13
00 12 00 63 01 00
```

The TLS record starts with a type field that comprises the value 0x16 (representing 22 in decimal notation, and hence standing for the Handshake Protocol), a version field that comprises the value 0x0301 (referring to TLS 1.0), and a length field that comprises the value 0x0041 (representing 65 in decimal notation). This means that the fragment of the TLS record is 65 bytes long, and that the following 65 bytes thus represent the CLIENTHELLO message. This message, in turn, starts with 0x01 standing for the TLS handshake message type 1 (referring to a CLIENTHELLO message), 0x00003d standing for a message length of 61 bytes, and 0x0301 again representing TLS 1.0. The subsequent 32 bytes—from 0x4947 to 0xd213—represent the random value chosen by the client (remember that the first 4 bytes represent the date and time). Because there is no TLS session to resume, the session ID length is set to zero (0x00) and no session ID is appended. Instead, the next value 0x0016 (representing 22 in decimal notation) indicates that the subsequent 22 bytes refer to the 11 cipher suites that are supported by the client. Each pair of bytes represents a cipher suite. For example, the first two cipher suites are referenced with the values 0x0004 and 0x0005 (i.e., TLS_RSA_WITH_RC4_128_MD5 and TLS_RSA_WITH_RC4_128_SHA). The second-to-last byte 01 indicates that there is a single compression method supported by the client, and the last byte 0x00 refers to this compression method (which actually refers to no compression).

After having received the CLIENTHELLO message, the server responds with a series of TLS handshake messages. If possible, then all messages are merged into a single TLS record and transmitted in a single TCP segment to the client. In our example, such a TLS record comprsies a SERVERHELLO, a CERTIFICATE, and a SERVERHELLODONE message. Similar to SSL, the TLS record starts with the following byte sequence:

```
16 03 01 0a 5f
```

Again, 0x16 refers to the TLS Handshake Protocol, 0x0301 refers to TLS 1.0, and 0x0a5f refers to the length of the TLS record (which is actually 2,655 bytes). The three above-mentioned messages are then encapsulated in the rest of the TLS record.

- The SERVERHELLO message looks as follows:

```
02 00 00 46 03 01 49 47    77 14 a2 fd 8f f0 46 2e
1b 05 43 3a 1f 6e 15 04    d3 56 1b eb 89 96 71 81
48 d4 87 10 6d e9 20 49    47 77 14 42 53 e0 5e bd
17 6a e9 35 31 06 f2 d2    30 28 af 46 19 d1 d2 e4
49 0a 0c cd 90 66 20 00    05 00
```

The message starts with 0x02 standing for the Handshake Protocol message type 2 (referring to a SERVERHELLO message), 0x000046 standing for a message length of 70 bytes, and 0x0301 standing for TLS 1.0. The subsequent 32 bytes

```
49 47 77 14 a2 fd 8f f0    46 2e 1b 05 43 3a 1f 6e
15 04 d3 56 1b eb 89 96    71 81 48 d4 87 10 6d e9
```

represent the random value chosen by the server (note again that the first 4 bytes represent the date and time). Afterwards, 0x20 refers to a session ID length of 32 bytes, and hence the subsequent 32 bytes

```
49 47 77 14 42 53 e0 5e    bd 17 6a e9 35 31 06 f2
d2 30 28 af 46 19 d1 d2    e4 49 0a 0c cd 90 66 20
```

represent the session ID. Remember that this ID is going to be used if the client wants to resume the TLS session at some later point in time (before the session expires). Following the session ID, 0x0005 refers to the selected cipher suite (which is TLS_RSA_WITH_RC4_128_SHA in this example) and 0x00 refers to the selected compression method (which is the null compression).

- Next, the CERTIFICATE message comprises the server's public key certificate. It is quite comprehensive and begins with the followiung byte sequence:

    0b 00 0a 0d 00 0a 0a

    In this byte sequence, 0x0b stands for the TLS Handshake Protocol message type 11 (referring to a CERTIFICATE message), 0x000a0d stands for a message length of 2573 bytes, and 0x000a0a stands for the length of the certificate chain. Note that the length of the certificate chain must equal the message length minus 3 (the length of the length field). The remaining 2570 bytes of the message then comprise the certificate chain required to validate the server's public key certificate (again, these bytes are not illustrated above).

- Last but not least, the TLS record also comprises a SERVERHELLODONE message. This message is very simple and only consists of 4 bytes:

    0e 00 00 00

    0x0e stands for the TLS Handshake Protocol message type 14 (referring to a SERVERHELLODONE message) and 0x000000 stands for a message length of zero bytes.

After having received the SERVERHELLODONE message, it is up to the client to submit a series of messages to the server. In our example, this series comprises a CLIENTKEYEXCHANGE, a CHANGECIPHERSPEC, and a FINISHED message. Each of these messages is transmitted in a TLS record of its own, but all three records can be transmitted in a single TCP segment to the server.

- The CLIENTKEYEXCHANGE message is transmitted in the first TLS record. In our example, this record looks as follows:

    ```
    16 03 01 00 86 10 00 00    82 00 80 ac 18 48 2e 50
    32 32 bb 5d 2b 35 39 f2    3d 32 cd 19 86 b4 57 e9
    c8 a5 5b ad da 29 24 22    90 bc d7 3d cd f8 94 8a
    4f 95 72 0c 13 52 52 82    e4 b0 25 f4 b8 b6 e1 7d
    2e d9 65 ce 6f 7c 33 70    12 41 63 87 b4 8b 35 71
    07 d1 0f 52 9d 3a ce 65    96 bc 42 af 2f 7b 13 78
    67 49 3e 36 6e d1 ed e2    1b b2 54 2e 35 bd cc 2c
    ```

```
88 b2 2d 0c 5c bb 20 9a    d4 c3 97 e9 81 a7 a8 39
05 1a 5d f8 06 af e4 ef    17 07 30
```

In the TLS record header, 0x16 stands for the Handshake Protocol, 0x0301 refers to TLS 1.0, and 0x0086 represents the length of the TLS record (134 bytes). After this header, the byte 0x10 stands for the Handshake Protocol message type 16 (referring to a CLIENTKEYEXCHANGE message), and the following three bytes 0x000082 refer to the message length (130 bytes). Consequently, the remaining 130 bytes of the message represent the premaster secret (as chosen by the client) encrypted under the server's public RSA key. The RSA encryption is line with PKCS #1.

- The CHANGECIPHERSPEC message is transmitted in the second TLS record. This record is very simple and consists of only 6 bytes:

```
14 03 01 00 01 01
```

In the TLS record header, 0x14 (20 in decimal notation) stands for the Change Cipher Spec Protocol, 0x0301 refers to TLS 1.0, and 0x0001 represents the message length of one single byte. This byte (i.e., 0x01), in turn, is the last byte in the record.

- The FINISHED message is the first message that is cryptographically protected according to the newly-negotiated cipher spec. Again, it is transmitted in a TLS record of its own. This record looks as follows:

```
16 03 01 00 24 fb 94 5f    ea 62 ec 90 04 36 5a f6
c7 c9 1e ae 5d da 70 31    cc 63 2f 81 87 97 60 46
d0 43 fa 6e 29 94 6c cd    17
```

In the TLS record header, 0x16 stands for the Handshake Protocol, 0x0301 refers to TLS 1.0, and 0x0024 represents the length of the TLS record (36 bytes). These 36 bytes are encrypted and look like gibberish to somebody not holding the appropriate decryption key.

After having received the CHANGECIPHERSPEC and FINISHED messages, the server must respond with the same pair of messages (not illustrated in our example). Afterwards, application data can be exchanged in TLS records. Such a record may start as follows:

```
17 03 01 02 13
```

In the TLS record header, 0x17 (23 in decimal notation) stands for the Application Data Protocol, 0x0301 stands for TLS 1.0, and 0x0213 (531) stands for the length of the encrypted data fragment. It goes without saying that an arbitrary number of TLS records can be exchanged between the client and the server.

5.6 SECURITY ANALYSIS

Due to the fact that the SSL and TLS protocols have a long history, they have been subject to many security analyses in the past (see Section 4.4). Some of these analyses led to the modifications incorporated in TLS 1.1 [5–7]. Since then, no serious cryptographic vulnerability or shortcoming has been found. This is good news and very much speaks in favor of the cryptographical strength of the current version of the TLS protocol. An informal security analysis of TLS 1.2 is given in appendix F of [3]. Since we have addressed most points raised in this analysis in previous parts of this chapter, there is no need to repeat them here. In spite of the assumed security of the SSL/TLS protocols, it may still be the case that specific implementations of the protocol have specific vulnerabilities or security flaws. In ths case of OpenSSL, for example, a corresponding list of vulnerabilities is publicly available[15] and open for discussion.

5.7 FINAL REMARKS

In this chapter, we overviewed, discussed, and put into perspective the (various versions of the) TLS protocol. With its latest modifications and extensions, the TLS protocol has slowly drifted away from the simple and straightforward cryptographic security protocol it used to be. Today, TLS 1.2 is quite involved and implementing it in an interoperable way is no longer a trivial task. On the other side, the modifications and extensions that have been incorporated also help making the TLS protocol more flexible and useful in nonstandard situations. In its current form, the TLS protocol is able to support all fancy technologies and techniques the cryptographic community has come up with in the recent past. This applies, for example, to the AES (in possibly new modes of operation), ECC, HMAC, and SHA-2. Whenever a new cryptographic technology or technique is proposed, there is strong incentive to write an RFC document that specifies the use of this technology or technique to make the TLS protocol more secure (the RFC document can be experimental, informational, or subject to the Internet Standards Track). One such example is the use of the SRP protocol specified in Informational RFC 5054 [21]. There have even been proposals to add cipher suites supporting quantum cryptography to the TLS protocol specification. This is not something to recommend, but it illustrates the

---

15 http://www.openssl.org/news/vulnerabilities.html.

point that any cryptographic technology or technique can be used in an SSL/TLS setting. It is possible and very likely that we will see many such proposals in the literature; it is then important to be able to put these proposals into perspective. This book should help you in this regard.

References

[1] Dierks, T., and C. Allen, "The TLS Protocol Version 1.0," Standards Track Request for Comments 2246, January 1999.

[2] Dierks, T., and E. Rescorla, "The Transport Layer Security (TLS) Protocol Version 1.1," Standards Track Request for Comments 4346, April 2006.

[3] Dierks, T., and E. Rescorla, "The Transport Layer Security (TLS) Protocol Version 1.2," Standards Track Request for Comments 5246, August 2008.

[4] Moriai, S., Kato, A., and M. Kanda, "Addition of Camellia Cipher Suites to Transport Layer Security (TLS)," Standards Track Request for Comments 4132, July 2005.

[5] Vaudenay, S., "Security Flaws Induced by CBC Padding—Applications to SSL, IPSEC, WTLS ... ," *Proceedings of EUROCRYPT '02*, Amsterdam, the Netherlands, Springer-Verlag, LNCS 2332, 2002, pp. 534–545.

[6] Canvel, B., Hiltgen, A., Vaudenay, S., and M. Vuagnoux, "Password Interception in a SSL/TLS Channel," *Proceedings of CRYPTO '03*, Springer-Verlag, LNCS 2729, 2003, pp. 583–599.

[7] Bard, G.V., "Vulnerability of SSL to Chosen-Plaintext Attack," Cryptology ePrint Archive, Report 2004/111, 2004.

[8] Medvinsky, A., and M. Hur, "Addition of Kerberos Cipher Suites to Transport Layer Security (TLS)," Standards Track Request for Comments 2712, October 1999.

[9] Chown, P., "Advanced Encryption Standard (AES) Ciphersuites for Transport Layer Security (TLS)," Standards Track Request for Comments 3268, June 2002.

[10] Narten, T., and H. Alvestrand, "Guidelines for Writing an IANA Considerations Section in RFCs," Request for Comments 2434 (BCP 26), October 1998.

[11] Blake-Wilson, S., Nystrom, M., Hopwood, D., Mikkelsen, J., and T. Wright, "Transport Layer Security (TLS) Extensions," Standards Track Request for Comments 4366, April 2006.

[12] Santesson, S., "TLS Handshake Message for Supplemental Data," Standards Track Request for Comments 4680, September 2006.

[13] Santesson, S., Medvinsky, A., and J. Ball, "TLS User Mapping Extension," Standards Track Request for Comments 4681, October 2006.

[14] Mavrogiannopoulos, N., "Using OpenPGP Keys for Transport Layer Security (TLS) Authentication," Experimental Request for Comments 5081, November 2007.

[15] Blake-Wilson, S., Bolyard, N., Gupta, V., Hawk, C., and B. Moeller, "Elliptic Curve Cryptography (ECC) Cipher Suites for Transport Layer Security (TLS)," Informational Request for Comments 4492, May 2006.

[16] Taylor, D., Wu, T., Mavrogiannopoulos, N., and T. Perrin, "Using the Secure Remote Password (SRP) Protocol for TLS Authentication," Informational Request for Comments 5054, November 2007.

[17] Salowey, Y., Zhou, H., Eronen, P., and H. Tschofenig, "Transport Layer Security (TLS) Session Resumption without Server-Side State," Standards Track Request for Comments 5077, January 2008.

[18] Standards for Efficient Cryptography, "SEC 2: Recommended Elliptic Curve Domain Parameteres," Version 1.0, September 2000.

[19] S.M. Bellovin, and M. Merritt, "Encrypted Key Exchange: Password-Based Protocols Secure Against Dictionary Attacks," *Proceedings of the 1992 IEEE Symposium on Security and Privacy*, IEEE Computer Society, Washington, D.C., 1992, pp. 72.

[20] S.M. Bellovin, and M. Merritt, "Augmented Encrypted Key Exchange: A Password-based Protocol Secure Against Dictionary Attacks and Password File Compromise," *Proceedings of 1st ACM Conference on Computer and Communications Security*, Fairfax, Virginia, November 1993, pp. 244–250.

[21] T. Wu, "The Secure Remote Password Protocol," *Proceedings of the 1998 Internet Society Network and Distributed System Security Symposium*, San Diego, CA, March 1998, pp. 97–111.

[22] T. Wu, "The SRP Authentication and Key Exchange System," Standards Track Request for Comments 2945, September 2000.

[23] Aura, T., and P. Nikander, "Stateless Connections," *Proceedings of the First International Conference on Information and Communication Security (ICICS 97)*, Springer-Verlag, LNCS 1334, 1997, pp. 87–97.

[24] Shacham, H., Boneh, D., and E. Rescorla, "Client-side caching for TLS," *Transactions on Information and System Security (TISSEC)*, Vol. 7, No. 4, 2004, pp. 553–575.

[25] Park, J.S., and R. Sandhu, "Secure Cookies on the Web," *IEEE Internet Computing*, Vol. 4, No. 4, 2000, pp. 36–44.

[26] McGrew, D., "An Interface and Algorithms for Authenticated Encryption," Standards Track Request for Comments 5116, January 2008.

[27] Dworkin, M., *Recommendation for Block Cipher Modes of Operation: The CCM Mode for Authentication and Confidentiality*, NIST Special Publication 800-38C, May 2004.

[28] Dworkin, M., *Recommendation for Block Cipher Modes of Operation: Galois/Counter Mode (GCM) and GMAC*, NIST Special Publication 800-38D, November 2007.

[28] Salowey, J., Choudhury, A., and D. McGrew, "AES Galois Counter Mode (GCM) Cipher Suites for TLS," Standards Track Request for Comments 5288, August 2008.

[30] Rescorla, E., "TLS Elliptic Curve Cipher Suites with SHA-256/384 and AES Galois Counter Mode (GCM)," Informational Request for Comments 5289, August 2008.

[31] Eronen, P., and H. Tschofenig (Eds.), "Pre-Shared Key Ciphersuites for Transport Layer Security (TLS)," Standards Track Request for Comments 4279, December 2005.

[32] Blumenthal, U., and P. Goel, "Pre-Shared Key (PSK) Ciphersuites with NULL Encryption for Transport Layer Security (TLS)," Standards Track Request for Comments 4785, January 2007.

[33] Hollenbeck, S., "Transport Layer Security Protocol Compression Methods," Standards Track Request for Comments 3749, May 2004.

[34] Deutsch, P., "DEFLATE Compressed Data Format Specification version 1.3," Informational Request for Comments 1951, May 1996.

Chapter 6

DTLS Protocol

As its name suggests, the DTLS protocol is the datagram version of the TLS protocol. This basically means that it can be used to secure UDP-based applications and application layer protocols. The DTLS protocol is picked out as a central theme in this chapter. We begin with an introduction in Section 6.1, focus on the specifics of the DTLS 1.0 and DTLS 1.2 protocols in Sections 6.2 and 6.3, briefly analyze their security in Section 6.4, and conclude with some final remarks in Section 6.5. Because the DTLS protocol is similar and not fundamentally different from the SSL/TLS protocols, this chapter mainly focuses on the differences between TLS and DTLS. It is therefore intentionally kept short.

6.1 INTRODUCTION

As mentioned several times so far, the SSL and TLS protocols are layered on top of a connection-oriented and reliable transport protocol, such as TCP in the case of the TCP/IP protocol stack. But there is an increasingly large body of applications and application layer protocols that are stacked on UDP (instead of TCP). Examples include media streaming, realtime communications (e.g., Internet telephony and video conferencing), multicast communications, online gaming, and gambling. UDP is a transport layer protocol that provides a best-effort datagram delivery service that is connectionless, and hence neither the SSL protocol nor any of the TLS protocol versions can be stacked on it (because they all require a connection-oriented and reliable transport layer data delivery service). The same is true for the the *Datagram Congestion Control Protocol* (DCCP) [1] that provides a best-effort datagram delivery service, similar to UDP, but with adaptive congestion control, similar to TCP or even the *Stream Control Transmission Protocol* (SCTP). DCCP can in fact be viewed equally well as either UDP-plus-congestion-control or TCP-minus-reliability (although, unlike TCP, DCCP offers multiple congestion control algorithms). As addressed later, the DTLS protocol can also be stacked on DCCP, and hence it also provides a solution to secure DCCP-based applications.

Having the inappropriateness of the SSL/TLS protocols to secure UDP-based (or DCCP-based) applications in mind, the designers of a corresponding application protocol are generally faced with three options:

- First, they can make sure that the application protocol is layered on top of TCP instead of UDP. Unfortunately, this is not always possible, and there are types of applications that perform poorly over TCP. This applies, for example, to applications that are latency and jitter sensitive, and that would suffer from TCP's loss and congestion correction algorithms.

- Second, they can use an Internet layer security protocol, such as IPsec/IKE, and make sure that the application protocol takes advantage of it. Unfortunately (as pointed out in Section 3.1), the use of Internet layer security protocols in general, and IPsec/IKE in particular, tends to be involved and error-prone. This also applies to the new versions of IPsec/IKE.

- Third, they can design a custom (and new) application layer security protocol. Unfortunately, although application layer security protocols generally provide superior security properties, they also require an unacceptably large amount of effort to design, implement, and deploy. This is in sharp contrast to the relatively small amount of effort required to run a protocol over SSL/TLS.

All three options have severe disadvantages and are therefore unsatisfactory when used in practice. The most desirable way to secure an application protocol would still be to use SSL/TLS or a similar transport layer security technology that can run in application space (without requiring any kernel modification). In the past, there have been a few proposals for a cryptographic security protocol that meets these requirements. For example, a few years ago, Microsoft proposed STLP (see Section 3.2) and the Wireless Application Protocol (WAP) Forum[1] proposed the Wireless TLS (WTLS). Both protocols have not been successful in the field and have silently sunk into oblivion. The reasons for these failures are design flaws. Most importantly, both protocols required an additional Web or proxy infrastructure for handheld use, which proved to be an unacceptable overhead and created some unacceptable network deployment constraints.

More importantly (at least for the purpose of this book), the IETF TLS WG became active and tried to adapt the TLS protocol for UDP-based applications at

---

1 The WAP Forum was founded in 1997 and was consolidated (along with many other forums of the industry) into the Open Mobile Alliance (OMA) in 2002.

the beginning of this century. The term coined to refer to the resulting protocol is datagram TLS, or DTLS in short [2]. The fact that DTLS is layered on top of UDP implies that the DTLS protocol must be able to deal with datagrams that are not reliably transmitted, meaning that they may get lost, reordered, or even replayed. Note that the TLS protocol has no internal facilities to handle this type of unreliability, and hence TLS implementations usually break when layered on top of UDP. This should be different with DTLS, and yet DTLS should be deliberately designed to be as similar to TLS as possible, both to minimize new security invention and to maximize the amount of code and infrastructure reuse.

In essence, the characteristics of UDP causes (at least) two problem areas that must be addressed in one way or another:

- First, UDP is a connectionless best-effort datagram delivery protocol that operates at the transport layer. This means that a UDP datagram is transmitted and processed independently from all other datagrams, and hence it must also be possible to encrypt and decrypt a DTLS record (that is transmitted in a UDP datagram) independently from all other records that have been encrypted and decrypted in the past. This severely limits the statefulness of the cryptographic operations in use. Note that TLS records are not processed independently, and that there are at least the following two types of interrecord dependencies:

    - In some cipher suites, cryptographic context is chained between subsequent TLS records. If, for example, a block cipher is used in CBC mode, then some former versions of the SSL/TLS protocols required that the last ciphertext block is the IV for the encryption of the next plaintext block. Also, if a stream cipher is used, then it is relevant which key bits from the stream are used to encrypt and decrypt a record. The key stream therefore represents the context and yields an interrecord dependency.

    - As addressed in Section 5.2, the TLP protocol provides protection agains replay and message reordering attacks by using a MAC that also comprises a sequence number (that is implicit to the record). It goes without saying that the sequence number is incremented for each TLS record, so the sequence number yields an interrecord dependency.

    These dependencies imply that TLS records cannot be treated independently. But with regard to DTLS, the dependencies can be overcome by either ignoring some cryptographic mechanisms or adding explicit state to the respective records. If, for example, stream ciphers are not used in DTLS, then stream cipher key state must not be maintained in the first place. This is why RC4-based cipher suites are not part of the DTLS protocol specification.[2] Also, TLS 1.1 has already added explicit CBC state to TLS records (see Section 5.3). DTLS borrows the same mechanism and adds an explicit sequence number field to the DTLS record format.

- Second, the TLS Handshake Protocol requires a reliable transport channel for the transmission of handshake messages. Due to this requirement, the TLS Handshake Protocol can be kept comparably simple. If UDP is used instead of TCP, then this requirement is no longer fulfilled, and the DTLS Handshake Protocol must therefore be modified to compensate for the missing reliability. In fact, the DTLS Handshake Protocol must incorporate controls for messages that are lost, reordered, or replayed.

Both problem areas are relevant and have implications for the design of the DTLS protocol. In April 2006, a companion RFC document to RFC 4346 [3] (that specifies TLS 1.1) was officially released as RFC 4347 [4] and submitted to the Internet Standards Track. It specified the first version of the DTLS protocol—or rather a delta from TLS 1.1—and it is sometimes referred to as DTLS 1.0. The combination of DTLS and UDP is simple and straightforward. The combination of DTLS and DCCP is slightly more involved and addressed in a separate Standards Track RFC [5]. DTLS 1.0 is currently being refined within the IETF TLS WG, and the next version of the DTLS protocol is going to be version 1.2 (DTLS 1.2). Consequently, there is no documented version 1.1 of the DTLS protocol. As of this writing, DTLS 1.2 is still work in progress and the DTLS 1.2 protocol specification is available only as an Internet-Draft.[3] In the following sections, we pick DTLS out as a central theme, and we overview, discuss, and put into perspective the evolution of the DTLS protocol from version 1.0 to version 1.2.

6.2 DTLS 1.0

The DTLS protocol is structurally similar to the SSL/TLS protocols. But instead of being stacked on TCP in the TCP/IP protocol stack, the DTLS protocol is actually stacked on UDP. This is illustrated in Figure 6.1 (compare this to Figure 4.1 that illustrates the situation for the SSL/TLS protocols).

---

2   Theoretically, it would be possible to use RC4 with a per-record seed. But this is fairly inefficient, especially considering the fact that the first 512 bytes of an RC4 keystream should be discarded (because they have bad, i.e., cryptographically weak, properties).
3   http://www.ietf.org/internet-drafts/draft-ietf-tls-rfc4347-bis-01.txt.

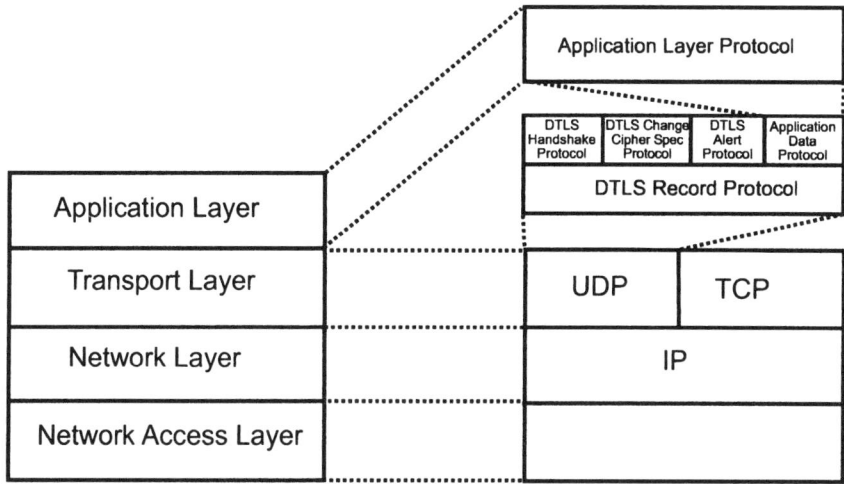

Figure 6.1 The placement of the DTLS protocol in the TCP/IP protocol stack.

Referring to the two problem areas mentioned above, the major differences between the TLS and DTLS protocols are related to the DTLS Record and Handshake Protocols. They are addressed separately.

6.2.1 Record Protocol

Every packet-switched network has a maximum transmission unit (MTU) size that refers to the size of the largest packet that can be transmitted in the network. This also applies to IP networks. Thus, if an IP packet needs to be transmitted that exceeds the size of the MTU, then the sender must fragment the packet and the recipient must reassemble the fragments to rebuild the original packet. In general, these steps (for packet fragmentation and reassembly) are computationally expensive. Also, if a fragment is lost, then the entire packet must be discarded (and eventually retransmitted). So for very large packets and small MTU sizes, this poses a real problem, and people are therefore trying to avoid IP fragmentation in the first place. This is particularly true for UDP-based applications, and hence it also applies to DTLS. Note that DTLS will still operate correctly with IP fragmentation and reassembly, since these operations are transparently performed by the kernel. But DTLS implementations should still try to avoid it and provide a way to determine the value of the path MTU (PMTU) or, alternatively, the maximum DTLS datagram size, which is the PMTU minus the DTLS per-record overhead. There are several algorithms that can be used to determine the PMTU value (e.g., [6–8]). If the DTLS implementation tries to send a record that is larger than this value, then the DTLS implementation should generate an error, thus avoiding IP fragmentation by default.

If IP fragmentation is avoided, then the maximum size of a DTLS record is bounded by the PMTU value. For example, a DTLS handshake message can be as large as $2^{24} - 1$ bytes, whereas the standard MTU size for Ethernet is only 1500 bytes. So handshake messages are routinely transmitted in multiple DTLS records. Due to the unreliability of UDP, these records can be lost, received out of order, or even replayed. It therefore makes a lot of sense to send an explicit sequence number along with the DTLS records. Because multiple DTLS records with similar sequence numbers may belong to different cipher states, each sequence number is zero-based (i.e., it starts at zero) but comes along with an epoch number. An alternative to epoch numbers would be to use randomly chosen initial sequence numbers for records (similar to the initial sequence numbers used by TCP). If the sequence numbers were sufficiently large, then the chance of collision of active sequence number ranges would be very small. The disadvantage of this approach would be that it would probably require more code to implement than the epoch strategy. To cut a long story short, a DTLS record comprises the following two additional fields (in addition to the type, version, length, and fragment fields of a "normal" TLS record):

- A 16-bit *epoch* field that comprises a counter value that is incremented on every cipher state change.

- A 48-bit *sequence number* field that comprises an explicit sequence number that is incremented for every DTLS record (sent in a given cipher state).

If several DTLS handshakes are performed simultaneously or in close succession, then there may coexist multiple DTLS records with the same sequence number but from different cipher states. As mentioned above, the epoch field is to allow recipients to distinguish these records. The epoch field is initially set to zero and is incremented each time a CHANGECIPHERSPEC message is sent. The sequence number field, in turn, always refers to a specific epoch and is incremented on a per-record basis. It is reset to zero after every CHANGECIPHERSPEC message that is sent. The DTLS record numbering scheme is illustrated in Figure 6.2. Using this general scheme, DTLS implementations must ensure that any given epoch/sequence number pair is unique (because TLS implementations rarely rehandshake, this should not pose a serious problem).

The sequence numbers of the DTLS records can also be used to provide replay protection. The corresponding sequence number verification process is similar to the one employed by IPsec: when a session is established, the receiver first initializes its record counter with zero. For each received record, the receiver then verifies

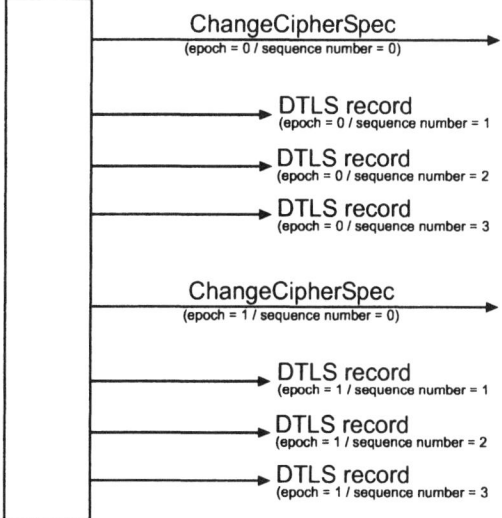

Figure 6.2 The DTLS record numbering scheme.

that the record contains a sequence number that does not duplicate the sequence number of any other record received in the past (during the session). Duplicates are detected (and hence, rejected) through the use of a sliding receive window. A minimum window size of 32 must be supported, but a window size of 64 is preferred and should be employed by default. Another window size may be chosen by the receiver. In either case, the right edge of the window represents the highest validated sequence number value received on this session, whereas records that contain sequence numbers lower than the left edge of the window are rejected. Records falling within the window are checked against a list of received records within the window. An efficient way of performing this task is based on the use of a bit mask. If the received record falls within the window and is new, or if the record is to the right of the window, then the receiver proceeds to MAC verification. If this verification fails, then the receiver must discard the record as invalid. Last but not least, the receive window is updated only if the MAC verification succeeds.

With regard to MAC generation and verification, we first note that the HMAC construction used by TLS also employs a sequence number seq_number (see Section 5.2), but that this sequence number is implicit, meaning that it must be maintained by the communicating peers. The sequence number employed by DTLS, in turn, is explicit, meaning that it is part of the DTLS record. If the concatenation of the epoch value and the sequence number value is taken as the new 64-bit value for seq_number, then the formula to compute a DTLS 1.0 MAC is exactly the same as the formula to compute a TLS MAC. In the case of DTLS, however, we can rewrite the formula as follows:

$$HMAC_K(DTLSCompressed) = \\ h(K \parallel opad \parallel h(K \parallel ipad \parallel epoch \parallel sequence\ number \parallel \\ type \parallel version \parallel length \parallel fragment))$$

Again, note that the bitstring $epoch \parallel sequence\ number$ in DTLS refers to seq_number in TLS. In either case, the length of the bitstring is 64. An important difference between TLS and DTLS is that in TLS MAC errors must result in connection termination, whereas in DTLS MAC errors need not result in connection termination. Instead, the receiving DTLS implementation may discard the offending record and continue with the transmission. This is possible because DTLS records are independent from each other. If a DTLS implementation chooses to generate an alert when it receives a record with an invalid MAC, then it must still generate a bad_record_mac (code 20) with level fatal and terminate its connection state accordingly.

Last but not least, we note that a subtle difference between the TLS and DTLS record format is related to the version field: in a DTLS record this field comprises the 1's complement of the DTLS version in use. If, for example, the DTLS version is 1.0, then the 1's complement of 1,0 is 254,255. So these bytes are included in the DTLS record's version field. For DTLS 1.2, the 1's complement of 1,2 is 254,253, and hence these bytes are included. The maximal spacing between TLS and DTLS version values is to ensure that records from the two protocols can be easily distinguished.

6.2.2 Handshake Protocol

As mentioned before, the differences between the TLS and DTLS protocols are kept as small as possible. This also applies to the handshake protocols, and hence the DTLS Handshake Protocol is very similar to that of TLS. There are only three major changes:

1. The header format of the DTSL Handshake Protocol is modified to handle message loss, reordering, and fragmentation.
2. The DTSL Handshake Protocol can retransmit a message if it is lost (or a timeout occurs).

3. A stateless cookie exchange is added to protect against denial of service (DoS) attacks (also known as resource clogging attacks).

Apart from these changes, the DTLS Handshake Protocol message formats, flows, and logic are essentially the same as those of the TLS protocol. Let us now briefly explore the three changes enumerated above.

6.2.2.1 Header Format

Beacause DTLS handshake messages may be too large to fit into a single DTLS record, the handshake messages may span multiple records. This means that it may be necessary to fragment and reassemble handshake messages. In order to do so, each DTLS handshake message header contains three new fields (in addition to the "normal" type and length fields):

- A 16-bit *message sequence* field that comprises a sequence number for the message that is sent. The first message each side transmits in a handshake has a value of zero, and every subsequent message has a message sequence value that is incremented by one. When a message is retransmitted, the same message sequence value is used. Note, however, that from the DTLS record layer's perspective, the retransmission of a message requires a new record. So the sequence number of the DTLS record will have a new value.
- A 24-bit *fragment offset* field that contains a value that refers to the number of bytes contained in previous fragments.
- A 24-bit *fragment length* field that contains a value that refers to the length of the fragment.

So the first handshake message that is sent has a message sequence field value of zero, a fragment offset field value of zero, and an appropriately valued fragment length field. If this value is n_1, then the second handshake message has a message sequence field value of one, a fragment offset field value of n_1, and a fragment length field value of n_2. The third handshake message has a message sequence field value of two, a fragment offset field value of $n_1 + n_2$, and a fragment length field value of n_3. This continues until the last handshake message is sent.

The message sequence, fragment offset, and fragment length fields are inserted after the message type and length fields in the DTLS handshake message header. The length field is the same as the length field of the original message. An unfragmented message is a degenerated case with a fragment offset of zero and a fragment length that equals the message length.

6.2.2.2 Message Retransmission

Due to the fact that the DTLS protocol is layered on top of UDP, handshake messages may get lost and the DTLS protocol must have means to deal with this situation. The usual approach to handle message loss is the use of acknowledgments of receipt. This means that the sender starts a timer when it sends out a message, and that it then waits for an acknowledgment of receipt before a timeout occurs. The DTLS protocol also envisions this approach: when a client sends an initial CLIENTHELLO message to the server, it starts a timer and it expects to receive a HELLOVERIFYREQUEST message back from the server within a reasonable amount of time. If the client does not receive such a message before a timeout occurs, then it knows that either the CLIENTHELLO or the HELLOVERIFYREQUEST message got lost. It then retransmits the CLIENTHELLO message to the server. The server also maintains a timer and retransmits the message when its timer expires. The DTLS protocol specification recommends a one-second timer (to improve latency for realtime applications).

The bottom line is that the DTLS protocol requires a new Handshake Protocol message—the HELLOVERIFYREQUEST message (type 3)—and that this message must not be included in the MAC computation for the CERTIFICATEVERIFY and FINISHED messages.

6.2.2.3 Cookie Exchange

Because the DTLS Handshake Protocol takes place over a datagram delivery service, it is susceptible to at least the following two denial of service (DoS) attacks (also known as resource clogging attacks):

- The first attack is obvious and refers to a standard resource clogging attack: the adversary initiates a handshake and this handshake clogs some computational and communicational resources at the victim.

- The second attack is less obvious and refers to an amplification attack: the adversary sends a CLIENTHELLO message apparently sourced by the victim to the server. The server then sends a potentially much longer CERTIFICATE message to the victim.

To mitigate these attacks, the DTLS protocol uses a *cookie exchange* [9] that has also been used in other protocols, such as the Photuris session key management protocol—a predecessor of IKE [10, 11]. Before the proper handshake begins, the server must provide a stateless cookie in the HELLOVERIFYREQUEST message and the client must replay it in the CLIENTHELLO message in order to demonstrate that it is capable of receiving packets at its claimed IP address. A cookie should be generated in such a way that it can be verified without retaining per-client state on the server. Ideally, it is a keyed one hash value of some client-specific parameters, such as the client IP address. The key in use needs to be known only to the server, so it is not a cryptographic key that must be established in some complicated and secure way. In DTLS 1.0, the cookie size is limited to 32 bytes.

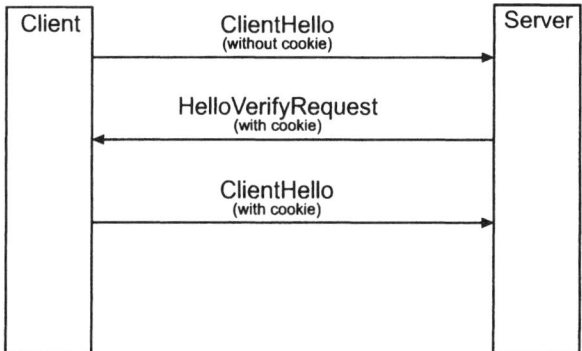

Figure 6.3 The cookie exchange mechanism used by the DTLS Handshake Protocol.

The cookie exchange mechanism used by the DTLS Handshake Protocol is illustrated in Figure 6.3. First, the client sends a DTLS CLIENTHELLO message without cookie to the server. The server then generates a cookie for this particular client and sends it to the client in the HELLOVERIFYREQUEST message (see above). Finally, the client resends the CLIENTHELLO message, but this time the message contains the cookie just received from the server. If the cookie is invalid, then the server should treat the CLIENTHELLO message as if it did not contain a cookie in the first place.

To accomodate the cookie exchange mechanism, the CLIENTHELLO message must be extended to additionally comprise a variable-length cookie field. If the client does not yet have a cookie (such as when sending the first CLIENTHELLO message), then the cookie field is left empty (i.e., it has a zero length). Needless to say that the HELLOVERIFYREQUEST message must also have room for a cookie. In addition to a cookie field, a HELLOVERIFYREQUEST message also comprises a protocol version field.

The bottom line of the cookie exchange mechanism is that it forces the client to be able to receive the cookie, which makes DoS attacks with spoofed IP addresses much more difficult to mount. Needless to say that this mechanism does not provide protection against DoS attacks mounted from anticipated IP addresses.

If, for example, an adversary collects a number of valid cookies from different IP addresses, then he or she can reuse them and attack the server accordingly. The server, in turn, can defend against this attack by changing the cryptographic key frequently, thus invalidating those cookies, but this defense makes the key management on the server side more involved.

The cookie exchange is optional. If it is performed, then the server has at least some assurance that the client is not trying to clog its resources from a randomly chosen IP address. Vice versa, if it is not perfomed, then resource clogging attacks become feasible. Reality will show whether this is problematic. In the case of IKE, for example, the cookie exchange is no longer mandatory in version 2. This means that the risk of resource clogging attacks has turned out to be smaller than originally anitipated (remember that the cookie exchange was mandatory in the first version of IKE). This is in line with the fact that the cookie exchange is optional for the DTLS protocol. Nevertheless, the DTLS protocol specification still suggests that servers should be configured to perform a cookie exchange whenever a new handshake is being performed (they may choose not to do a cookie exchange when a session is resumed). DTLS clients must be prepared to do a cookie exchange with every DTLS handshake. Again, if the HELLOVERIFYREQUEST message is used, then the first CLIENTHELLO message and the HELLOVERIFYREQUEST message must not be included in the MAC computation for the CERTIFICATEVERIFIY and FINISHED messages.

6.3 DTLS 1.2

As mentioned before, the IETF TLS WG is currently working on bringing the DTLS protocol in line with TLS 1.2. The resulting DTLS protocol version 1.2 is currently being specified. In spite of its unfinished nature, there are only a few substantial changes related to DTLS 1.2:

- Remember from Section 5.4 that TLS 1.2 introduces a couple of cipher suites that implement AEAD. These cipher suites can also be used with DTLS. Also, upon registration, new TLS cipher suites must indicate whether they are suitable for DTLS usage and what, if any, adaptations must be made.
- DTLS 1.2 increases the cookie size limit of DTLS 1.0 from 32 to 255 bytes. This should increase the flexibility for future applications.

All other changes are either editorial or of minor concern. It is, however, possible and very likely that more changes will be incorporated in future versions of the protocol specification.

6.4 SECURITY ANALYSIS

Fairly little is known about the real security of the DTLS protocol. Its designers argue that DTLS does not reveal any additional information beyond TLS during the handshake or application data transfer phase [2]. For example, at the record layer, the DTLS protocol reveals the epoch and sequence numbers (in addition to the usual header fields). Both pieces of information seem to be harmless, and there is no known vulnerability due to the fact that a passive adversary may learn them. Similarly, at the handshake layer, messages reveal the message sequence number, the fragment offset, and the fragment length. Again, these pieces of information seem to be harmless and can easily be derived by an eavesdropper monitoring a handshake. Also with regard to side channel attacks, it does not seem to be the case that the DTLS protocol is inherently different from the TLS protocol. Both protocols must be implemented with care in order to defeat side channel attacks. There is nothing special about DTLS at this point.

Maybe the biggest worry is that DTLS is stacked on UDP (instead of TCP), and that specific vulnerabilities or security problems may be inherited from this fact. Note that the properties of UDP and TCP are inherently different, and that some security technologies have problems when faced with the characteristics of UDP. For example, proxy-based firewalls have not been designed to handle UDP-based applications, and hence these firewalls usually have a hard time when dealing with such applications. Obviously, they can always trigger some intrusion detection and/or prevention heuristics, but the ultimate goal of a proxy-based firewall is to proxy TCP connections. If an application is not using such connections in the first place, then the proxy-based firewall cannot be used in its originally intended way. DTLS therefore has some inherent boundaries and limitations that have not been sufficiently explored so far.

The bottom line is that one can have a reasonably good feeling about the security of the DTLS protocol. The good feeling is inherited from the security analyses that are available for the SSL/TLS protocols and the belief that the SSL/TLS and DTLS protocols have very similar security characteristics (because their differences are so small). It is, however, still a belief, and whether this belief is justified in some reasonable way is still an open research question. Any analysis in the field is missing.

6.5 FINAL REMARKS

In this chapter, we have elaborated on the DTLS protocol, which is basically a UDP version of the SSL/TLS protocols. The differences are minor and mainly due to the characteristics of UDP, being a connectionless best-effort datagram delivery protocol that operates at the transport layer. This requires some minor modifications in the DTLS Record and Handshake Protocols. The modifications are so minor that it is unlikely that they negatively influence the security of the DTLS protocol. In fact, we expect the DTLS protocol to be equally secure as the SSL/TLS protocols.

There are a couple of DTLS implementations available on the market. Most importantly, OpenSSL (since version 0.9.8) and Cisco's VPN client AnyConnect support DTLS 1.0, and there are even a few complementary products that also claim to support DTLS (refer to the corresponding product sheets). For all these prodcuts, it is important to verify the claims and check whether the DTLS protocol is implemented properly. Implementing DTLS is not rocket science, but it is still leading edge technology that is just about to leave standardization. Consequently, many things must be clarified over time, and there is not a lot of experience in the field. This is likely to change, as the DTLS protocol is about to become a standard technology for newer Internet applications (as mentioned at the beginning of this chapter). Most importantly, the DTLS protocol is frequently discussed in the realm of Internet telephony and voice over IP (VoIP) technologies. This is certainly the area where we will see the DTLS protocol being deployed first.

The lack of implementation experience goes hand in hand with the fact that there are only a few studies about the optimal deployment of DTLS. As DTLS allows finer control of timers and record sizes, it is worthwhile doing additional analyses, for example, to determine the optimal values and backoff strategies. This is certainly a research challenge for the future. As of this writing, it is absolutely not clear what values and backoff strategy values are optimal for the deployment of DTLS. The same is true for the firewall traversal of the DTLS protocol. As we will see in the following chapter, many firewall technologies are well-suited for TCP-based applications, but they are less well-suited for UDP-based applications. Consequently, the secure firewall traversal of the DTLS protocol is another research challenge for the future. The firewall traversal of the SSL/TLS protocols is addressed next.

References

[1] Kohler, E., Handley, M., and S. Floyd, "Datagram Congestion Control Protocol (DCCP)," Standards Track Request for Comments 4340, March 2006.

[2] Modadugu, N., and E. Rescorla, "The Design and Implementation of Datagram TLS," *Proceedings of the Network and Distributed System Security Symposium (NDSS)*, Internet Society, 2004.

[3] Dierks, T., and E. Rescorla, "The Transport Layer Security (TLS) Protocol Version 1.1," Standards Track Request for Comments 4346, April 2006.

[4] Rescorla, E., and N. Modadugu, "Datagram Transport Layer Security," Standards Track Request for Comments 4347, April 2006.

[5] Phelan, T., "Datagram Transport Layer Security (DTLS) over the Datagram Congestion Control Protocol (DCCP)," Standards Track Request for Comments 5238, May 2008.

[6] Mogul, J., and S. Deering, "Path MTU Discovery," Standards Track Request for Comments 1191, November 1990.

[7] McCann, J., Deering, S., and J. Mogul, "Path MTU Discovery for IP version 6," Standards Track Request for Comments 1981, August 1996.

[8] Mathis, M., and J. Heffner, "Packetization Layer Path MTU Discovery," Standards Track Request for Comments 4821, March 2007.

[9] Oppliger, R., "Protecting Key Exchange and Management Protocols Against Resource Clogging Attacks," *Proceedings of the IFIP TC6 and TC11 Joint Working Conference on Communications and Multimedia Security*, September 1999, Kluwer Academic Publishers, Norwell, MA, pp. 163–175.

[10] Karn, P., and W. Simpson, "Photuris: Session-Key Management Protocol," Experimental Request for Comments 2522, March 1999.

[11] Karn, P., and W. Simpson, "Photuris: Extended Schemes and Attributes," Experimental Request for Comments 2523, March 1999.

Chapter 7

Firewall Traversal

Firewalls are omnipresent today, but their use and interplay with the SSL/TLS protocols is somehow tricky if not contradictory. On the one hand, the SSL/TLS protocols are used to provide end-to-end security services, and hence secure end-to-end connectivity. On the other hand, firewalls are to restrict or at least control end-to-end connectivity on the Internet. Against this background, it is not obvious if and how the SSL/TLS protocols can effectively traverse a firewall. This is the topic of this chapter. We provide an introduction in Section 7.1, elaborate on SSL/TLS tunneling and proxying in Sections 7.2 and 7.3, and conclude with some final remarks in Section 7.4. A lot has been done to leverage the SSL/TLS protocols in proxy firewalls and application gateways, not only for HTTP but also for many other messaging and streaming media protocols. You may refer to [1] to get a comprehensive overview. In this book, we scratch the surface and address only the tip of the iceberg.

7.1 INTRODUCTION

There are many possibilities to define the term *Internet firewall*, or *firewall* in short. For example, according to RFC 2828 [2], a firewall refers to "an internetwork gateway that restricts data communication traffic to and from one of the connected networks (the one said to be 'inside' the firewall) and thus protects that network's system resources against threats from the other network (the one that is said to be 'outside' the firewall)." This definition is fairly broad and not very precise.

In the early days of the firewall technology, William R. Cheswick and Steven M. Bellovin defined a firewall (system) as a collection of components placed between two networks that collectively have the following three properties [3]:

1. All traffic from inside to outside, and vice versa, must pass through the firewall.
2. Only authorized traffic, as defined by the local security policy, is allowed to pass through.
3. The firewall itself is immune to penetration.

Note that these properties are design goals. This means that a failure in one aspect does not necessarily mean that the collection is not a firewall, simply that it is not a good one. Consequently, there are different grades of security a firewall may achieve. As indicated in property 2 (with the notion of "authorized traffic"), there must be a security policy in place that specifies what traffic is authorized for the firewall, and this policy must also be enforced. In fact, it turns out that the specification of a security policy is key to the successful deployment of a firewall, or, alternatively speaking, any firewall without an explicitly specified security policy is next to useless in practice (because it tends to get holey over time).

There are many technologies to implement a firewall. They range from *static* and *dynamic*[1] *packet filtering* to *proxies*—or gateways—that operate at the transport or applicaton layer. In some literature, the former are called *circuit-level gateways*, whereas the latter are called *application-level gateways* [3]. Also, there are many possibilities to combine these technologies in real-world configurations, and to operate them in some centralized or decentralized way. In fact, there are increasingly many firewalls—so-called *personal firewalls*—that are operated decentrally, typically at the desktop level. For the purpose of this book, we don't delve into the design and deployment of a firewall configuration. There are many books that elaborate on these issues (among the many books on firewalls, I particularly recommend [4] and [5]). Instead, we assume a firewall to exist, and we further assume that this firewall at least comprises an HTTP proxy server. If a firewall did not comprise an HTTP proxy server, then it it would be condemned to use "only" packet filters and/or circuit-level gateways. Such a firewall is not optimal with regard the secuirty it is able to provide.

If an HTTP proxy server is in place and a client[2] wants to use HTTP to connect to an origin Web server, then the corresponding HTTP request is delivered to the HTTP proxy server and forwarded from there. The HTTP proxy server acts as a mediator for the HTTP connection, meaning that the client and server talk to the proxy server, whereas they both think that they are talking directly to each other. Hence, the HTTP proxy server represents (and can be seen as) a legitimate MITM. Whether this is acceptable or even desired mainly depends on the application setting.

1   Dynamic packet filtering is also known as *stateful inspection*.
2   In this chapter, we use the term *client* to refer to an HTTP client, which is basically a browser. Consequently, we could have also used the term *browser* instead of client.

In general, different application protocols have different requirements for proxy servers. On a high level of abstraction, an application protocol can either be proxied or tunneled through a proxy server.

- When we say that an application protocol is being *proxied*, we actually mean that the corresponding proxy server is aware of the specifics of the protocol and can understand what is going on at the protocol level. This allows such things as protocol-level filtering (including, for example, protocol header anomaly detection), access control, accounting, and logging. Examples of protocols that are usually proxied include Telnet, FTP, SMTP, and HTTP.
- Contrary to that, we say that an application protocol is being *tunneled* when we actually mean that the corresponding proxy server (which is basically acting as a circuit-level gateway) is not aware of the specifics of the protocol and cannot understand what is going on at the protocol level. It is simply relaying—or "tunneling"—data between the client and the server, and it does not necessarily understand the protocol in use. Consequently, it cannot perform such things as protocol-level filtering, access control, accounting, and logging to the same extent as is possible for a full-fledged proxy server. Examples of protocols that are sometimes tunneled by proxy servers or circuit-level gateways include proprietary protocols, protocols for which a proxy server is unavailable, or encrypted protocols (e.g., SSL/TLS protocols).

With regard to the SSL/TLS protocols, the two possibilities itemized above are illustrated in Figure 7.1. Note that in the case of SSL/TLS tunneling, there exists a single SSL/TLS connection from the client to the server, whereas in the case of SSL/TLS proxying there exist two SSL/TLS connections (one from the client to the proxy server and another one from the proxy server to the server). In SSL/TLS tunneling, the proxy server is passive in the sense that it yet provides connectivity, but it does not interfere with the data transmission. Contrary to that, in SSL/TLS proxying, the proxy server is active and fully controls the data transmission.

In the past, it has been been common practice to tunnel outbound SSL/TLS connections and proxy inbound SSL/TLS connections. This practice, however, is about to change as the deployment settings are getting more and more involved. For example, SSL/TLS tunneling may be used between the client and a company's proxy server, whereas the proxy server itself may define a secure perimeter demarcation point. It is then often assumed that the path between the demarcation point and the server is trusted and need not be protected by SSL/TLS. This is common, for example, in SSL/TLS VPNs, secure VoIP configurations (again, refer to [1]), and server farm deployments. Let us more thoroughly discuss SSL/TLS tunneling and SSL/TLS proxying next.

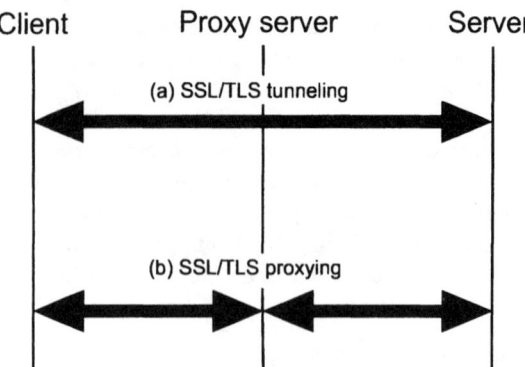

Figure 7.1 SSL/TLS tunneling (a) and proxying (b).

7.2 SSL/TLS TUNNELING

In an early attempt to address the problem of having SSL or HTTPS traffic traverse a proxy-based firewall, Ari Luotonen from Netscape Communications proposed a simple mechanism that allowed an HTTP proxy server to act as a tunnel for SSL-enhanced protocols (see, for example, [6] for an early reference). The mechanism was named *SSL tunneling*, and it was effectively specified in a series of Internet-Drafts.[3] Today, the mechanism—or rather the HTTP CONNECT method it suggests—is also used for the TLS protocol and it is part of the HTTP specification.

In short, SSL/TLS tunneling allows an SSL (or HTTPS) client to open a secure tunnel through an HTTP proxy server that resides on a firewall. When tunneling SSL or TLS, the HTTP proxy server must not have access to the data being transferred in either direction (for the sake of confidentiality). The HTTP proxy server need only know the source and destination IP addresses and port numbers, as well as the name of the requesting user (if the HTTP proxy server is configured to require user authentication). Consequently, there is a handshake between the client and the HTTP proxy server to establish the connection between the client and the origin server through the intermediate proxy server. To make SSL/TLS tunneling be backward-compatible, the handshake must be in the same format as normal HTTP requests,

---

[3] The first four versions of the Internet-Draft entitled "Tunneling SSL Through a WWW Proxy" are available from http://tools.ietf.org/html/draft-luotonen-ssl-tunneling-XX (where XX stands for 00, 01, 02, or 03), whereas the second two versions of the Internet-Draft more generally entitled "Tunneling TCP based protocols through Web proxy servers" are available from http://tools.ietf.org/html/draft-luotonen-web-proxy-tunneling-XX (where XX stands for 00 or 01). Note that the most recent version dates back to August 1998.

so that proxy servers without support for this feature can still determine the request as impossible for them to service, and provide proper error notification. As such, SSL/TLS tunneling is not really SSL/TLS-specific. Instead, it is a general way to have a third party establish a connection between two endpoints, after which bytes are simply copied back and forth by this intermediary.

More specifically, SSL/TLS tunneling uses the HTTP CONNECT method to have the HTTP proxy server connect to the origin server. To invoke the method, the client must specifiy the hostname and port number of the origin server (separated with a colon), followed by a space, a string specifying the HTTP version number (e.g., HTTP/1.0), and a line terminator. After that, there is a series of zero or more HTTP request header lines, followed by an empty line. Consequently, the first line of a fictitious HTTP CONNECT request message may look as follows:

```
CONNECT www.esecurity.ch:443 HTTP/1.0
```

This example requires an SSL/TLS-enabled Web server running at port 443 (default value) of www.esecurity.ch. This server does not exist, but the example may still give you an idea.

This message is sent out by the client and it is received by the HTTP proxy server. The proxy server, in turn, tries to establish a TCP connection to port 443 on the server www.esecurity.ch. If the server accepts the TCP connection, then the HTTP proxy server starts acting as a relay between the client and the server. This means that is copies back and forth data sent through the connection. It is then up to the client and the server to perform an SSL/TLS handshake to establish a secure connection between them. This handshake is opaque to the HTTP proxy server, meaning that the proxy server need not be aware of the fact that the client and the server actually perform an SSL/TLS handshake.

SSL/TLS tunneling can also be combined with the "normal" authentication and authorization mechanisms employed by an HTTP proxy server. For example, if a client invokes the HTTP CONNECT method but the proxy server is configured to require user authentication and authorization, then the proxy server does not immediately set up a tunnel to the origin server. Instead, the proxy server responds with a 407 status code and a Proxy-Authenticate response header to request user credentials. The corresponding HTTP response message may begin with the following two lines:

```
HTTP/1.0 407 Proxy authentication required
Proxy-Authenticate: ...
```

In the first line, the proxy server informs the client that it has not been able to serve the request, because it still requires client (or user) authentication. In the second line, the proxy server challenges the client with a `Proxy-Authenticate` response header and a challenge that refers to the authentication scheme and the parameters applicable to the proxy for this request (not displayed above). It is then up to the client to send the requested authentication information to the proxy server. Hence, the next HTTP request that it sends to the proxy server must comprise the credentials (containing the authentication information). The corresponding HTTP request message may begin with the following two lines:

```
CONNECT www.esecurity.ch:443 HTTP/1.0
Proxy-Authorization: ...
```

In the first line, the client repeats the request to connect to port 443 on the server `www.esecurity.ch`. This is the same message as before. In the second line, however, the client provides a `Proxy-authorization` request header that comprises the credentials as requested by the proxy server. Only if these credentials are correct does the proxy server connect to the origin server and hot wire the client with this server accordingly.

Note that the CONNECT method provides a lower level function than the other HTTP methods. Think of it as some kind of an "escape mechanism" for saying that the proxy server should not interfere with the transaction, but merely serve as a circuit-level gateway and forward the data stream accordingly. In fact, the proxy server should not need to know the entire URL that is being requested—only the information that is needed to serve the request, such as the hostname and port number of the origin Web server. Consequently, the HTTP proxy server cannot verify that the protocol being spoken is really SSL/TLS, and the proxy server configuration should therefore explicitly limit allowed (tunneled) connections to well-known SSL/TLS ports, such as 443 for HTTPS (or any other port number assigned by the IANA).

As of this writing, SSL/TLS tunneling is supported by almost all commercially or freely available HTTP clients and proxy servers. If, for example, you are located behind a corporate firewall and connect to an HTTPS server located on the Internet (e.g., to do Internet banking), then it is very likely that your client and the firewall's HTTP proxy server employ SSL/TLS tunneling to interconnect the client and the origin server. The HTTPS connection is then established end-to-end, meaning that the HTTP proxy server is not able to interfere with the data transmission. In principle, this is advantageous, but it also reveals a disadvantage of SSL/TLS tunneling: because the cryptographic protection is end-to-end, the requested resources are useful only for the requesting client. The HTTP proxy server "sees" the resources only in encrypted form, so it can do neither content screening nor caching in some meaningful way. Because content screening and caching are increasingly important today, SSL/TLS tunneling and its use are getting more and more problematic in many practically relevant settings.

7.3 SSL/TLS PROXYING

The end-to-end characteristic of SSL/TLS tunneling comes along with a few distinct disadvantages. First and foremost, we mentioned above that an HTTP proxy server cannot do content screening or caching in some meaningful way. Similarly, an HTTP proxy server cannot ensure that the application protocol used on top of SSL/TLS is really HTTP. It can verify the port number in use, but the port number does not reliably tell what application protocol is in actual use. If, for example, the client and the origin server have agreed to use port 443 for some proprietary protocol, then the client can have the proxy server establish an SSL/TLS tunnel to this port and use the tunnel to transmit arbitrary application data. The HTTP proxy server can neither control the protocol in use nor the data that is actually transmitted. Many companies and organizations therefore support SSL/TLS tunneling only for outgoing connections. In this case, it is less important to restrict the possible port numbers for external servers.

In theory, SSL/TLS tunneling could also be used for incoming connections, namely, to make internal HTTPS servers visible and accessible to the outside world (i.e., users located on the Internet). In this case, the HTTP proxy server must act as an inbound proxy[4] for the SSL/TLS connection. What this basically means is that HTTPS connections originating from the outside are relayed by the inbound proxy to the internal HTTPS servers, where the requesting users need to be strongly authenticated. Therefore, the internal Web servers need to implement the SSL/TLS protocols. Unfortunately, this is not always the case and most internal Web servers are not SSL/TLS-enabled (and do not represent HTTPS servers accordingly). There are a few software solutions that can be plugged in to act as SSL/TLS wrappers. Most importantly, *stunnel*[5] is a program that can map SSL/TLS connections to TCP connections that belong to specific services.

In spite of the fact that it is technically feasible, SSL/TLS tunneling is seldom used for incoming connections. Instead, SSL/TLS proxying is used, meaning that there is an SSL/TLS proxy server running at the firewall. This proxy server accepts SSL/TLS connection requests from the outside world, authenticates and

---

4   In the literature, inbound proxies are also called *reverse proxies* most of the time. In this book, however, we use the term "inbound proxy," as there is no reverse functionality involved. In fact, a reverse proxy is doing nothing differently than a normal HTTP proxy server. The only difference is that it primarily serves inbound connections (instead of outbound connections).

5   http://stunnel.mirt.net.

authorizes the requesting client, and—in the positive case—establishes a secondary SSL/TLS connection to the (internal) origin server. In some cases, it may not be necessary to establish a secondary SSL/TLS connection, and a TCP connection is sufficient enough. In either case, the SSL/TLS proxy server copies back and forth the application data. Because the data is not encrypted when processed by the proxy server, it can do content screening and caching.

To the best of our knowledge, the first SSL/TLS proxy server or gateway was developed by a group of researchers at the DEC Systems Research Center back in 1998. They basically used a combination of SSL client authentication (at the inbound proxy) and URL rewriting techniques in a technology called *secure Web tunneling*[6] [7]. A similar technology to access internal Web servers was developed and complemented with a one-time password system by a group of researchers at AT&T Laboratories [8]. During the last decade, many companies and organizations have developed similar ideas and brought corresponding products to market. Today, there is such a huge diversity of SSL/TLS proxy servers and gateways with distinct features that it makes no sense (for this book) to discuss them all.

It is, however, worthwhile mentioning that an SSL/TLS proxy server need not be operated centrally. Instead, it is possible (and sometimes makes a lot of sense) for a user to run his or her local SSL/TLS proxy server. During the old days of U.S. export controls, for example, such proxy servers were used to locally turn export-grade cryptography into strong cryptography (remember, for example, C2Net Software's SafePassage Web Proxy mentioned in Section 4.2.2.4). In this case, no matter how crippled the cryptography of the clients was, all communications went through a local SSL/TLS proxy server that empowered the use of strong cryptography between the proxy server and the origin server. Needless to say that the client was still using weak cryptography to exchange data with the proxy server, but this data exchange occured within the client system and was therefore assumed to be reasonably secure. Today, the situation is quite different and many malware-based attacks work this way (i.e., they establish a compromising proxy server between the client and the "real" proxy or origin server). The compromising proxy server then represents a MITM. There are few technologies that can be used to protect against a MITM; some of them are mentioned in Section 9.2.2.

7.4 FINAL REMARKS

In this chapter, we have addressed the practically relevant problem of how the SSL/TLS protocols can (securely) traverse a firewall. There are basically two possibilities: SSL/TLS tunneling and SSL/TLS proxying. In the past, most companies

---

6   Note that, in spite of its name, the technology refers to SSL/TLS proxying and not tunneling.

and organizations used SSL/TLS tunneling for oubound connections and SSL/TLS proxying for inbound connections (with or without restrictions regarding the allowable port numbers). Due to the huge amount of content-driven attacks (e.g., malware attacks), however, this strategy is about to change. Today, many security professionals opt for proxying outbound SSL/TLS connections, as well. SSL/TLS proxying enables content screening and this possibility is valued highly today. In fact, there are many Web application firewalls that basically represent SSL/TLS proxy servers that are additionally able to do content screening based on heuristics and an up-to-date rule base. From a performance point of view, SSL/TLS proxying has the additional advantage that the contents are decrypted and can therefore be cached for the delivery to some other clients.

In a typical real-world setting for an e-* application, both the client and the server are located on local area network (LAN) segments that are interconnected through the Internet. Both the client-side LAN and the server-side LAN are protected with a firewall. In this setting, there are typically multiple intermediate devices between the client and server. The most important intermediate device is the server-side firewall that may host an SSL/TLS proxy server. In such a setting, SSL/TLS tunneling is usually used between the client and the SSL/TLS proxy server, and SSL/TLS proxying is used between the SSL/TLS proxy server and the origin server. Whether the server-side firewall uses HTTP or HTTPS to communicate with the origin server is less important (because this communications occur in a trusted environment).

Due to the connectionless and best-effort nature of UDP, making the DTLS protocol traverse a firewall is conceptually more challenging. In particular, proxy-based firewalls do not natively work, and hence it is not at all obvious how to effectively implement a DTLS proxy server. Dynamic packet filtering and stateful inspection techniques may be used instead. At the time of this writing, the DTLS protocol is just being standardized, and hence firewall traversal in not yet a big issue. But if the DTLS protocol is successful (what we expect), then dynamic packet filtering and stateful inspection techniques for the DTLS protocol to securely traverse a firewall will become important topics in the future.

References

[1] Johnston, A.B., and D.M. Piscitello, *Understanding Voice over IP Security*. Artech House Publishers, Norwood, MA, 2006.

[2] Shirey, R., "Internet Security Glossary," Informational Request for Comments 2828 (FYI 36), May 2000.

[3] Cheswick, W.R., and S.M. Bellovin, "Network Firewalls," *IEEE Communications Magazine*, September 1994, pp. 50–57.

[4] Zwicky, E.D., Cooper, S., and D.B. Chapman, *Building Internet Firewalls*, 2nd edition. O'Reilly, Sebastopol, CA, 2000.

[5] Cheswick, W.R., Bellovin, S.M., and A.D. Rubin, *Firewalls and Internet Security: Repelling the Wily Hacker*, 2nd edition. Addison-Wesley, Reading, MA, 2003.

[6] A. Luotonen, and K. Altis, "World-Wide Web Proxies," *Computer Networks and ISDN Systems*, Vol. 27, No. 2, 1994, pp. 147–154.

[7] M. Abadi, et al., "Secure Web Tunneling," *Proceedings of 7th International World Wide Web Conference*, Elsevier Science Publishers B.V., Amsterdam, the Netherlands, 1998, pp. 531–539.

[8] Gilmore, C., Kormann, D., and A.D. Rubin, "Secure Remote Access to an Internal Web Server," *Proceedings of ISOC Symposium on Network and Distributed System Security*, February 1999.

Chapter 8

Public Key Certificates and PKIs

In previous chapters, we mentioned that the SSL/TLS protocols yet require public key certificates, but that the management of these certificates is not addressed in the corresponding protocol specifications. Consequently, the management of public key certficates must be addressed outside the scope of SSL/TLS, for example, as part of a PKI. This is the topic of this chapter. More specifically, we introduce the topic in Section 8.1, elaborate on server and client certificates in Sections 8.2 and 8.3, and conclude with some final remarks in Section 8.4. Again, this chapter is intentionally kept short and readers who want to get more information about public key certificates and PKIs are referred to the many books that are available on the topic (e.g., [1–4]).

8.1 INTRODUCTION

According to RFC 2828 [5], the term *certificate* refers to "a document that attests to the truth of something or the ownership of something." Historically, the term certificate was coined and first used by Loren M. Kohnfelder to refer to a digitally signed record holding a name and a public key [6]. As such, the certificate attests to the legitimate ownership of a public key and attributes a public key to a principal, such as a person, a hardware device, or any other entity. The resulting certificates are called *public key certificates*. They are used by many cryptographic security protocols, such as IPsec/IKE, SSL/TLS, S/MIME, and many more. Again referring to RFC 2828, a public key certificate is special case of a certificate, namely one "that binds a system entity's identity to a public key value, and possibly to additional data items." As such, it is a digitally signed data structure that attests to the true ownership of a public key.

More generally (but still in accordance with RFC 2828), a certificate can not only be used to attest to the legitimate ownership of a public key as in the case of a public key certificate, but also to attest to the truth of any property attributable to the certificate owner. This more general class of certificates is commonly referred to as *attribute certificates*. The major difference between a public key certificate and an attribute certificate is that the former includes a public key (i.e., the public key that is certified), whereas the latter includes a list of attributes (i.e., the attributes that are certified). In either case, the certificates are issued (and possibly revoked) by authorities that are recognized and trusted by a community of users.

- In the case of public key certificates, the authorities are called *certification authorities* (CAs[1]) or—more related to digital signature legislation—*certification service providers* (CSPs).
- In the case of attribute certificates, the authorities are called *attribute authorities* (AAs).

It goes without saying that a CA and a AA may in fact be the same organization. As soon as attribute certificates start to take off, it is possible and very likely that CAs will also try to establish themselves as AAs. It also goes without saying that a CA can have one or several *registration authorities* (RAs)—sometimes also called *local registration authorities* or *local registration agents* (LRAs). The functions an RA carries out varies from case to case, but they typically include the registration and authentication of the principals that become certificate owners. In addition, the RA may also be involved in tasks like token distribution, certificate revocation reporting, key generation, and key archival. In fact, a CA can delegate some of its authorities (apart from certificate signing) to an RA. Consequently, RAs are optional components that are transparent to the users. Also, the certificates that are generated by the CAs may be made available in online directories and certificate repositories.

In short, a PKI consists of one (or several) CA(s). According to RFC 2828, a PKI is "a system of CAs that perform some set of certificate management, archive management, key management, and token management functions for a community of users" that employ public key cryptography. Another way to look at a PKI is as an infrastructure that can be used to issue, validate, and revoke public keys and public key certificates. As such, a PKI comprises a set of agreed-upon standards, CAs, structures among multiple CAs, methods to discover and validate certification paths, operational and management protocols, interoperable tools, and supporting legislation. A PKI and the operation thereof are therefore quite involved. In the last couple of years, PKIs have experienced hype and many companies and organizations have announced that they are willing to provide certification services

---

1   In the past, CAs were often called trusted third parties (TTPs). This is particularly true for CAs that are operated by government bodies.

on a commercial basis. As discussed towards the end of this chapter, most of these service providers have not been commercially successful.

Many standardization bodies are working in the field of public key certificates and PKIs. Most importantly, the Telecommunication Standardization Sector of the International Telecommunication Union (ITU-T) has released and is periodically updating a recommendation that is commonly referred to as ITU-T X.509 [7], or X.509 in short (the corresponding certificates are addressed in Section 8.1.2). Meanwhile, the ITU-T X.509 has also been adopted by many other standardization bodies, including, for example, the ISO/IEC JTC1 [8]. Furthermore, a few other standardization bodies also work in the field of "profiling" ITU-T X.509 for specific application environments.[2]

In 1995, for example, the IETF recognized the importance of public key certificates, and chartered an IETF Public-Key Infrastructure X.509 (PKIX[3]) WG with the intent of developing Internet Standards needed to support an X.509-based PKI for the Internet community. The PKIX WG has initiated and stimulated a lot of standardization and profiling activities within the IETF. It is closely aligned with the respective activities within the ITU-T. In spite of the practical importance of the specifications of the IETF PKIX WG, we do not delve into the details in this book. This would be a topic for a book of its own. Feel free to browse through the IETF PKIX WG's Web site and the corresponding RFCs and Internet-Drafts; it provides a rich flora and fauna on the topic.

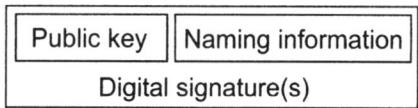

Figure 8.1 A public key certificate comprising three pieces of information.

As illustrated in Figure 8.1, a public key certificate comprises at least the following three pieces of information:

- A public key;
- Some naming information;
- One or more digital signatures.

---

2 To "profile" ITU-T X.509—or any general standard or recommendation—basically means to fix the details with regard to a specific application environment. The result is a profile that elaborates on how to use and deploy ITU-T X.509 in the environment.

3 http://www.ietf.org/html.charters/pkix-charter.html.

The *public key* is the raison d'être for the public key certificate, meaning that it is necessary because the certificate only exists to certify the public key in the first place.

The *naming information* is used to identify the owner of the public key certificate, such as his or her name and first name. In the past, there has been some confusion about the naming scheme that is appropriate for the global Internet. For example, the ITU-T recommendation X.500 introduced the notion of a distinguished name (DN) that can be used to uniquely identify an entity, such as a public key certificate owner, in a globally unique namespace. There are other examples of globally unique namespaces on the Internet, the most prominent being the DNS. The existence and usefulness of globally unique namespaces, however, has also been challenged in the research community (e.g., [9]). In fact, the Simple Distributed Security Infrastructure (SDSI) architecture and initiative [10] have evolved from the argument that a globally unique namespace is not appropriate for the global Internet, and that logically linked local namespaces provide a simpler and more realistic model [11]. As such, work on SDSI inspired the establishment of a Simple Public Key Infrastructure (SPKI) WG within the IETF. The WG was tasked with producing a certificate infrastructure and operating procedure to meet the needs of the Internet community for trust management in as easy, simple, and extensible a way as possible. This was partly in contrast and in competition to the IETF PKIX WG. The IETF SPKI WG published a pair of experimental RFCs [12, 13], before its activities were finally abandoned in 2001. Consequently, the SDSI and SPKI initiatives have turned out to be dead ends for the Internet, and hence they are not further addressed in this book.

Last but not least, the *digital signature(s)* is (are) used to attest to the fact that the other two pieces of information (i.e., the public key and the naming information) actually belong together. This basically turns the certificate into a data structure that is actually useful.

Today, there are two practically relevant types of public key certificates: *PGP certificates* (i.e., certificates used for Pretty Good Privacy (PGP) or OpenPGP) and *X.509 certificates* (i.e., certificates that conform to ITU-T X.509). As addressed next, the two types use slightly different certificate formats and trust models. A *trust model*, by the way, refers to the set of rules a system or application uses to decide whether a certificate is valid. In the direct trust model, for example, a user trusts a public key certificate because he or she knows where it came from and considers this entity as trustworthy. In addition to the direct trust model, there is a cumulative trust model employed, for example, by PGP, and a hierarchical trust model employed, for example, by ITU-T X.509.

8.1.1 PGP Certificates

As outlined, for example, in [14], PGP refers to both a standard and a software package for secure messaging on the Internet. OpenPGP, in turn, is an open specification of PGP developed within the IETF, so for the purpose of this book, PGP and OpenPGP are essentially the same. In particular, they both use the same certificate format and the same cumulative trust model.

8.1.1.1 Certificate Format

One of the distinguishing features of a PGP certificate is that it can have multiple user identities (user IDs) and signatures. This basically means that a PGP certificate is yet issued for a public key, but that multiple user IDs can be associated with that particular key (meaning that the naming information of Figure 8.1 may comprise multiple user IDs). Also, multiple signatures can certify the fact that a specific user ID is associated with the public key. Consequently, there is a one-to-many relationship between the public key of a PGP certificate and the user IDs associated with it, and there is another one-to-many relationship for each of these user IDs and the signatures that are associated with it. Contrary to that, we will see below that an X.509 certificate is structurally simpler, as it allows only one user ID associated with a public key and one signature that attests for this association.

Technically speaking, a PGP certificate is a data structure that includes six pieces of information and corresponding fields.

- *Version number:* This field is used to identify which version of PGP was used to create the public key pair.

- *Public key:* This field is used to hold the public key and the corresponding algorithm identifier (i.e., RSA, Diffie-Hellman, or DSA).

- *Certificate owner information:* This field is used to hold identity information about the certificate owner and the holder of the corresponding private key. As mentioned above, this field may include several user IDs and signatures.

- *Self-signature:* This field is used to hold a self-signature for the certificate. As its name suggests, a self-signature is generated by the certificate owner using the private key that corresponds to the public key associated with the certificate. Note that X.509 certificates normally do not include self-signatures (except for root CA certificates).

- *Validity period:* This field is used to determine the start and expiration date and time of the certificate (if they are specified at all). As such, it may specify the validity period or lifetime of the certificate.
- *Preferred encryption algorithm:* This field is used to identify the encryption algorithm of choice for the certificate owner (e.g., DES, 3DES, or IDEA). This is a remnant that bears witness to the fact that PGP has evolved from a secure messaging setting (in which the sender of a message needs to know in advance what encryption algorithm to use).

One may think of a PGP certificate as a public key with one or more labels attached to it. For example, several user IDs may be attached to it, each of which may contains different means of identifying the certificate owner (e.g., the certificate owner's name and corporate e-mail address or the certificate owner's first name and private e-mail address). Typically, a user ID includes the name of the user and one of his e-mail addresses put in angle brackets (< and >), such as `Rolf Oppliger <rolf.oppliger@esecurity.ch>`. The e-mail address basically makes the user ID unique. Also, one or several photographs may be attached to a PGP certificate to simplify visual authentication. Again, this is a feature that is not known and does not exist in the realm of X.509 certificates.

8.1.1.2 Cumulative Trust Model

The fact that PGP uses a *cumulative trust model* basically means that there is no central CA trusted by all users by default, and hence every user must decide for himself or herself whom to trust. If a user trusts another user, then this other user acts as *introducer*, meaning that any PGP certificate signed by him or her will be accepted by the user (needless to say that different users typically have different introducers). There are various degrees of trust that can be distinguished. PGP, for example, originally distinguished between marginal and full trust, but more fine-grained distinctions are possible, as well (e.g., [15]). The trust model is cumulative in the sense that more than one introducer can vouch for the validity and trustworthiness of a certificate. The bottom line is that the association of a user ID and a public key may be testified by one or several people, each of them generating a digital signature attached to the certificate. This way, many people can sign a PGP certificate to attest to their own assurance that the public key included in the certificate actually belongs to the claimed user ID. The more people to sign a certificate, the more likely it is going to be trusted by a third party. The resulting certification and trust infrastructure is highly distributed—it is sometimes called a *web of trust*. The PGP web of trust is discussed in many references and books, including, for example, Chapter 8 of [14]. Because it is not relevant for SSL/TLS, we don't delve deeper into the topic.

8.1.2 X.509 Certificates

The ITU-T recommendation X.509 specifies both a certificate format and a certificate distribution scheme [7]. It was first published in 1988 as part of the X.500 directory recommendations. The X.509 version 1 (X.509v1) format was extended in 1993 to incorporate two new fields, resulting in the X.509 version 2 (X.509v2) format. In addition, and as a result of attempting to deploy certificates on the global Internet, X.509v2 was revised to allow for additional extension fields. The resulting X.509 version 3 (X.509v3) specification was officially released in June 1996. Meanwhile, the ITU-T recommendation X.509 has been approved by the ISO/IEC JTC1 [8] and many other standardization bodies.

Again, we have a look at the X.509 certificate format and the trust model in use, which now is a hierarchical one.

8.1.2.1 Certificate Format

The format of an X.509v3 certificate is specified in the abstract syntax notation one (ASN.1[4]) and the resulting certificates are encoded according to specific encoding rules[5] to produce a series of bits and bytes suitable for transmission. Independent from the way it is specified and encoded, an X.509 public key certificate always contains the following fields:

- *Version:* This field is used to specify the X.509 version in use (i.e., version 1, 2, or 3).

- *Serial number:* This field is used to specify a serial number for the certificate. The serial number, in turn, is a unique integer value assigned by the certificate issuer.

- *Algorithm ID:* This field is used to specify the object identifier (OID) of the algorithm that is used to digitally sign the certificate. For example, the OID 1.2.840.113549.1.1.5 refers to sha1RSA, standing for the combined use of SHA-1 and RSA.

- *Issuer:* This field is used to specify the DN of the issuer (i.e., the DN of the CA that actually signs the issues the certificate).

- *Validity:* This field is used to specify a validity period for the certificate. The period, in turn, is defined by two dates, a start date and a finish date.

---

4 ASN.1 is officially specified in ITU-T X.680 and ISO/IEC 8824.
5 There are three standardized encoding rules, namely the basic encoding rules (BER), the distinguished encoding rules (DER), and the packet encoding rules (PER). Obviously, anybody can specify and use his or her own set of encoding rules.

- *Subject:* This field is used to specify the DN of the subject (i.e., the owner of the certificate).
- *Subject Public Key Info:* This field is used to specify the public key (together with the algorithm) that is actually certified.
- *Issuer Unique Identifier:* This field can be used to specify some optional information related to the issuer of the certificate (only in X.509 versions 2 and 3).
- *Subject Unique Identifier:* This field can be used to specify some optional information related to the subject (only in X.509 versions 2 and 3).
- *Extensions:* This field can be used to specify some optional extensions that may be critical or not (only in X.509 version 3).

The existence of the three above-mentioned extension fields makes X.509v3 certificates very flexible, but also very difficult to deploy in an interoperable manner. Anyway, the certificate must come along with a digital signature that conforms to the digital signature algorithm specified in *Algorithm ID* field.

8.1.2.2 Hierarchical Trust Model

In spite of the fact that we characterize the trust model employed by ITU-T X.509 as being hierarchical, it is not so in a strict sense. The possibility to define cross-certificates, as well as forward and reverse certificates enable the construction of a mesh (rather than a hierarchy). This means that something similar to PGP's web of trust can also be established using ITU-T X.509. The misunderstanding occurs, because the X.509 trust model is mapped to the directory information tree (DIT), which is hierarchic in nature (in fact each DN represents a leaf in the DIT).

In the X.509 trust model, the user must define a number of trusted CAs and corresponding certificates (i.e., certificates that are trusted by default) from which trust may extend. At this point, a subtle distinction is sometimes made between between a trusted root CA and an intermediate CA.

- A *trusted root CA* is trusted by default, meaning that a client is preconfigured with this CA being trusted. The certificate of the root CA needs to be self-signed, meaning that the issuer and the subject of the certificate are the same. Note that from a theoretical point of view, self-signed certificates are not particularly useful. Anybody can claim something and issue a certificate for this claim. Consequently, a self-signed certificate basically says: "Here is my public key, trust me." But to bootstrap hierarchical trust, one or several root

CAs with self-signed certificates are unavoidable (because the hierarchy is finite and must have a top level).

- Unlike a trusted root CA, an *intermediate CA* is not trusted by default. Instead, it is trusted because its certificate is issued by a trusted root CA. The corresponding certificates are not self-signed. The aim of considering trusted intermediate CAs is to simplify the handling of certifcation chains (as discussed below).

In a typical setting, a CSP operates a CA that represents a trusted root CA, and several subordinate CAs that represent intermediate CAs. Note, however, that not all clients make the distinction between between trusted root CAs and intermediate CAs. Microsoft Internet Explorer and all browsers that rely on the certificate management functions of the Windows operating system (e.g., Google Chrome) make the distinction and can take advantage of it. On the other side, for example, the Firefox browser does not support intermediate CAs.

Equipped with one or several root CAs with root certificates, a user can try to find a *certification path* (or *certification chain*) from a root certificate to a leaf certificate (i.e., a certificate that is issued for a user or system). Formally speaking, a certification path or chain is defined in a tree or wood of CAs (root CAs and intermediate CAs) and refers to a sequence of one or more certificates that lead from a trusted root certificate to a leaf certificate. Each certificate certifies the public key of its successor. Finally, the leaf certificate is typically issued for a person or an end system. Let's assume that CA_{root} is a root certificate and B is an entity for which a certificate must be verified. In this case, a certification path or chain with n intermediate CAs (i.e., $CA_1, CA_2, \ldots, CA_n$) would look as follows:

$$CA_{root} \ll CA_1 \gg$$
$$CA_1 \ll CA_2 \gg$$
$$CA_2 \ll CA_3 \gg$$
$$\ldots$$
$$CA_{n-1} \ll CA_n \gg$$
$$CA_n \ll B \gg$$

If a client supports intermediate CAs, then it may be sufficient to find a sequence of certificates that lead from a trusted intermediate CA's certificate to the leaf certificate. This may shorten certification chains considerably.

The simplest model one may think of is a certification hierarchy representing a tree with a single root CA. In practice, however, more general structures are possible, using multiple root CAs, intermediate CAs, and CAs that issue cross certificates.

In such a general structure, a certification path may not be unqiue and multiple certification paths may exist. In such a situation, it is required to have metrics in place that can handle multiple certification paths. Again, this is a highly challenging research topic (e.g., [16]).

As mentioned above, each X.509 certificate has a validity period, meaning that it is well-defined from when to when the certificate is supposedly valid. But in spite of this information, it may still be possible that a certificate needs to be revoked ahead of time. For example, it may be the case that a user's private key gets compromised or a CA goes out of business. For situations like these, it is necessary to address certificate revocation in one way or another. The simplest way is to have the CA periodically issue a CRL (as already briefly mentioned in Section 5.4.1.6). The CRL is basically a black list that enumerates all certificates (by their serial numbers) that have been revoked so far or since the issuance of the last CRL in the case of a delta CRL. In either case, CRLs can be tremendously large and impractical to handle. Due to the CRLs' practical disadvantages, the trend goes to retrieving online status information about the validity of a certificate. The protocol of choice to retrieve this information is OCSP. In fact, an increasingly large number of CAs support OCSP requests and operate corresponding OCSP servers. But certificate revocation remains a challenge on the client side. In fact, many application clients that employ public key certificates either do not care about certificate revocation or handle it incompletely or even improperly. This is also true for some HTTP clients and Web browsers. Fortunately, things are gradually improving and many browsers are nowadays able to properly address certificate revocation.

8.2 SERVER CERTIFICATES

As mentioned in previous chapters of this book, all nonanonymous key exchange methods of the SSL/TLS protocols require the server to provide a public key certificate—or rather a certificate chain since SSL 3.0—in a respective CERTIFICATE message. The certificate type must be in line with the key exchange method in use. Typically, it is an X.509 certificate that conforms to the profiles specified by the IETF PKIX WG. If the server provides a certificate chain, then it must lead from a trusted root certificate (or a certificate from an intermediate CA, respectively) to a leaf certificate, representing the actual server certificate. In this case, the certificate is implicitly accepted and the user need not explicitly confirm the acceptance of the certificate. If, however, there is at least one certificate in the chain not issued by a trusted root or intermediate CA, then the server certificate cannot be accepted automatically. In this case, the client must inform the user that the verification process for the server certificate poses some problems, and that he or she is asked to manually confirm or refuse its acceptance. The GUI for this user dialog varies from client to client, but the general idea is always the same. Unfortunately, all empirical investigations reveal the embarrassing fact that most users click through any such dialog, meaning that they almost certainly click "OK" when they are asked to confirm acceptance of a certificate. This is independent from the fact that they theoretically have to verify the server certificate's fingerprint prior to confirming it (which is seldom if ever done in practice). This user behavior gives room and enables some sophisticated attacks, such as MITM attacks (as further addressed in Section 9.2.2).

In order to avoid user dialogs and corresponding inconveniences, SSL/TLS-enabled Web servers are usually equipped and configured with a certificate issued by a root CA that is commonly trusted by most browsers in use today. In fact, most browser manufacturers have a program for CAs to include their root certificates in their browsers' certificate stores. In the case of Microsoft, for example, this program is called the Microsoft Root Certificate Program.[6] To become a trusted CA, the CSP must show conformance with international standards and best practices, such as

- WebTrust[7];
- ETSI TS 101 456 [17];
- ETSI TS 102 042 [18];[8]
- ISO 21188 [19].

Other browser manufacturers have similar programs and criteria. In either case, including a root certificate in a browser's certificate store is a lengthly process and there are good reasons for it to be so.

In spite of the fact that the Microsoft Root Certificate Program and the similar programs of the other browser manufacturers comprise many dozens of trusted CAs, the market for server certificates is actually dominated by only a few internationally operating CSPs. Most importantly, there is VeriSign,[9] thawte,[10] Geotrust[11] (including its subsidiary RapidSSL[12] that owns an Equifax[13] root certificate), Comodo,[14] and a few others. Typically, the validity period of a server certificate is a few years

6 http://support.microsoft.com/kb/931125/EN-US/.
7 http://www.webtrust.org.
8 Note that [17] addresses policy requirements for CAs issuing qualified certificates, whereas [18] does the same for CAs issuing public key certificates.
9 http://www.verisign.com.
10 http://www.thawte.com.
11 http://www.geotrust.com.
12 http://rapidssl.com.
13 Note that Equifax digital certificate services became GeoTrust in 2001.
14 http://www.instantssl.com.

(e.g., 1–5 years), and its cost is in the range of a few hundred U.S. dollars per year (except RapidSSL that provides low-end certificates with simplified validation and certificate issuance processes). In addition to these "normal" certificates, there are a few other types of server certificates with unique features and a generally higher price tag. Most importantly, there are wildcard certificates, International Step-Up and SGC certificates, as well as extended validation certificates.

8.2.1 Wildcard Certificates

To be applicable to the SSL/TLS protocols, a server certificate is usually issued to a fully qualified domain name (FQDN), such as secure.esecurity.ch. Such a certificate cannot be used for another subdomain of esecurity.ch, such as www.esecurity.ch or books.esecurity.ch. This is certainly fine from a security viewpoint, but it is sometimes unfortunate from a more practically oriented viewpoint. This is because it requires a domain owner to procure muliple certificates. In addition to higher costs, this means that several certificates must be managed simultaneously. To get over these practical disadvantages, many CSPs offer wildcard certificates. As its name suggests, a *wildcard certificate* is a server certificate that has a wildcard in its domain name, meaning that it can be used to secure multiple subdomains at the expense of a generally higher price tag. If, for example, there is a wildcard certificate issued for *.esecurity.ch, then this certificate can be used for all subdomains mentioned above (and optionally also other subdomains of esecurity.ch). This simplifies certificate management considerably and is particularly well suited for server farms that support load balancing. The security implications, however, cannot be ignored, because it may be confusing for a user not to know exactly to which server he or she is connecting to.

8.2.2 International Step-Up and SGC Certificates

In Section 4.2.2.4, we introduced the notion of International Step-Up[15] and SGC certificates. The former were employed by Netscape Communications, whereas the latter were (and sometimes still are) employed by Microsoft. Either type of certificates was relevant in the 1990s, when the U.S. export controls were still in place. They allowed an international browser to invoke and make use of strong cryptography (otherwise it was restricted to crippled export-grade cryptography). Only a few CSPs (e.g., VeriSign) were authorized and approved by the U.S. government to issue International Step-Up and SGC certificates.

---

15 In favor of brevity, International Step-Up certificates are sometimes only called "Step-up" or "Step up" certificates.

As mentioned in Section 2.1.6, the legal situation today is completely different and browser manufacturers are generally allowed to ship their products incorporating strong cryptography overseas. In such a situation, International Step-Up and SGC certificates do not make a lot of sense anymore. This is particularly true for International Step-Up certificates, because hardly anybody is using the Netscape Navigator anymore. Nevertheless, there are still a few CAs, such as thawte and Comodo, that still sell SGC certificates. Consequently, there seems to be a market for these certificates, and hence not everybody is using a browser that natively supports strong cryptography.

8.2.3 Extended Validation Certificates

Due to the fact that phishing and Web spoofing have become increasingly popular on the Internet, a group of commercial CA operators, browser manufacturers, and WebTrust assessors have joined together to form the *CA/Browser Forum*.[16] Members of the forum have worked closely together in defining the guidelines and means of implementation for the *extended validation* (EV) SSL certificate standard as a way of providing a heightened security for Internet transactions and creating a more intuitive method of displaying secure sites to Internet users. EV SSL certificates are sometimes also called *high assurance* (HA) certificates. This term, however, is less frequently used in the literature; it is therefore not used in this book.

Today's browsers support EV SSL certificates and use different indicators on their GUIs. For example, the Microsoft Internet Explorer (since version 7) displays a green address bar if the server is equipped with an EV SSL certificate. Also, the security status bar alternately displays the name of the server and the CA that issued the EV SSL certificate.[17] Similarly, Mozilla Firefox (since version 3) displays the name of the server in green, and if the user drags the mouse over the server's name, the name of the certificate-issuing CA is also displayed. Other browsers still use different indicators on their GUIs.

As of this writing, most CSPs already offer EV SSL certificates, and it is possible and very likely that all will do so in the near future. In fact, we expect EV SSL certificates to silently replace "normal" server certificates in the field. EV SSL certificates tend to be a little bit more expensive, but except from that there

---

16 http://www.cabforum.org.
17 To make sure that all Internet Explorer (version 7 or higher) users can take advantage of EV SSL certificates, VeriSign offers a server-side solution called EV Upgrader that enforces that requesting browsers update their VeriSign SSL root certificates of their local certificate stores. The update is done transparently and is invisible for the user. It is part of the VeriSign Secured seal. More information about VeriSign EV SSL certificates, the EV Upgrader, and the VeriSign Secured seal is available at http://www.verisign.com as well as https://extended-validation-ssl.verisign.com.

is hardly any disadvantage for the service providers that want to show their high security standards to their customers.

8.3 CLIENT CERTIFICATES

In theory, an X.509 certificate is independent from its owner, meaning that it does not really matter whether it is issued for a server or a client. The format and the fields are essentially the same (only the contents differ). In practice, however, there is a fundamental difference between a server certificate and a client certificate in the way it is issued: while the former is typically issued by an internationally operating trusted CA (as discussed above), the latter can be issued by any locally operating CA that is trusted by the server(s). This makes the issuance of client certificates conceptually simple and straightfoward. There is, however, a scalability issue. Typically, there are many clients involved that need to be equipped with a certificate. For example, if we consider an Internet bank that wants to employ certificate-based client authentication in SSL/TLS, then literally all customers of the bank need to be equipped with a certificate. If the bank is large, then we are talking about a couple hundred thousands or even millions of certificates that need to be rolled out. This is by far not a simple task. In fact, it refers to the task of rolling out an entire PKI that has proven to be difficult (to say the least). Nevertheless, there are many companies that sell client certificates to the general public. The companies mentioned above are certainly also in the client certificate business, but many other companies (many of them only locally operating) also compete.

As long as client certificates are only used for authentication (as is the case in SSL/TLS), one may be skeptical about the success of a PKI. In fact, public key certificates are hardly competitive when it comes to client (or user) authentication. One-time password and challenge-response systems are generally simpler and cheaper to deploy. There is, however, an exception to be mentioned here. If a client certificate can be automatically rolled out (i.e., without any user registration and identification process), then things look better for client certificates. Let's assume for a moment that we can automatically equip users with anonymous certificates, and that we already have a mechanism in place to authenticate users once in a simple way. For example, if they already have a password, then we can use this password for authentication. Otherwise, we can always provide users with a one-time password or PIN sent by a postal mail delivery service. The user can authenticate himself or herself using this mechanism, and he or she can then be equipped with an anonymous certificate that gets personalized at this point in time (i.e., the certificate's serial number is attributed to the user in a database). From this moment on, the user can always use this certificate to authenticate himself or herself to the server. This idea is further explored in [20]. The corresponding certificates (that are first anonymous and then personalized) are called *certinyms*— an acronym derived from "anonymous certificates." One can argue that certinyms (or somthing conceptually similar with a different name) have a large potential when it comes to the use of low-end certificates to establish trust in large-scale computing environments.

8.4 FINAL REMARKS

In this chapter, we elaborated on public key certificates and PKIs as far as they are relevant for SSL/TLS in general, and the SSL/TLS potocols in particular. The standard of choice in this area is ITU-T X.509,[18] meaning that most (server and client) certificates in use today are X.509 certificates—this particularly also applies to SSL/TLS. Hence, there are many CSPs that provide commercial certification services to the general public. Most of them make a living from selling server certificates to Web site operators. The marketing of client certificates has turned out to be more involved than originally anticipated. In fact, many CSPs that have focused on client certificates in the past have gone out of business (for the reasons discussed, for example, in [21]). The bottom line is that we are far away from having a full-fledged PKI that we can use for SSL/TLS support on the the client-side, and that Web application providers are therefore condemned to use other client or user authentication technologies instead. Ideally, these technologies are part of the TLS protocol specification and implemented accordingly. As of this writing, however, this is not yet the case, and client or user authentication is typically done at the application layer (i.e., on top of SSL/TLS). The main problem with this approach is that it is susceptible to MITM attacks (this point is further addressed in Section 9.2.2).

When it comes to using public key certificates, trust is a major issue. Each browser comes along with a preconfigured set of trusted CAs (root CAs and intermediate CAs). If a Web server provides a certificate issued by such a CA, then the browser accepts the certificate (after proper validation) without user interaction. This is convenient and certainly the preferred choice from a usability perspective. From a security perspective, however, the preferred choice is to empty the set of trusted CAs and selectively include only the CAs that are really trustworthy. Needless to say that most users are overextended with such a procedure, and hence we don't see it happen in practice. Sometimes companies and organizations distribute browser software with a customized set of trusted CAs. This is certainly an approach that is recommended and should be considered seriously. It allows a

---

18 Note that technically speaking, ITU-T X.509 is not a standard but a recommendation.

company or organization to control the user interaction dialogs. Note, however, that the danger of users clicking through the dialogs remains unsolved—even if the set of trusted CAs is customized. To solve this problem, certificate validation processes need to be strengthened and (user) awareness raising needs to be improved. These are not trivial tasks and they require an interdisciplinary course of action.

References

[1] Feghhi, J., Feghhi, J., and P. Williams, *Digital Certificates: Applied Internet Security*. Addison-Wesley, Reading, MA, 1998.

[2] Housley, R., and T. Polk, *Planning for PKI: Best Practices Guide for Deploying Public Key Infrastructure*. John Wiley & Sons, New York, 2001.

[3] Adams, C., and S. Lloyd, *Understanding PKI: Concepts, Standards, and Deployment Considerations*, 2nd edition. Addison-Wesley, Reading, MA, 2002.

[4] Vacca, J.R., *Public Key Infrastructure: Building Trusted Applications and Web Services*. Auerbach Publications, 2004.

[5] Shirey, R., "Internet Security Glossary," Request for Comments 2828, May 2000.

[6] Kohnfelder, L.M., "Towards a Practical Public-Key Cryptosystem," Bachelor's thesis, Massachusetts Institute of Technology (MIT), Cambridge, MA, May 1978.

[7] ITU-T, *Recommendation X.509: The Directory—Authentication Framework*, 1988.

[8] ISO/IEC 9594-8, *Information Technology—Open Systems Interconnection—The Directory—Part 8: Authentication Framework*, 1990.

[9] Ellison, C., "Establishing Identity Without Certification Authorities," *Proceedings of the 6th USENIX Security Symposium*, 1996, pp. 67–76.

[10] Rivest, R.L., and B. Lampson, "SDSI—A Simple Distributed Security Infrastructure," September 1996, http://people.csail.mit.edu/rivest/sdsi10.html.

[11] Abadi, M., "On SDSI's Linked Local Name Spaces," *Proceedings of 10th IEEE Computer Security Foundations Workshop*, June 1997, pp. 98–108.

[12] Ellison, C., "SPKI Requirements," Experimental Request for Comments 2692, September 1999.

[13] Ellison, C. et al., "SPKI Certificate Theory," Experimental Request for Comments 2693, September 1999.

[14] Oppliger, R., *Secure Messaging with PGP and S/MIME*. Artech House Publishers, Norwood, MA, 2001.

[15] Haenni, R., and J. Jonczy, "A New Approach to PGP's Web of Trust," *Proceedings of the European e-Identity Conference (EEMA 2007)*, 2007.

[16] Reiter, M.K., and S.G. Stubblebine, "Authentication Metric Analysis and Design," *ACM Transactions on Information and System Security*, Vol. 2, No. 2, May 1999, pp. 138–158.

[17] ETSI TS 101 456, *Electronic Signatures and Infrastructures (ESI); Policy Requirements for Certification Authorities Issuing Qualified Certificates*, 2007.

[18] ETSI TS 102 042, *Policy Requirements for Certification Authorities Issuing Public Key Certificates*, 2004.

[19] ISO 21188, *Public Key Infrastructure for Financial Services—Practices and Policy Framework*, 2006.

[20] Oppliger, R., and R. Rytz, "Certinyms—Low-End Certificates to Establish Trust in Large-Scale Computing Environments," unpublished manuscript (available from the author).

[21] Lopez, J., Oppliger, R., and G. Pernul, "Why Have Public Key Infrastructures Failed So Far?" *Internet Research*, Vol. 15, No. 5, 2005, pp. 544–556.

Chapter 9

Conclusions and Outlook

In this chapter, we conclude the book and provide an outlook. More specifically, we elaborate on the deployment of the SSL/TLS protocols in Section 9.1, address a few research challenges in Section 9.2, and (try to) predict some future developments in Section 9.3. While most contents of this book are based on facts and solid ground, this chapter is speculative in nature. This also means that some statements may turn out to be wrong in the future—this is the risk of being predictive.

9.1 DEPLOYMENT

In the preceding parts of this book, we have claimed (1) that the SSL/TLS protocols are widely deployed, and (2) that the protocols provide cryptographic strength to Web servers and corresponding sites. We now provide some evidence for these claims.

- With regard to the first claim (i.e., that the SSL/TLS protocols are widely deployed), it is sufficient to look at some major Internet sites. Many of these sites provide support for SSL/TLS, be it for specific pages (e.g., login pages) or for the entire site. This applies, for example, to almost all Internet banking and auction sites, but it also applies to many other e-commerce sites. Using SSL/TLS to secure Internet transactions has in fact become best practice, and users have become accustomed to the use of SSL/TLS (as far as they need to be aware of the use of SSL/TLS in the first place).

- With regard to the second claim (i.e., that the SSL/TLS protocols provide cryptographic strength to Web servers and corresponding sites), empirical studies were done in 2001[1] and 2006 [1]. The first study is not representative, mainly because the SSL/TLS protocols started to take off at exactly the same time as the study was done. The 2006 study, however, is more representative and its outcome is characteristic for the current state of Internet security. The study was done with a specifically designed and developed tool named Probing SSL Security Tool (PSST) that was applied to more than 19,000 Web servers. The corresponding results revealed some rather astonishing facts:

- Eighty-five percent of the servers supported the SSL 2.0 protocol, whereas a small number of these servers only supported SSL 2.0.

- Ninety-three percent of the servers still supported DES, despite the fact that this cipher is susceptible to an exhaustive key search. Similarly, many servers still supported export-grade encryption levels. This, by the way, provides evidence for the fact that SGC certificates are still needed today (see Section 8.2.2).

- Almost 4 percent of the servers supported RSA-based authentication with only 512-bit keys, even though this key length is too small today.

- Over 57 percent of the servers supported AES. Out of these, about 94 percent default to AES when presented with all options (and the vast majority of them even default to AES-256).

During the period of the study (February 2005 to November 2006), the situation improved, and the authors argued that it is likely that the situation will further improve in the future. This is likely to be true, and we are looking forward to hearing from more recent studies.

We note that—in spite of the fact that the SSL/TLS protocols are widely deployed and provide cryptographic strength to Web servers and corresponding sites—the use of the SSL/TLS protocols also comes along with a few disadvantages and practical problems. For example, the use of the SSL/TLS protocols generally makes caching difficult (or in the case of SSL/TLS tunneling, even impossible), and this may slow down the responsiveness and efficiency of Web applications considerably. To make things worse, the use of the SSL/TLS protocols also requires that a client download a complete resource and verify it entirely before it can start rendering and displaying it. This all-or-nothing behavior results in a different (and typically less comfortable) user experience. This sounds innocent and not really relevant, but for the daily use of the corresponding applications it is highly relevant and disturbing.

1   http://www.usenix.org/events/sec01/murray/.

Against this background, many commercial Web service providers, such as Google (GMail), Microsoft (Hotmail), Yahoo, and Facebook, employ the SSL/TLS protocols only to secure the transmission of the users' passwords at login time, meaning that an HTTPS connection is established only to securely transmit the password. Once the user is authenticated, the HTTPS session is dropped and a "normal" HTTP session is used instead. HTTP session management is then done traditionally, using, for example, session tokens transmitted in cookies. In this case, the cookie is transmitted in every single request, even when the application falls back to HTTP. If an adversary is able to eavesdrop on HTTP request messages sent to a Web server, then he or she can also extract session tokens and use them to hijack the respective sessions. This is particularly true in a wireless environment. At BlackHat 2007, for example, Robert Graham and David Maynor gave a talk and demonstrated how to hijack a GMail session that was previously authenticated using SSL/TLS.[2] They employed two specifically crafted tools, named *Ferret* and *Hamster*, and coined the term *sidejacking* to refer to this type of session hijacking attack. The talk was well received in the trade press, and the term sidejacking made the headlines (once again, the security industry had created a new term for an already existing and well-known attack).

There are a couple of defense strategies against sidejacking and related session hijacking attacks. The most obvious defense strategy is to use the SSL/TLS protocols not only to securely transmit the user credentials, but to secure the entire session. If all HTTP requests were protected with SSL/TLS, then eavesdropping could not reveal any session token. Unfortunately (as mentioned above), the use of the SSL/TLS protocols comes along with a few complications and practical problems, and hence there is room for alternative and more low-weight technologies or techniques to protect against sidejacking and related session hijacking attacks. In 2008, for example, Ben Adida came up with a simple approach—named *SessionLock*—to protect Web sessions without extending the use of SSL/TLS [2]. More specifically, SessionLock uses SSL/TLS in exactly the same way as before, namely to secure the session on which the user credentials are transmitted. But in addition to a session identifier, SessionLock also generates a session secret that is never sent in the clear (i.e., over an HTTP session). Instead, the session secret is used to generate a MAC for every single HTTP request message that is sent. The secret is passed from the HTTPS login page to the HTTP portion of the site, and from one page to another under HTTP, by way of the URL fragment identifier. Thus, although all URLs after the user login are requested over HTTP, the session secret is never transmitted in the clear. We think that SessionLock populates an important niche between no security and the full—but sometimes prohibitively expensive—security of SSL/TLS. Consequently,

2   http://www.erratasec.com/BH_DC_07_Data_seepage.ppt.

we expect SessionLock to be used and similar technologies and techniques to be developed and proposed in the future.

In the following section, we elaborate on a few research challenges that are more deeply intertwined with the SSL/TLS protocol.

9.2 RESEARCH CHALLENGES

In spite of the fact that the standardization level of the SSL/TLS protocols is quite mature, meaning that the protocols are well specified and standardized, there are still a few research challenges and opportunities for further studies. We already mentioned that there are research challenges related to the DTLS protocol (see Section 6.5). In addition (but without claim for completeness), we introduce, overview, and briefly discuss a few others. If you are a scientist, then you may be stimulated by the ideas and you may even bring in your own thoughts. The field is open for innovative thinking.

9.2.1 Performance Optimization

The early versions of the SSL/TLS protocols were rather narrow in terms of supported options and cipher suites. This no longer applies for the more recent versions of the TLS protocol. Remember, for example, that TLS 1.2 comes along with many possible extensions that may be used for various things. Against this background, SSL/TLS performance optimization—both in theory and practice—has become an increasingly important topic and research challenge.

To the best of our knowledge, the first comprehensive study of the performance costs of TLS was done in 2001 (a first publication appeared in 2002, but the journal version of the paper was published in 2006 [3]). The study releavled that TLS Web servers incur a significant perfomance penalty relative to a regular Web server running on the same platform (a factor between 3.4 and 9 was reported in the study). The perfomance penalty is mainly caused by the public key operations that are part of the TLS Handshake Protocol. This is particularly true for RSA. Consequently, researchers have tried to design and come up with algorithms and approaches to accelerate RSA operations. One approach is to perform RSA operations together in batches [4]; another approach is to offload the RSA operations from Web servers to dedicated servers with hardware optimized for RSA computations [5]. A similar approach is to distribute the TLS processing stages among multiple machines (e.g., [6]). In all of these approaches, hardware accelerators may be used additionally to further speed up RSA computations.

Looking more deeply into the performance issues related to RSA, it is important to note that RSA operations are expensive, but that the connection pattern of a typical client also yields a possibility for optimization. In fact, clients normally connect and reconnect to only a few Web servers, and this characteristic behavior can be exploited using caching in several ways. For example, it is always possible to have an SSL/TLS connection resume an earlier SSL/TLS session and thus reuse the result of an earlier RSA computation. More specifically, some early research results suggest that session caching may help improving Web server performance considerably (e.g., [7]). Based on these results, people have started to propose changes in the TLS protocol (e.g., [8]) or cache as much TLS handshake information as possible on the client side (e.g., [9, 10]). There are at least two possibilities to implement the second proposal:

- The client can cache information related to the server's public parameters and negotiated paramteres for future use (so they need not be renegotiated in subsequent handshakes).
- The server can store an encrypted version of the session information on the client side.

The first possibility leads to a *fast-track* mechanism [9] that allows a client to make well-informed guesses about parameters the server is likely to select. For example, if the client caches the server's certificate (chain), then the server no longer has to send this paramter. Similarly, it is possible and very likely that a server always selects the same Diffie-Hellman group (if a Diffie-Hellman key exchange is performed in the first place), as well as the same preferred cipher suite and the same compression method. The overall goal of the fast-track mechanism is to reduce both network traffic and the number of round trips without requiring additional server state. These savings are most useful in high latency environments, such as wireless networks.

The second possibility leads to a *client-side session cache* mechanism that allows a server to maintain a much larger number of sessions for a given memory size. This mechanism is conceptually similar and the logical predecessor of the SessionTicket extension for TLS as introduced and discussed in Section 5.4.1.12.

Mechansims like fast track and client-side session cache are important when it comes to the large-scale deployment of SSL/TLS-enabled Web servers. If most connections of a Web server are secured using SSL/TLS, then it is important to have mechanisms in place that minimize the server's workload and state considerably. Hence, we expect many other mechanisms and heuristics to be developed and proposed in the future.

9.2.2 Protection Against MITM Attacks

According to RFC 2828 [11], a MITM attack refers to "a form of active wiretapping attack in which the attacker intercepts and selectively modifies communicated data in order to masquerade as one or more of the entities involved in a communication association." Consequently, the major characteristics of an MITM attack are: (1) that it represents an active attack, and (2) that it targets the association between the communicating entities (rather than the entities or the communication channel between them). Note that in some literature, an MITM that carries out an active attack in real-time is also called adaptive. We don't use this term and assume that an MITM attack is already adaptive by default.

There are many possibilities to implement MITM attacks. Examples include Address Resolution Protocol (ARP) cache poisoning and DNS spoofing.[3] In either case, an MITM attack is very powerful; the attacker can do literally everything the user is authorized to do on the server side (or everything the server is authorized to do on the client side, respectively). In a typical setting, the attacker places himself between the user and the server in a way that he can talk to the user and the server separately, whereas the user and the server think that they are talking directly with each other. The best way to think about an MITM attack in an SSL/TLS setting is to consider an adversary that represents an SSL/TLS proxy server (or relay) between the user and the server. Neither the user nor the server are aware of the MITM. Cryptography makes no difference here as the MITM is in the loop and can decrypt and reencrypt all messages that are sent back and forth. If the user wants to authenticate himself to an application server, then he reveals his credentials to the MITM. Afterwards, the MITM may choose to use the credentials fairly or to misuse them to illegitimately spoof the user. If, for example, the user employs a SecurID token to authenticate himself or herself to a server, then the MITM can grab the SecurID string (that is typically valid for a couple of seconds up to a minute) and reuse it to spoof the user. If the user employs a challenge-response authentication system, then the MITM can simply send back and forth the challenge and response messages. Even if the user employed a zero-knowledge authentication protocol [12, 13], then the MITM would still be able to forward the messages and spoof the user accordingly. The zero-knowledge property of an authentication protocol does not, by itself, protect against MITM attacks—it only protects against information leakage related to the user's secret.[4]

---

3   Recently, the term pharming has been coined to refer to DNS spoofing attacks, such as local DNS cache poisoning.
4   Note, however, that there is a general construction that can be used to immunize a zero-knowledge authentication protocol against MITM attacks [14].

Against this background, we make a case that most currently deployed user authentication mechanisms fail to provide protection against MITM attacks, even when they run on top of the SSL/TLS protocols. There are basically two reasons for this failure:

1. SSL/TLS server authentication is usually done poorly by the naïve user, if done at all.
2. SSL/TLS session establishment is usually decoupled from user authentication.

The first reason leads to a situation in which the user talks to the MITM, thereby revealing his or her credentials. The second reason means that the credentials revealed by the user can now be used by the MITM to spoof the user to the server. Consequently, any effective countermeasure against MITM attacks in an SSL/TLS setting must address these problems by either enforcing proper server authentication or combining user authentication with SSL/TLS session establishment.

- With regard to proper server authentication, there are attempts to improve the quality of the server certificates, such as EV certificates (see Section 8.2.3), as well as attempts to assist the users in properly validating the certificates. For example, it is possible to associate the certificate or its fingerprint (i.e., a 128- or 160-bit cryptographic hash value) with an image or a meaningful word. For example, Petname[5] is a Firefox add-on that allows a user to associate a server certificate with the name of a pet. When the user establishes an SSL/TLS session to this particular server, he or she must make sure that the proper name of the pet is displayed by the browser. If this is not the case, then either the server has a new certificate, or the SSL/TLS session is established to a foreign server (that may represent an MITM). There are other attempts to visually or textually represent the server certificate or its fingerprint, such as public passwords, visual fingerprints, or snowflakes. The idea is always the same: if a certificate or its fingerprint is associated with an image or a meaningful text, then it is simpler for the user to properly validate it. Along a similar line of argumentation, it is possible to include visual representations of names (so-called logotypes) in X.509 public key certificates. Such logotypes are, for example, employed by TrustBar.[6] Last but not least, a new approach is implemented in a system called Perspectives [15].[7] It is a system that uses a collection of notary hosts to observe a server's public key via multiple network vantage points (detecting localized attacks) and keep a record of the server's key over time (recognizing short-lived attacks). Perspectives has advantages

5 https://addons.mozilla.org/de/firefox/addon/957.
6 http://trustbar.mozdev.org.
7 http://www.cs.cmu.edu/~perspectives.

and disadvantages that need to be explored more thoroughly before the system can be widely deloyed. This yields an interesting research challenge of its own.

- With regard to combining user authentication with SSL/TLS session establishment, there is some work to secure tunneled authentication protocols against MITM attacks [16]. More recently, similar ideas were explored in SSL/TLS session-aware (TLS-SA) user authentication [17]. The basic idea of TLS-SA is to make it possible for a server to recognize the fact that the client and server employ different SSL/TLS connections to send and receive the user credentials. If this is the case, then it is possible and likely that an MITM (with two distinct SSL/TLS connections to the client and server) is in place.

To the best of our knowledge, the first approach to make the SSL/TLS protocols resistant against MITM attack was proposed by Bodo Möller in a posting to the OpenSSL mailing list: after the client and server have exchanged CHANGECIPHERSPEC and FINISHED messages, they can exchange additional messages that include a MAC for the respective FINISHED message. The MAC, in turn, is keyed with a shared secret, such as a password. Unfortunately, this approach requires the SSL/TLS protocols to be modified.

There are also some attempts to provide protection against MITM attacks that are independent from SSL/TLS. Examples include the Interlock protocol [18] that was shown to be vulnerable when used for authentication [19], delayed password disclosure (DPD) [20], and the password protection module (PPM[8]), as well as the simultaneous use of multiple communication channels and channel hopping (e.g., [21]). Furthermore, there are some applications—especially in Europe—that authenticate users by sending out short messaging system (SMS) messages that contain TANs and require that users enter these TANs when they login. While it has been argued that this mechanism protects against MITM attacks, unfortunately, this is not the case. If a MITM is located between the user and the server, then he need not eavesdrop on the SMS messages; all he needs to do to spoof the user is to forward the TAN submitted by the user on the SSL/TLS session. If one wants to work with TANs distributed via SMS messages, then one has to work with transaction-based TANs. For each transaction submitted by the user, a summary is returned to the user together with a TAN in an SMS message. To confirm the transaction, the user must enter the corresponding TAN. There are several other systems that implement similar ideas. Examples include Phoolproof [22] and AXSionics' AXS tokens.[9] The downside of this proposal is that transaction-based TANs are expensive (perhaps prohibitively so) and not particularly user-friendly. Hence, another approach is to have a token

---

8 http://www.wipo.int/pctdb/en/wo.jsp?wo=2006014358.
9 http://www.axsionics.ch.

that implements an SSL/TLS proxy server. Whenever critical information is sent to a server, the user is asked to confirm this information on the token. The IBM Zone Trusted Information Channel (ZTIC) is an example of this type. Taking all of these systems into account, it is possible and very likely that we will pass through a phase of consolidation. It is highly unlikely that all of these systems will survive on the market. In a few years, we will know more.

9.2.3 Trust Management

In Chapter 8, we elaborated on public key certificates and PKI requirements that are key for the successful deployment of the SSL/TLS protocols. Ten years ago, this topic was hot and the few companies that were around at this time were either bought by larger companies or went out of business. In the more recent past, the discussion has shifted away from authentication-centric public key certificates and PKIs to the authorization-centric notion of *trust management*. In fact, trust management has established itself as a new and very active area of research in the computer network and distributed system security space. This is particularly true for distributed trust management. There are many initiatives and research projects that focus on distributed trust management (e.g., [23, 24]). More recently, people have also started to investigate using X.509 attribute certificates for distributed trust management (e.g., [25]). The resulting infrastructure is known as *privilege management infrastructure* (PMI). In order to set up and employ a PMI in an SSL/TLS setting, it is necessary that future versions of the TLS protocol provide support for attribute certificates. This basically means that clients and servers must use heuristics to provide the attribute certificates that are relevant in a given context in respective handshake messages. The use of attribute certificates and PMIs in an SSL/TLS setting is not yet sufficiently addressed by international standardization, at least not within the IETF. This is about to change, but it requires a nonnegligible amount of time.

9.3 FUTURE DEVELOPMENTS

In this book, we saw that SSL/TLS is a broad topic, and that the successful deployment of the SSL/TLS protocols depends on many factors that need to be resolved and may even need to be standardized. Meanwhile, the deployment of the SSL/TLS protocols will continue, and many Internet applications will be empowered to make use of SSL/TLS. In fact, there is no reason not to layer a TCP-based application protocol on top of SSL/TLS and a UDP-based application protocol on top of DTLS. For a relatively small surcharge, the corresponding application protocols can be secured in terms of data confidentiality, integrity, and authenticity. The research challenges mentioned above can be addressed while the SSL/TLS protocols are being deployed (i.e., there is no need to solve the challenges before the SSL/TLS protocols are being deployed).

Given the current situation, it is relatively simple and straightforward to predict that the SSL/TLS protocols will become a key security technology in the future, probably causing other security technologies to disappear. We mentioned before that this process is already going on in virtual private networking (as IPsec-based VPNs are being replaced with SSL/TLS-based VPNs). The tremendous success of the SSL/TLS protocols goes hand in hand with further developments. Many people are working in the field, and these people are constantly making proposals, implementations, and applications. Consequently, the TLS protocol is subject to change and represents a moving target. This also means that you have to make yourself familiar with the most recent version of the TLS protocol. This book can only give you the starting stimulus—it is up to you to take advantage of it.

References

[1] Lee, H.K., Malkin, T., and E. Nahum, "Cryptographic Strength of SSL/TLS Servers: Current and Recent Practices," *Proceedings of the 7th Internet Measurement Conference (IMC 2007)*, San Diego, CA, ACM Press, October 2007, pp. 83–92.

[2] Adida, B., "SessionLock: Securing Web Sessions Against Eavesdropping," *Proceeding of the 17th International Conference on World Wide Web (WWW 2008)*, Beijing, China, ACM Press, April 2008, pp. 517–524.

[3] Coarfa, C., Druschel, P., and D.S. Wallach, "Performance Analysis of TLS Web Servers," *ACM Transactions on Computer Systems (TOCS)*, Vol. 24, No. 1, February 2006, pp. 39–69.

[4] Boneh, D., H. Shacham, H., "Improving SSL Handshake Performance via Batching," *Proceedings of the RSA Conference*, Springer-Verlag, LNCS 2020, 2001, pp. 28–43.

[5] Dean, D., Berson, T., Franklin, M., Smetters, D., and M. Spreitzer, "Cryptology as a Network Service," *Proceedings of the 7th ISOC Network and Distributed Systems Security Symposium (NDSS '01)*, San Diego, CA, The Internet Society, February 2001.

[6] Mraz, R., "Secure Blue: An Architecture for a Scalable, Reliable High Volume SSL Internet Server," *Proceedings of the 17th Computer Security Applications Conference (ACSAC 2001)*, December 2001, pp. 391–398.

[7] Goldberg, A., Buff, R., and A. Schmitt, "Secure Web Server Performance Dramatically Improved by Caching SSL Session Keys," *Proceedings of the Workshop on Internet Server Performance*, June 1998.

[8] Apostolopoulos, G., Peris, V., and D. Saha, "Transport Layer Security: How Much Does It Really Cost?" *Proceedings of IEEE INFOCOM*, 1999, pp. 717–725.

[9] Shacham, H., and D. Boneh, "Fast-Track Session Establishment for TLS," *Proceedings of the 8th ISOC Network and Distributed Systems Security Symposium (NDSS '02)*, San Diego, CA, February 2002.

[10] Shacham, H., Boneh, D., and E. Rescorla, "Client-Side Caching for TLS," *Transactions on Information and System Security (TISSEC)*, Vol. 7, No. 4, 2004, pp. 553–575.

[11] Shirey, R., "Internet Security Glossary," Informational Request for Comments 2828 (FYI 36), May 2000.

[12] Fiat, A., and A. Shamir, "How to Prove Yourself: Practical Solutions to Identification and Signature Problems," *Proceedings of CRYPTO '86*, Springer-Verlag, LNCS 263, 1987, pp. 186–194.

[13] Guillou, L.C., and J.J. Quisquater, "A Practical Zero-Knowledge Protocol Fitted to Security Microprocessor Minimizing Both Transmission and Memory," *Proceedings of EUROCRYPT '88*, Springer-Verlag, LNCS 330, 1988, pp. 123–128.

[14] Cramer, R., and I. Damgård, "Fast and Secure Immunization Against Adaptive Man-in-the-Middle Impersonation," *Proceedings of EUROCRYPT '97*, Springer-Verlag, LNCS 1233, May 1997, pp. 75–87.

[15] Wendlandt, D., Andersen, D.G., and A. Perrig, "Perspectives: Improving SSH-Style Host Authentication with Multi-Path Probing," *Proceedings of the USENIX Annual Technical Conference*, 2008, pp. 321–334.

[16] Asokan, N., Niemi, V., and K. Nyberg, "Man-in-the-Middle in Tunneled Authentication Protocols," *Proceedings of the International Workshop on Security Protocols*, 2003, pp. 15–24 (also available as IACR ePrint 2002/163).

[17] Oppliger, R., Hauser, R., and D. Basin, "SSL/TLS Session-Aware User Authentication," *IEEE Computer*, Vol. 41, No. 3, March 2008, pp. 59–65.

[18] Rivest, R.L., and A. Shamir, "How to Expose an Eavesdropper," *Communications of the ACM*, Vol. 27, No. 4, 1984, pp. 393–395.

[19] Bellovin, S.M., and M. Merritt, "An Attack on the Interlock Protocol When Used for Authentication," *IEEE Transactions on Information Theory*, Vol. 40, No. 1, January 1994, pp. 273–275.

[20] Jakobsson, M., and S. Myers, "Delayed Password Disclosure," *International Journal of Applied Cryptography*, Vol. 1, No. 1, February 2008, pp. 47–59.

[21] Alkassar, A., Stüble, C., and A.-R. Sadeghi, "Secure Object Identification—or: Solving the Chess Grandmaster Problem," *Proceedings of the 2003 Workshop on New Security Paradigms*, Ascona, Switzerland, ACM Press, NY, 2003, pp. 77–85.

[22] Parno, B., Kuo, C., and A. Perrig, "Phoolproof Phishing Prevention," *Proceedings of Financial Cryptography and Data Security*, Springer-Verlag, LNCS 4107, 2006, pp. 1–19.

[23] Blaze, M., Feigenbaum, J., and J. Lacy, "Decentralized Trust Management," *Proceedings of the 1996 IEEE Symposium on Security and Privacy*, IEEE Computer Society Press, 1996, pp. 164–173.

[24] Blaze, M., Feigenbaum, J., and A.D. Keromytis, "KeyNote: Trust Management for Public-Key Infrastructures," *Proceedings of the International Workshop on Security Protocols*, Springer-Verlag, LNCS 1550, 1998, pp. 59–63.

[25] Chadwick, D., Otenko, A., and E. Ball, "Role-Based Access Control with X.509 Attribute Certificates," *IEEE Internet Computing*, Vol. 7, No. 2, 2003, pp. 62–69.

Appendix

Standardized TLS Cipher Suites

TLS_NULL_WITH_NULL_NULL	{ 0x00, 0x00 }
TLS_RSA_WITH_NULL_MD5	{ 0x00, 0x01 }
TLS_RSA_WITH_NULL_SHA	{ 0x00, 0x02 }
TLS_RSA_WITH_RC4_128_MD5	{ 0x00, 0x04 }
TLS_RSA_WITH_RC4_128_SHA	{ 0x00, 0x05 }
TLS_RSA_WITH_IDEA_CBC_SHA	{ 0x00, 0x07 }
TLS_RSA_WITH_DES_CBC_SHA	{ 0x00, 0x09 }
TLS_RSA_WITH_3DES_EDE_CBC_SHA	{ 0x00, 0x0A }
TLS_DH_DSS_WITH_DES_CBC_SHA	{ 0x00, 0x0C }
TLS_DH_DSS_WITH_3DES_EDE_CBC_SHA	{ 0x00, 0x0D }
TLS_DH_RSA_WITH_DES_CBC_SHA	{ 0x00, 0x0F }
TLS_DH_RSA_WITH_3DES_EDE_CBC_SHA	{ 0x00, 0x10 }
TLS_DHE_DSS_WITH_DES_CBC_SHA	{ 0x00, 0x12 }
TLS_DHE_DSS_WITH_3DES_EDE_CBC_SHA	{ 0x00, 0x13 }
TLS_DHE_RSA_WITH_DES_CBC_SHA	{ 0x00, 0x15 }
TLS_DHE_RSA_WITH_3DES_EDE_CBC_SHA	{ 0x00, 0x16 }
TLS_DH_anon_WITH_RC4_128_MD5	{ 0x00, 0x18 }
TLS_DH_anon_WITH_DES_CBC_SHA	{ 0x00, 0x1A }
TLS_DH_anon_WITH_3DES_EDE_CBC_SHA	{ 0x00, 0x1B }
TLS_KRB5_WITH_DES_CBC_SHA	{ 0x00, 0x1E }
TLS_KRB5_WITH_3DES_EDE_CBC_SHA	{ 0x00, 0x1F }
TLS_KRB5_WITH_RC4_128_SHA	{ 0x00, 0x20 }
TLS_KRB5_WITH_IDEA_CBC_SHA	{ 0x00, 0x21 }
TLS_KRB5_WITH_DES_CBC_MD5	{ 0x00, 0x22 }
TLS_KRB5_WITH_3DES_EDE_CBC_MD5	{ 0x00, 0x23 }
TLS_KRB5_WITH_RC4_128_MD5	{ 0x00, 0x24 }

TLS_KRB5_WITH_IDEA_CBC_MD5	{ 0x00, 0x25 }
TLS_PSK_WITH_NULL_SHA	{ 0x00, 0x2C }
TLS_DHE_PSK_WITH_NULL_SHA	{ 0x00, 0x2D }
TLS_RSA_PSK_WITH_NULL_SHA	{ 0x00, 0x2E }
TLS_RSA_WITH_AES_128_CBC_SHA	{ 0x00, 0x2F }
TLS_DH_DSS_WITH_AES_128_CBC_SHA	{ 0x00, 0x30 }
TLS_DH_RSA_WITH_AES_128_CBC_SHA	{ 0x00, 0x31 }
TLS_DHE_DSS_WITH_AES_128_CBC_SHA	{ 0x00, 0x32 }
TLS_DHE_RSA_WITH_AES_128_CBC_SHA	{ 0x00, 0x33 }
TLS_DH_anon_WITH_AES_128_CBC_SHA	{ 0x00, 0x34 }
TLS_RSA_WITH_AES_256_CBC_SHA	{ 0x00, 0x35 }
TLS_DH_DSS_WITH_AES_256_CBC_SHA	{ 0x00, 0x36 }
TLS_DH_RSA_WITH_AES_256_CBC_SHA	{ 0x00, 0x37 }
TLS_DHE_DSS_WITH_AES_256_CBC_SHA	{ 0x00, 0x38 }
TLS_DHE_RSA_WITH_AES_256_CBC_SHA	{ 0x00, 0x39 }
TLS_DH_anon_WITH_AES_256_CBC_SHA	{ 0x00, 0x3A }
TLS_RSA_WITH_NULL_SHA256	{ 0x00, 0x3B }
TLS_RSA_WITH_AES_128_CBC_SHA256	{ 0x00, 0x3C }
TLS_RSA_WITH_AES_256_CBC_SHA256	{ 0x00, 0x3D }
TLS_DH_DSS_WITH_AES_128_CBC_SHA256	{ 0x00, 0x3E }
TLS_DH_RSA_WITH_AES_128_CBC_SHA256	{ 0x00, 0x3F }
TLS_DHE_DSS_WITH_AES_128_CBC_SHA256	{ 0x00, 0x40 }
TLS_RSA_WITH_CAMELLIA_128_CBC_SHA	{ 0x00, 0x41 }
TLS_RSA_WITH_CAMELLIA_128_CBC_SHA	{ 0x00, 0x41 }
TLS_DH_DSS_WITH_CAMELLIA_128_CBC_SHA	{ 0x00, 0x42 }
TLS_DH_RSA_WITH_CAMELLIA_128_CBC_SHA	{ 0x00, 0x43 }
TLS_DHE_DSS_WITH_CAMELLIA_128_CBC_SHA	{ 0x00, 0x44 }
TLS_DHE_RSA_WITH_CAMELLIA_128_CBC_SHA	{ 0x00, 0x45 }
TLS_DH_anon_WITH_CAMELLIA_128_CBC_SHA	{ 0x00, 0x46 }
TLS_DHE_RSA_WITH_AES_128_CBC_SHA256	{ 0x00, 0x67 }
TLS_DH_DSS_WITH_AES_256_CBC_SHA256	{ 0x00, 0x68 }
TLS_DH_RSA_WITH_AES_256_CBC_SHA256	{ 0x00, 0x69 }
TLS_DHE_DSS_WITH_AES_256_CBC_SHA256	{ 0x00, 0x6A }
TLS_DHE_RSA_WITH_AES_256_CBC_SHA256	{ 0x00, 0x6B }
TLS_DH_anon_WITH_AES_128_CBC_SHA256	{ 0x00, 0x6C }
TLS_DH_anon_WITH_AES_256_CBC_SHA256	{ 0x00, 0x6D }
TLS_RSA_WITH_CAMELLIA_256_CBC_SHA	{ 0x00, 0x84 }
TLS_DH_DSS_WITH_CAMELLIA_256_CBC_SHA	{ 0x00, 0x85 }
TLS_DH_RSA_WITH_CAMELLIA_256_CBC_SHA	{ 0x00, 0x86 }
TLS_DHE_DSS_WITH_CAMELLIA_256_CBC_SHA	{ 0x00, 0x87 }

TLS_DHE_RSA_WITH_CAMELLIA_256_CBC_SHA	{ 0x00, 0x88 }
TLS_DH_anon_WITH_CAMELLIA_256_CBC_SHA	{ 0x00, 0x89 }
TLS_PSK_WITH_RC4_128_SHA	{ 0x00, 0x8A }
TLS_PSK_WITH_3DES_EDE_CBC_SHA	{ 0x00, 0x8B }
TLS_PSK_WITH_AES_128_CBC_SHA	{ 0x00, 0x8C }
TLS_PSK_WITH_AES_256_CBC_SHA	{ 0x00, 0x8D }
TLS_DHE_PSK_WITH_RC4_128_SHA	{ 0x00, 0x8E }
TLS_DHE_PSK_WITH_3DES_EDE_CBC_SHA	{ 0x00, 0x8F }
TLS_DHE_PSK_WITH_AES_128_CBC_SHA	{ 0x00, 0x90 }
TLS_DHE_PSK_WITH_AES_256_CBC_SHA	{ 0x00, 0x91 }
TLS_RSA_PSK_WITH_RC4_128_SHA	{ 0x00, 0x92 }
TLS_RSA_PSK_WITH_3DES_EDE_CBC_SHA	{ 0x00, 0x93 }
TLS_RSA_PSK_WITH_AES_128_CBC_SHA	{ 0x00, 0x94 }
TLS_RSA_PSK_WITH_AES_256_CBC_SHA	{ 0x00, 0x95 }
TLS_ECDH_ECDSA_WITH_NULL_SHA	{ 0xC0, 0x01 }
TLS_ECDH_ECDSA_WITH_RC4_128_SHA	{ 0xC0, 0x02 }
TLS_ECDH_ECDSA_WITH_3DES_EDE_CBC_SHA	{ 0xC0, 0x03 }
TLS_ECDH_ECDSA_WITH_AES_128_CBC_SHA	{ 0xC0, 0x04 }
TLS_ECDH_ECDSA_WITH_AES_256_CBC_SHA	{ 0xC0, 0x05 }
TLS_ECDHE_ECDSA_WITH_NULL_SHA	{ 0xC0, 0x06 }
TLS_ECDHE_ECDSA_WITH_RC4_128_SHA	{ 0xC0, 0x07 }
TLS_ECDHE_ECDSA_WITH_3DES_EDE_CBC_SHA	{ 0xC0, 0x08 }
TLS_ECDHE_ECDSA_WITH_AES_128_CBC_SHA	{ 0xC0, 0x09 }
TLS_ECDHE_ECDSA_WITH_AES_256_CBC_SHA	{ 0xC0, 0x0A }
TLS_ECDH_RSA_WITH_NULL_SHA	{ 0xC0, 0x0B }
TLS_ECDH_RSA_WITH_RC4_128_SHA	{ 0xC0, 0x0C }
TLS_ECDH_RSA_WITH_3DES_EDE_CBC_SHA	{ 0xC0, 0x0D }
TLS_ECDH_RSA_WITH_AES_128_CBC_SHA	{ 0xC0, 0x0E }
TLS_ECDH_RSA_WITH_AES_256_CBC_SHA	{ 0xC0, 0x0F }
TLS_ECDHE_RSA_WITH_NULL_SHA	{ 0xC0, 0x10 }
TLS_ECDHE_RSA_WITH_RC4_128_SHA	{ 0xC0, 0x11 }
TLS_ECDHE_RSA_WITH_3DES_EDE_CBC_SHA	{ 0xC0, 0x12 }
TLS_ECDHE_RSA_WITH_AES_128_CBC_SHA	{ 0xC0, 0x13 }
TLS_ECDHE_RSA_WITH_AES_256_CBC_SHA	{ 0xC0, 0x14 }
TLS_ECDH_anon_WITH_NULL_SHA	{ 0xC0, 0x15 }
TLS_ECDH_anon_WITH_RC4_128_SHA	{ 0xC0, 0x16 }
TLS_ECDH_anon_WITH_3DES_EDE_CBC_SHA	{ 0xC0, 0x17 }
TLS_ECDH_anon_WITH_AES_128_CBC_SHA	{ 0xC0, 0x18 }
TLS_ECDH_anon_WITH_AES_256_CBC_SHA	{ 0xC0, 0x19 }
TLS_SRP_SHA_WITH_3DES_EDE_CBC_SHA	{ 0xC0, 0x1A }

TLS_SRP_SHA_RSA_WITH_3DES_EDE_CBC_SHA	{ 0xC0 , 0x1B }
TLS_SRP_SHA_DSS_WITH_3DES_EDE_CBC_SHA	{ 0xC0 , 0x1C }
TLS_SRP_SHA_WITH_AES_128_CBC_SHA	{ 0xC0 , 0x1D }
TLS_SRP_SHA_RSA_WITH_AES_128_CBC_SHA	{ 0xC0 , 0x1E }
TLS_SRP_SHA_DSS_WITH_AES_128_CBC_SHA	{ 0xC0 , 0x1F }
TLS_SRP_SHA_WITH_AES_256_CBC_SHA	{ 0xC0 , 0x20 }
TLS_SRP_SHA_RSA_WITH_AES_256_CBC_SHA	{ 0xC0 , 0x21 }
TLS_SRP_SHA_DSS_WITH_AES_256_CBC_SHA	{ 0xC0 , 0x22 }

Abbreviations and Acronyms

AA	attribute authority
AAI	authentication and authorization infrastructure
ACM	Association for Computing Machinery
AEAD	authenticated encryption with additional data
AES	Advanced Encryption Standard
API	application programming interface
ARP	Address Resolution Protocol
ASCII	American Standard Code for Information Interchange
ASN.1	abstract syntax notation one
AtE	authenticate-then-encrypt
BBS	Blum, Blum, and Shub
BCP	best current practice
BER	basic encoding rules
BIS	Bureau of Industry and Security
CA	certification authority
CBC	cipherblock chaining
CCA	chosen ciphertext attack
CCA2	adaptive chosen ciphertext attack
CCM	counter with CBC-MAC mode
CFB	cipher feedback
COCOM	Coordinating Committee for Multilateral Export Controls
CRC	cyclic redundancy check
CRL	certificate revocation list
CSP	certification service provider

CTR	counter mode encryption
DAC	discretionary access control
DCCP	Datagram Congestion Control Protocol
DEA	Data Encryption Algorithm
DER	distinguished encoding rules
DES	Data Encryption Standard
DH	Diffie-Hellman
DHE	ephemeral Diffie-Hellman
DIT	directory information tree
DN	distinguished name
DoC	Department of Commerce
DoD	Department of Defense
DoS	denial of service
DPD	delayed password disclosure
DSA	Digital Signature Algorithm
DSS	Digital Signature Standard
DTLS	datagram TLS
E&A	encrypt-and-authenticate
EAR	Export Administration Regulations
ECB	electronic code book
ECC	elliptic curve cryptography
ECDH	elliptic curve Diffie-Hellman
ECDHE	elliptic curve ephemeral Diffie-Hellman
ECDSA	elliptic curve digital signature algorithm
ECMQV	elliptic curve Menezes-Qu-Vanstone
EIT	Enterprise Integration Technologies
EKE	encrypted key exchange
EKM	exported keying material
EtA	encrypt-then-authenticate
ETSI	European Telecommunications Standards Institute
EV	extended validation
FIPS	Federal Information Processing Standard
FQDN	fully qualified domain name
FSUIT	Federal Strategy Unit for Information Technology
FTP	File Transfer Protocol
FYI	for your information

GCM	Galois/counter mode
GMT	Greenwich Mean Time
GNU	GNU's not Unix
GUI	graphical user interface
HA	high assurance
HMAC	hashed MAC
HTTP	Hypertext Transfer Protocol
IACR	International Association for Cryptologic Research
IANA	Internet Assigned Numbers Authority
ICSI	International Computer Science Institute
ID	identity (identifier)
IDEA	International Data Encryption Algorithm
IEC	International Electrotechnical Commission
IEEE	Institute of Electrical and Electronics Engineers
IETF	Internet Engineering Task Force
IESG	Internet Engineering Steering Group
IFIP	International Federation for Information Processing
IIOP	Internet InterORB Protocol
IKE	Internet key exchange
IMAP	Internet Message Access Protocol
IP	Internet Protocol
IPES	Improved PES
IPsec	IP security
IRC	Internet relay chat
IRTF	Internet Research Task Force
ISO	International Organization for Standardization
ISOC	Interent Society
IT	information technology
ITU	International Telecommunication Union
ITU-T	ITU Telecommunication Standardization Sector
IV	initialization vector
JTC1	Joint Technical Committee 1
KDC	key distribution center
KEA	key exchange algorithm
L2TP	Layer 2 Tunneling Protocol

LAN	local area network
LDAP	Lightweight Directory Access Protocol
LEAF	law enforcement access field
LFSR	linear feedback shift register
LRA	local registration authority (or agent)
LSB	least significant bit
MAC	mandatory access control
	media access control
	message authentication code
MIC	message integrity code
MIME	multipurpose Internet mail extensions
MIT	Massachusetts Institute of Technology
MITM	man-in-the-middle
MTU	maximum transmission unit
NCSA	National Center for Supercomputing Applications
NIST	National Institute of Standards and Technology
NNTP	Network News Transfer Protocol
NSA	National Security Agency
NTT	Nippon Telegraph and Telephone Corporation
OAEP	optimal asymmetric encryption padding
OCSP	online certificate status protocol
OFB	output feedback
OID	object identifier
OMA	Open Mobile Alliance
OSI	Open Systems Interconnection
PCT	Private Communication Technology
PER	packet encoding rules
PES	Proposed Encryption Standard
PGP	Pretty Good Privacy
PKCS	public key cryptography standard
PKI	public key infrastructure
PKIX	Public-Key Infrastructure X.509
PMI	privilege management infrastructure
PMTU	path MTU
POP3	Post Office Protocol
PPM	password protection module

PPTP	Point-to-Point Tunneling Protocol
PRBG	pseudorandom bit generator
PRF	pseudorandom function
PSK	preshared key
PSRG	Privacy and Security Research Group
PSST	Probing SSL Security Tool
PUB	Publication
RA	registration authority
RBAC	role-based access control
RC2	Rivest Cipher 2
RC4	Rivest Cipher 4
RFC	request for comments
RSA	Rivest, Shamir, and Adleman
SCTP	Stream Control Transmission Protocol
SDSI	simple distributed security infrastructure
SECG	Standards for Efficient Cryptography Group
SGC	server gated cryptography
SHA	Secure Hash Algorithm
SHS	Secure Hash Standard
SIP	Session Initiation Protocol
S/MIME	Secure MIME
SMS	short messaging system
SMTP	Simple Mail Transfer Protocol
SPI	security parameter index
SPKI	simple public key infrastructure
SRP	secure remote password
SSH	secure shell
SSL	secure sockets layer
STLP	Secure Transport Layer Protocol
S-HTTP	Secure HTTP (also known as SHTTP)
TC11	Technical Committee 11
TCP	Transmission Control Protocol
TEK	token encryption key
TFTP	Trivial FTP
TLS	transport layer security
TLS-SA	SSL/TLS session-aware
TTP	trusted third party

UDP	User Datagram Protocol
URL	uniform resource locator
UTC	Coordinated Universal Time (in French)
VoIP	voice over IP
VPN	virtual private network
W3C	World Wide Web Consortium
WAP	Wireless Application Protocol
WEP	wired equivalent privacy
WG	Working Group
WLAN	wireless local area network
WTLS	wireless TLS
WTS	Web transaction security
WWW	World Wide Web
XML	eXtensible Markup Language
XOR	exclusive or
ZTIC	Zone Trusted Information Channel

About the Author

Rolf Oppliger received his M.Sc. and Ph.D. degrees in computer science from the University of Berne, Switzerland, in 1991 and 1993, respectively. After spending one year as a postdoctoral researcher at the International Computer Science Institute (ICSI) in Berkeley, California, he joined the Federal Authorities of the Swiss Confederation in 1995 and continued his research and teaching activities at several universities in Switzerland and Germany. In 1999, he received the venia legendi (also known as Habilitation) for computer science from the University of Zürich, Switzerland, where he was appointed as an adjunct professor in 2007. Also in 1999, he founded eSECURITY Technologies (http://www.esecurity.ch) to provide scientific and state-of-the-art consulting, education, and engineering services related to IT security, and started to serve as the series editor for the Artech House Information Security and Privacy Series. He has published numerous scientific papers, articles, and books on security-related topics. He is a senior member of the Association for Computing Machinery (ACM) and a member of the Institute of Electrical and Electronics Engineers (IEEE) Computer Society and the International Association for Cryptologic Research (IACR). He also served as the vice-chair of the International Federation for Information Processing (IFIP) Technical Committee 11 (TC11) Working Group 4 (WG4) on network security.

Index

abstract syntax notation one, 215
access control, 5
access control mechanism, 8
access control service, 5
access right, 8
accountability, 5
Achilles' heel, 43, 53
ACM Turing Award, 48
active attack, 13
adaptive, 232
Address Resolution Protocol, 232
Advanced Encryption Standard, 37
alert description, 119
alert level, 118
algorithm, 19
anonymous Diffie-Hellman key exchange, 84
application layer, 66
application programming interface, 66
application-level gateways, 200
ARC4, 39
ARCFOUR, 39
ARP, 232
art, 25
asymmetric encryption system, 30, 46, 47
attribute authority, 210
attribute certificate, 210, 235
authenticated encryption, 169
authenticated encryption with additional data, 169
authentication and authorization infrastructure, 5
authentication and key distribution system, 54
authentication exchange mechanisms, 9
authentication function, 43
authentication service, 5
authentication tag, 42
authenticity, 42
Authorization, 5
AXS token, 234
AXSionics, 234

basic encoding rules, 215
basic reference model, 3
BBS generator, 45
big endian, 80
bit security, 126
BlackHat, 229
block cipher, 37
browser, 200
Bureau of Industry and Security, 27

CA/Browser Forum, 221
cache poisoning, 232
Caesar cipher, 25
Camellia, 143
certificate, 209
certificate distribution scheme, 215
certificate repository, 210
certificate revocation list, 157
certification authority, 210
certification chain, 217
certification path, 217
certification service provider, 210
certinym, 223
chosen-protocol attack, 20
cipher, 35
cipher feedback, 37
cipher spec, 89
cipher suite, 89
cipherblock chaining, 37
ciphertext, 35

ciphertext space, 35
circuit-level gateways, 200
client, 200
client-side session cache, 231
collision resistant, 31
collision resistant hash function, 31
Comodo, 219
computational complexity theory, 22
computational security, 22
computationally secure, 37
conditional, 22
conditional security, 22
confidentiality protection, 35
connection confidentiality service, 6
connection integrity service with recovery, 6
connection integrity service without recovery, 6
connectionless confidentiality service, 6
connectionless integrity service, 7
cookie exchange, 192
Coordinated Universal Time, 100
Coordinating Committee for Multilateral Export Controls, 27
CRL, 218
cryptanalysis, 18
cryptographic, 31
cryptographic algorithm, 20
cryptographic hash function, 28
cryptographic protocol, 20
cryptographic scheme, 19
cryptographic system, 19
cryptographically secure, 45
cryptography, 18
cryptology, 17
cryptosystem, 19
cumulative trust model, 212, 214
cyclic redundancy check, 69

Danvers Doctrine, 71
data confidentiality service, 6
Data Encryption Algorithm, 37
Data Encryption Standard, 37
data integrity mechanism, 9
data integrity protection, 31
data integrity service, 6
data origin authentication service, 5
Datagram Congestion Control Protocol, 183
datagram TLS, xvi, 185

decrypt, 35
decryption, 35
decryption function, 36
delayed password disclosure, 234
delta CRL, 218
denial of service, 191, 192
Department of Commerce, 27
Department of Defense, 26
deterministic, 20
differential, 38
differential power analysis, 24
Diffie-Hellman key exchange protocol, 55
Diffie-Hellman problem, 56
digest, 31
digital fingerprinting, 19
digital signature, 49
digital signature algorithm, 53
digital signature giving message recovery, 50
digital signature mechanism, 8
digital signature scheme, 19
digital signature standard, 53
digital signature system with appendix, 51
digital signature system, 19, 30
digital signature with appendix, 49
digital signature, 31
digital watermarking, 19
directory information tree, 216
discrete exponentiation function, 29
discretionary access control, 8
distinguished encoding rules, 215
distinguished name, 212
DNS spoofing, 232
Dolev-Yao model, 13
domain, 30
Double DES, 38
double handshake technique, 158

e-business, xv
e-commerce, xv, 7
e-government, xv
eSECURITY Technologies, 249
easy, 28
ECDH key exchange, 160
ECDSA, 53
ECMQV, 57
electronic business, xv
electronic code book, 37
electronic commerce, xv

electronic government, xv
Elgamal asymmetric encryption system, 56
elliptic curve cryptography, 57
elliptic curve Diffie-Hellman, 57
elliptic curve Menezes-Qu-Vanstone, 57
encipherment, 8
encrypt, 35
Encrypted Key Exchange, 163
encryption, 35
encryption function, 36
end-to-end argument, 67
endianness, 80
Enterprise Integration Technologies, 67
ephemeral Diffie-Hellman key exchange, 84
epoch, 188
ethical hacking, 2
ETSI TS 101 456, 219
ETSI TS 102 042, 219
EV certificate, 233
EV Upgrader, 221
event detection, 11
expected running time, 29
Export Administration Regulations, 27
Exported Keying Material, 141
export, 27
extended validation, 221

Facebook, 229
fast-track, 231
fault analysis, 24
Ferret, 229
fingerprint, 31
finite state machine, 45
firewall, 199
firewall traversal, xvi
fixed Diffie-Hellman key exchange, 84
flight, 95
Fortify, 106
fragment, 134
fragment length, 191
fragment offset, 191
fully qualified domain name, 220

gateway, 206
Geotrust, 219
GMail, 229
Google, 229
graphical user interface, xvii

Habilitation, 249
Hamster, 229
hard, 28
hash function, 30
hashed MAC, 43
hidden volume, 19
hierarchical trust model, 212
high assurance, 221
Hotmail, 229
HTTP CONNECT method, 203
hybrid cryptosystem, 46
Hypertext Transfer Protocol, xv

ideal system, 23
IEEE 802.1AE, 66
IETF Concensus, 154
Improved PES, 40
inbound proxy, 205
information theory, 22, 25
information-theoretic security, 22
information-theoretically secure, 37
initiator, 81
integrity, 42
intermediate CA, 217
International Computer Science Institute, 249
International Data Encryption Algorithm, 40
International Electrotechnical Commission, 3
International Organization for Standardization, 3
International Step-Up, 27, 105, 220
International Telecommunication Union, 3, 211
Internet Assigned Numbers Authority, 79, 151
Internet Engineering Steering Group, 152
Internet Engineering Task Force, 3
Internet firewall, 199
Internet Key Exchange, 66
Internet layer, 66
Internet Research Task Force, 3
introducer, 214
invisible ink, 19
IP fragmentation, 187
IP security, 66
ISO/IEC 7498, 3
issuer, 215
ITU-T, 3, 211

Joint Technical Committee 1, 3

Kerberos, 54, 66
Kerckhoffs' principle, 24
key agreement protocol, 30, 54
key distribution center, 54
key distribution protocol, 54
key establishment protocol, 54
key length, 36
key space, 35, 43

law enforcement access field, 41
layer 2 tunneling protocol, 66
least significant bit, 126
length, 94, 134
linear crytanalysis, 38
linear feedback shift register, 39
local area network, 207
local namespace, 212
local registration agent, 210
local registration authority, 210
logotype, 233
Lucifer, 37

MAC, 35, 43
man-in-the-middle attack, 56
mandatory access control, 8
maximum transmission unit, 187
media access control, 66
meet-in-the-middle attack, 38
message authentication, 31
message authentication code, 43
message authentication system, 43
message integrity code, 42
message sequence, 191
message space, 43
Microsoft Root Certificate Program, 219
MITM attack, 232
modular power function, 29
modular square function, 29
multientity, 20
multiple entities cryptosystem, 20

National Center for Supercomputing Applications, 68
network access layer, 66
network byte order, 80
Network News Transfer Protocol, 79
non-secret encryption, 25

nonrepudiation service with proof of delivery, 7
nonrepudiation service with proof of origin, 7
nonrepudiation service, 7, 75
nonrepudiation with proof of delivery, 75
nonrepudiation with proof of origin, 75
notarization mechanisms, 10

object identifier, 215
object, 8
OCSP, 218
OID, 215
one-way, 28, 29, 30
one-way function, 28, 31
Online Certificate Status Protocol, 157
Open Systems Interconnection, 3
OpenPGP, 213
OpenSSL, xvi
optimal asymmetric encryption padding, 128
OSI security architecture, 3
output feedback, 37

packet encoding rules, 215
packet filtering, 200
passive attack, 13
password protection module, 234
path MTU, 187
peer entity authentication service, 5
perfect forward secrecy, 84
permissions, 5
personal firewall, 200
Perspectives, 233
Petname, 233
PGP, 213
PGP certificate, 212
Phoolproof, 234
PKCS #1 conforming, 127
plaintext, 35
plaintext message, 35
plaintext message space, 35
plausible deniability, 19
point-to-point tunneling protocol, 66
polynomial, 29
PRBG, 35, 44
preimage resistant, 30
preshared key, 170
Pretty Good Privacy, 40
Privacy and Security Research Group, 3

Index 255

Private Communication Technology, 69
private key, 45
private use, 152
privilege management infrastructure, 235
privilege, 5
probabilistic, 20
probability theory, 22
Probing SSL Security Tool, 228
Proposed Encryption Standard, 40
protocol, 20
provable security, 22
proxied, 201
proxy, 200
pseudorandom bit generator, 21
pseudorandom bit sequence, 44
PSK identity, 172
PSK identity hint, 172
PSST, 228
public key, 45
public key certificate, xvi, 209
public key cryptography, 46
public key cryptosystem, 21, 45
public key infrastructure, xvi
public password, 233
Public-Key Infrastructure X.509, 211

random bit generator, 28, 34, 44
random oracle methodology, 23
random oracle model, 23
randomized, 20
RapidSSL, 219
RC4, 37
real system, 23
recommendation X.800, 3
reexport, 27
registration authority, 210
regulation, 26
resource clogging, 191, 192
responder, 81
reverse proxy, 205
Rijndael, 38
Rivest Cipher 4, 39
role, 9
role-based access controls, 9
routing control mechanism, 9
RSA family, 48
RSA public key cryptosystem, 48
running time, 29

SafePassage Web Proxy, 106, 206
science, 25
SDSI, 212
second-preimage resistant, 31
secret key cryptography, 46
secret key cryptosystem, 21, 35
secret parameter, 45
secure, 13
secure cookie, 168
Secure Hash Algorithm, 32
Secure Hash Standard, 33
Secure Hypertext Transfer Protocol, 67
Secure MIME, 66
Secure Remote Password, 164
Secure Sockets Layer, 68
secure system, 13
Secure Transport Layer Protocol, 71
secure Web tunneling, 206
SecurID, 232
security architecture, 1, 3
security association, 81
security audit, 3
security audit trail, 11
security label, 10
security parameter index, 81
security recovery, 11
seed, 44
selected field connection integrity service, 7
selected field connectionless integrity service, 7
selective field confidentiality service, 6
self-signature, 213
separate port strategy, 78
sequence number, 188
Server Gated Cryptography, 27
SessionLock, 229
SGC, 105
SGC certificates, 220, 228
SHA-1, 33
short messaging system, 234
side channel attack, 24
sidejacking, 229
signatory, 50
signer, 50
Simple Distributed Security Infrastructure, 212
Simple Mail Transfer Protocol, 79
Simple Public Key Infrastructure, 212
single-entity cryptosystem, 20

snowflakes, 233
Specification Required, 152
SSL, xv
SSL Alert Protocol, 77, 87, 118
SSL Application Data Protocol, 77, 87, 120
SSL Change Cipher Spec Protocol, 77, 87, 116, 117
SSL connection, 81
SSL Handshake Protocol, 77, 87, 94
SSL patent, 69
SSL protocol, 77
SSL record, 76
SSL Record Protocol, 77, 87
SSL session, 81
SSL tunneling, 202
SSL/TLS proxy server, 206, 232
SSL/TLS session-aware, 234
Standards Action, 152
Standards for Efficient Cryptography Group, 163
stateful inspection, 200
steganography, 18
stream cipher, 37
Stream Control Transmission Protocol, 183
strong collision resistant, 31
stunnel, 205
subject, 8, 216
super-polynomial, 29
symmetric encryption, 35
symmetric encryption system, 35

tag space, 43
Telecommunication Standardization Sector, 3, 211
Thawte, 219
threat and risk analysis, 3
threats model, 12
timing attack, 24
TLS, xv
TLS Alert Protocol, 134
TLS Application Data Protocol, 134
TLS Change Cipher Spec Protocol, 134
TLS connection, 135
TLS extension, xvi
TLS Handshake Protocol, 134
TLS protocol, 134
TLS Record Protocol, 133
TLS session, 135

token encryption key, 59
traffic analysis, 6
traffic flow confidentiality service, 6
traffic padding mechanisms, 9
Transmission Control Protocol, 66
transport layer, 66
trapdoor, 29
trapdoor function, 25, 29
trapdoor one-way function, 29
Triple DES, 38
TrueCrypt, 19
trust, 223
trust management, 235
trust model, 212
TrustBar, 233
trusted CA, 223
trusted functionality, 10
trusted party, 10
trusted root CA, 216
trusted third party, 10, 210
tunneled, 201
type, 93, 133

unconditional, 22
Unconditional security, 22
unkeyed cryptosystem, 21, 28
upward negotiation strategy, 78
URL fragment identifier, 229
User Datagram Protocol, 68
user ID, 214

validity period, 215
verification functions, 43
verifier, 50
VeriSign, 219
version, 93, 134
virtual hosting, 155
virtual private network, 130
visual fingerprint, 233
voice over IP, 196

Wassenaar Arrangement, 27
weak collision resistant, 31
web of trust, 214
WebTrust, 219
wildcard certificate, 220
wired equivalent privacy, 39
Wireless Application Protocol, 184

wireless local area network, 39
Wireless TLS, 184
Wireshark, xvii
World Wide Web, xv
World Wide Web Consortium, 68
wrapper, 205

X.500 directory, 215
X.509, 211
X.509 certificate, 212
X.509 version 1 (X.509v1), 215
X.509 version 2 (X.509v2), 215
X.509 version 3 (X.509v3), 215
XML signatures, 68

Yahoo, 229

zero-knowledge authentication protocol, 232
Zone Trusted Information Channel, 235

Recent Titles in the Artech House Information Security and Privacy Series

Rolf Oppliger, Series Editor

Bluetooth Security, Christian Gehrmann, Joakim Persson and Ben Smeets

Computer Forensics and Privacy, Michael A. Caloyannides

Computer and Intrusion Forensics, George Mohay, et al.

Defense and Detection Strategies against Internet Worms, Jose Nazario

Demystifying the IPsec Puzzle, Sheila Frankel

Developing Secure Distributed Systems with CORBA, Ulrich Lang and Rudolf Schreiner

Electric Payment Systems for E-Commerce, Second Edition, Donal O'Mahony, Michael Peirce, and Hitesh Tewari

Evaluating Agile Software Development: Methods for Your Organization, Alan S. Koch

Implementing Electronic Card Payment Systems, Cristian Radu

Implementing the ISO/IEC 27001 Information Security Management System Standard, Edward Humphreys

Implementing Security for ATM Networks, Thomas Tarman and Edward Witzke

Information Hiding Techniques for Steganography and Digital Watermarking, Stefan Katzenbeisser and Fabien A. P. Petitcolas, editors

Internet and Intranet Security, Second Edition, Rolf Oppliger

Introduction to Identity-Based Encryption, Luther Martin

Java Card for E-Payment Applications, Vesna Hassler, Martin Manninger, Mikail Gordeev, and Christoph Müller

Multicast and Group Security, Thomas Hardjono and Lakshminath R. Dondeti

Non-repudiation in Electronic Commerce, Jianying Zhou

Outsourcing Information Security, C. Warren Axelrod

Privacy Protection and Computer Forensics, Second Edition, Michael A. Caloyannides

Role-Based Access Control, Second Edition, David F. Ferraiolo, D. Richard Kuhn, and Ramaswamy Chandramouli

Secure Messaging with PGP and S/MIME, Rolf Oppliger

Security Fundamentals for E-Commerce, Vesna Hassler

Security Technologies for the World Wide Web, Second Edition, Rolf Oppliger

SSL and TLS: Theory and Practice, Rolf Oppliger

Techniques and Applications of Digital Watermarking and Content Protection, Michael Arnold, Martin Schmucker, and Stephen D. Wolthusen

User's Guide to Cryptography and Standards, Alexander W. Dent and Chris J. Mitchell

For further information on these and other Artech House titles, including previously considered out-of-print books now available through our In-Print-Forever® (IPF®) program, contact:

Artech House
685 Canton Street
Norwood, MA 02062
Phone: 781-769-9750
Fax: 781-769-6334
e-mail: artech@artechhouse.com

Artech House
16 Sussex Street
London SW1V 4RW UK
Phone: +44 (0)20 7596-8750
Fax: +44 (0)20 7630-0166
e-mail: artech-uk@artechhouse.com

Find us on the World Wide Web at:
www.artechhouse.com